Spring 2.5 Aspect-Oriented Programming

Create dynamic, feature-rich, and robust enterprise applications using the Spring framework

Massimiliano Dessì

PUBLISHING

BIRMINGHAM - MUMBAI

Spring 2.5 Aspect-Oriented Programming

First published: February 2009

Production Reference: 1170209

Published by Packt Publishing Ltd.
32 Lincoln Road
Olton
Birmingham, B27 6PA, UK.

ISBN 978-1-847194-02-2

www.packtpub.com

Cover Image by Parag Kadam (paragvkadam@gmail.com)

Credits

Author

Massimiliano Dessì

Reviewer

Stefano Sanna

Acquisition Editor

Rashmi Phadnis

Development Editor

Dhiraj Chandiramani

Technical Editor

Abhinav Prasoon

Copy Editor

Sneha Kulkarni

Editorial Team Leader

Akshara Aware

Project Manager

Abhijeet Deobhakta

Project Coordinator

Neelkanth Mehta

Indexer

Rekha Nair

Proofreader

Chris Smith

Production Coordinator

Aparna Bhagat

Cover Designer

Aparna Bhagat

About the Author

Massimiliano Dessì is an experienced Java developer who started developing JEE applications in 2000. In 2004 he discovered the Spring Framework 1.0, and since then he has been one of its most enthusiastic users.

Massimiliano is specialized in design and development of enterprise Web-based applications, such as portals, content management systems and banking applications. JEE technology and applied agile methodologies like eXtreme Programming are his core skills. He currently works as a Software Architect and Engineer for Sourcesense (`www.sourcesense.com`), one of the leading European Open Source System Integrators. He have a strong background as a community supporter and open-source software contributor. He's also an active technical writer, author of various articles, publications, and reviews availables on `http://www.jugsardegna.org/vqwiki/jsp/Wiki?MassimilianoDessi` and on `http://wiki.java.net/bin/view/People/MassimilianoDessi`.

Massimiliano also speaks regurarly at Users Groups conferences (including Java Users Groups, Spring Framework User Group, Javaday, and Linux Users Groups).

He is one of the founders of Java User Group Sardinia (`http://www.jugsardegna.org`), as well as the founder of "Spring Framework Italian User Group", "Jetspeed Italian user Group" and "Groovy Italian User Group".

He maintains a personal weblog at: `http://jroller.com/page/desmax`.

Massimiliano lives in Cagliari, Sardinia with his family.

About the Reviewer

Stefano Sanna is senior engineer and Java ME Tech Lead at Beeweeb Technologies (Rome), where his activities are focused on mobile multimedia applications (JME, iPhone, Android). His experience on Java for mobile devices began in 1999 on a Psion handheld computer. He is author of the Italian book "Java Micro Edition", targeted on developing network-oriented applications for mobile phones and published by Hoepli (Nov 2007). He has written more than 50 technical articles on Java ME, mobile technologies, and Linux. He has presented more than 30 seminars on the same topics, including Sun SPOTs and Arduino sensor networks. Stefano supports some Italian communities: JUG Sardegna, Java Mobile Developers Forum, and Java Italian Association. Before joining Beeweeb, he was a software engineer at CRS4 (Sardinia) in the Network Distributed Applications group, where he worked on multimodal applications and mobile cartography. He regularly writes about mobile computing, Java, embedded systems, and good Italian food on his blog: http://www.gerdavax.it.

This book is dedicated to my wife Monica and my children Michele, Mattia and Chiara

Table of Contents

Preface

In software engineering, mostly low-level languages were used for many years, which were closer to the computer machine code than to human language. In the 70s, Brian Kernighan and Dennis Ritchie created the language C. It was quite similar to human language, making it easier and faster to write code, while keeping a high level of abstraction. This allowed the realization of concepts and ideas, which was not possible for the previous languages as they were forced to focus on the processor's language. Later, Smalltalk and C++ permitted the shaping of concepts and ideas through objects, providing a new way to structure applications and write programs. With the object-oriented languages, any system could be created with increasing complexity in a more manageable way, thanks to the modeling of entities in the form of types and the collaboration between them. In some cases, object-oriented programming introduces or causes inefficiencies, and aspect-oriented programming helps in filling these gaps. The aim of Aspect-Oriented Programming (AOP) is not to replace Object-Oriented Programming (OOP), but to complement it, allowing you to create clearer and better structured programs. Gregor Kiczales, one of the founders of AOP, said (an extract from `http://www.cs.ubc.ca/~gregor/ papers/kiczales-ECOOP1997-AOP.pdf`) "We have found many programming problems for which neither procedural nor object-oriented programming techniques are sufficient to clearly capture some of the important design decisions the program must implement. This forces the implementation of those design decisions to be scattered throughout the code, resulting in tangled code that is excessively difficult to develop and maintain." Neither aspect-oriented programming nor object-oriented programming can make up for a bad design: The first assumption is that a software system is well-designed. There is no solution for a badly designed system, and also none for a badly implemented system. There is only one good strategy: to change it. The difference between a good and a bad design is the capacity to evolve and adapt to new requirements without being twisted. Object-oriented programming, supported by aspect-oriented programming, helps designers and developers in this direction.

What this book covers

Chapter 1 introduces the ideas that led to Aspect-Oriented Programming. An overview of main concepts of AOP is used to describe components and features provided by Spring AOP, while a set of concise yet clear examples lets the reader discover what can actually be done with AOP.

Chapter 2 describes in detail the fundamentals of AOP in Spring, presenting interfaces and classes introduced in early 1.x versions of the framework. This chapter shows how to use AOP programmatically, to let the reader discover the basis of Spring AOP and the components that implement Aspect-Oriented Programming in Spring.

Chapter 3 explains how the weaving of AOP components is done using the proxy pattern and JDK or CGLIB implementations. It describes the purpose of proxies and how to use them effectively. Some practical examples show how to use the proxies programmatically, with annotations and with XML; they explain the ProxyFactoryBean and how to make the programmer's work easier with AutoProxy. The chapter describes also some smart techniques on target sources.

Chapter 4 explains how Spring AOP is supported by AspectJ. Configuration activity is made simpler, more flexible and more powerful, thanks to annotations and the syntax of AspectJ on pointcuts (without which those costructs would not be available). All examples show how to use AspectJ with both annotations and XML. The chapter contains practical recipes for specific cases, such as the injection of dependencies on domain objects, the management of aspects' priority, the use of different life cycles for Aspects and how to use Load Time Weaving. The chapter ends with some strategies on how to choose different AOP approaches to fulfil specific requirements.

Chapter 5 describes the design alternatives that can be implemented using AOP. These alternatives are solutions for common requirements: concurrency, caching, and security. Using AOP, they can be achieved in a very elegant and easy way, being at the same time totally transparent for the system where they are applied.

Chapter 6 introduces Domain-Driven Development as a alternative way to design applications. The prototype example presented in this chapter is a typical Three-Layer application, where DDD is used for design and AOP is used to inject the dependencies on domain objects. iBatis is used for persistence to the database.

Chapter 7 completes the prototype application started in Chapter 6, showing the application layer and the user interface. The latter is implemented with Spring MVC using annotations. Integration and unit tests are used to verify the correctness of the classes; DBUnit is used to test persistence classes, while some Mock classes are used to test the UI. The chapter contains the configurations for the prototype infrastructure, including autentication and authorization with Spring Security and the JUnit 4.5 test suite.

Chapter 8 describes the development tools needed to include Spring AOP and AspectJ in the Eclipse IDE. The reader can find here detailed istructions on how to configure Eclipse with the plug-ins for Spring and for the AspectJ Development Tool, and how to install the PostgreSQL database and the Apache Tomcat servlet engine. All installation procedures are described for the three main operating systems: Ubuntu Linux, Apple Mac OS X, and Microsoft Windows XP.

What you need for this book

The book requires a basic knowledge of Spring and it's configuration. It needs software like Java Development Kit (JDK) 1.5 or higher, Spring 2.5.6 (at the time of writing on this book), Eclipse (3.4.1 or higher version), Eclipse plug-ins, Tomcat Apache (Tomcat 6.x), and PostgreSQL (version 8.3).

Who this book is for

This book is written for software architects, engineers, and developers that want be able to write applications in a more modular and concise way, without learning AspectJ or using languages other than Java and frameworks other than Spring.

Conventions

In this book, you will find a number of styles of text that distinguish between different kinds of information. Here are some examples of these styles, and an explanation of their meaning.

Code words in text are shown as follows: "We can include other contexts through the use of the `include` directive."

A block of code will be set as follows:

```
package org.springaop.target;
public class ExceptionTarget {

    public void errorMethod() throws Exception {
        throw new Exception("Fake exception");
    }

    public void otherErrorMethod() throws IllegalArgumentException {
        throw new NullPointerException("Other Fake exception");
    }

}
```

When we wish to draw your attention to a particular part of a code block, the relevant lines or items will be made bold:

```
package java.lang.reflect;
public interface InvocationHandler {

public Object invoke(Object proxy, Method method, Object[] args)
    throws Throwable;
}
```

Any command-line input and output is written as follows:

java -javaagent:<path_on_your_machine>/spring-framework-X.X/lib/aspectj/ aspectjweaver.jar

<package>.<yourclass>.Main

New terms and **important words** are introduced in a bold-type font. Words that you see on the screen, in menus or dialog boxes for example, appear in our text like this: "clicking the **Next** button moves you to the next screen".

 Warnings or important notes appear in a box like this.

 Tips and tricks appear like this.

Reader feedback

Feedback from our readers is always welcome. Let us know what you think about this book, what you liked or may have disliked. Reader feedback is important for us to develop titles that you really get the most out of.

To send us general feedback, simply drop an email to feedback@packtpub.com, making sure to mention the book title in the subject of your message.

If there is a book that you need and would like to see us publish, please send us a note in the **SUGGEST A TITLE** form on www.packtpub.com or email suggest@packtpub.com.

If there is a topic that you have expertise in and you are interested in either writing or contributing to a book, see our author guide on www.packtpub.com/authors.

Customer support

Now that you are the proud owner of a Packt book, we have a number of things to help you to get the most from your purchase.

Downloading the example code for the book

Visit http://www.packtpub.com/files/code/4022_Code.zip to directly download the example code.

The downloadable files contain instructions on how to use them.

Errata

Although we have taken every care to ensure the accuracy of our contents, mistakes do happen. If you find a mistake in one of our books—maybe a mistake in text or code—we would be grateful if you would report this to us. By doing this you can save other readers from frustration, and help to improve subsequent versions of this book. If you find any errata, report them by visiting http://www.packtpub.com/support, selecting your book, clicking on the **let us know** link, and entering the details of your errata. Once your errata are verified, your submission will be accepted and the errata added to the list of existing errata. The existing errata can be viewed by selecting your title from http://www.packtpub.com/support.

Piracy

Piracy of copyright material on the Internet is an ongoing problem across all media. At Packt, we take the protection of our copyright and licenses very seriously. If you come across any illegal copies of our works in any form on the Internet, please provide the location address or web site name immediately so we can pursue a remedy.

Please contact us at `copyright@packtpub.com` with a link to the suspected pirated material.

We appreciate your help in protecting our authors, and our ability to bring you valuable content.

Questions

You can contact us at `questions@packtpub.com` if you are having a problem with some aspect of the book, and we will do our best to address it.

1

Understanding AOP Concepts

This chapter presents an overview of Aspect-Oriented Programming concepts, and explains their capabilities and features. Here is a brief outline of the topics covered in this chapter:

- Limits of Object-Oriented Programming
- The AOP solutions
- Spring AOP components
- Spring AOP 2.5

In this chapter we will see what the designing and realization process of an application or software system consists of.

We have to stop and think about the problems that we will see, beginning from the designing phase: how to structure the application, what are the problems in the implementation phase if we use only object-oriented programming, and in which forms they show themselves. We will also see how aspect-oriented programming can support object-oriented programming to solve problems in the implementation phase. We will finally see what Spring provides to allow us to use aspect-oriented programming with **Inversion of Control (IoC)**.

If we use a method such as the **Extreme Programming**, we iteratively focus hard on the functionalities and improve them following the clients' feedback.

Therefore, who does what is described so that the functionalities that the system provides to the user are clear.

After having found these entities, we model them as classes that contain data and have behavior.

To do this, we use some features of the object-oriented languages, such as inheritance, polymorphism, encapsulation, and interfaces, to create a model that helps us solve the domain problem in the simplest way possible.

Drawing, structuring, and building software systems in this way is now considered a common practice. Nevertheless, there are some inefficiencies that emerge at the moment of realizing the project. In fact, however accurately the design may have been made with highly cohesive classes and low coupling, there are still some situations where we have to make compromises.

Limits of object-oriented programming

The object-oriented paradigm provided the concepts and the right instruments for the creation of complex programs and had a great impact on the development of new disciplines in the domain of software design. In this sense, both engineering and software design disciplines developed greatly. Particularly important has been the development of the so-called **Design Patterns** that allow a certain degree of systemization of the activity of software design and development.

The concept of a class that includes data and functions that change its values allows for the realization of cohesive and independent entities (high cohesion, low coupling). This in turn realizes the required business functionalities through the exchange of messages.

Using design patterns and object-oriented programming, the development of an application can be realized by dividing the activities into independent groups of functionalities. In fact, as soon as the interfaces of every entity of the application have been defined, their implementation can be realized independently by different groups of developers.

Another advantage is the reliability offered by the object. If we consider that the access to an object's data and its modification can happen only by means of the methods that it exposes through its interface, no user can unpredictably corrupt this data and make that object's state inconsistent.

Finally, the concept of inheritance allows the definition of new classes that extend the functionality of the classes from which they derive. In this sense, we obtain the extendibility and the reuse of software.

After the advantages of the new instruments given by the object-oriented programming paradigm, we have to consider the limits that occurred in practical application.

The main problem is to manage to control the complexity. To face it, we will have to choose modularization: "divide et impera", according to the Latin maxim.

If architects look at the previous projects on which they have worked, they will notice that a common feature is the constant increase in the systems' complexity.

Separating the functionalities that have to be implemented into simpler and more manageable modules helps to control the complexity. Software systems are conceptually complex by their very nature, and increasing their complexity in the implementation means increasing the expense and the probability of its failure.

The code needed to integrate a complex implementation is expensive. The cost would be even higher if new features are required. In fact, those features imply deep changes in several parts of the implementation.

If we didn't take the way of modularization and simplification, we would have a monolithic system that would be unmanageable to modify.

First of all, we have to single out the modules that will implement the core business that justifies the design and the implementation of the software. Once we have completely understood how to implement the core business, we can think about designing the rest of the application so that the core business supports the system's users.

We are used to take the best practice of dividing the application into logical layers (presentation layer, business layer, and data layer). But, there are some functionalities that cross these layers transversally. They are named **crosscutting concerns.**

A crosscutting concern is, therefore, an independent entity that transversally crosses other functionalities of software. Take a look at the following figure:

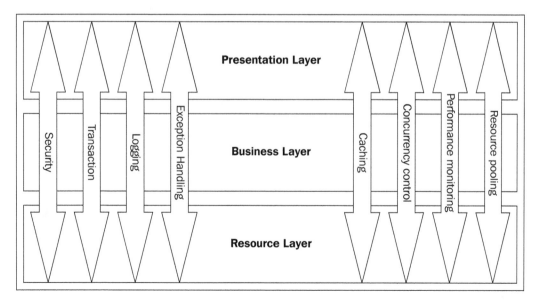

The most common crosscutting concerns are: security, logging, transactions management, caching, performance checking, concurrency control, and exception management.

These crosscutting concerns, if implemented only with object-oriented programming, realize a bad matching between the core business and the modules that implement its functionalities. We are forced to deal with the implementation of these transversal functionalities into various modules, moreover, adding other transversal modules or modifying the existing ones. We are also forced to modify the code in which these modules are used. This is owing to the undesired, but necessary, matching that the object-oriented implementation unavoidably brings with it.

The followings graphs (extracts from `http://www.parc.com/research/projects/aspectj/downloads/SDWest2002-BetterJavaWithAJ.ppt`), show the code of Servlet Engine Tomcat 4 divided in modules:

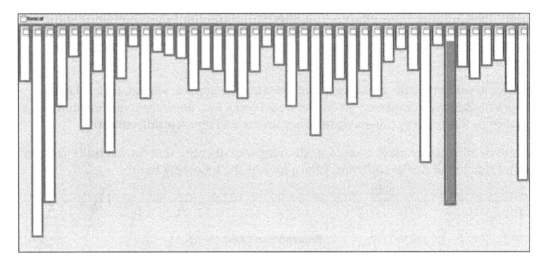

In the figure above, XML parsing fits in one module.

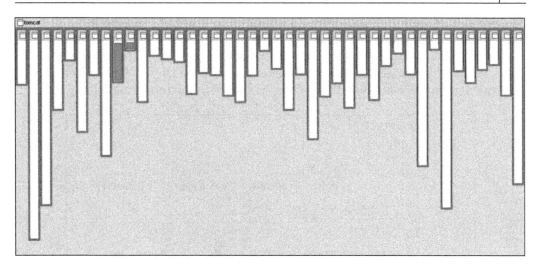

In the figure above, the URL pattern matching fits in two modules.

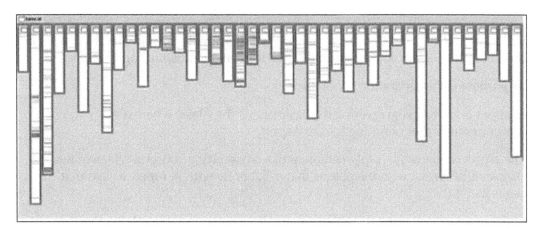

In the figure above, logging is scattered in too many modules.

This figure shows the points where Tomcat classes' logging functionalities are called (underlined in red). As we can see, they are scattered in the points of the modules where the functionality is required.

The problem of scattering code derived from the crosscutting concerns in object-oriented programming arises due to its transversality to the crosscutting concerns, which is implemented in the classes. More correctly, the crosscutting concerns should be analysed as a third dimension of the design. Whereas in the implementation there are two dimensions, as shown in the following figure:

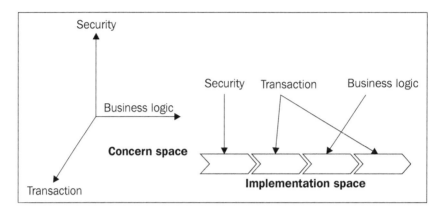

In these situations, aspect-oriented programming provides support to object-oriented programming for uncoupling modules that implement crosscutting concerns.

Its purpose is the separation of concerns.

In object-oriented programming the basic unit is the **Class,** whereas in aspect-oriented programming it's the **Aspect.**

The aspect contains the implementation of a crosscutting concern, which in the class should coexist with the objects that collaborate with it, for each class that needs it.

In this way, we can write the object-oriented classes without involving the crosscutting concerns in the implementation.

So, classes can freely evolve without taking into account this dependency.

The functionalities provided by the crosscutting concerns in the aspects will be applied to the objects through an aspect weaver or through some proxy classes. We will deal with this in the later chapters.

Now we will see how the problems we exposed, arise in the code.

Code scattering

Code scattering appears when the functionality is scattered because it's implemented in several modules.

There are two sorts of code scattering:

- Blocks of duplicated code (that is, the same code appears in different modules)
- Blocks of complementary code, and different modules implementing complementary parts of the concern (for example, in Access Control, one module performs authentication and a second performs authorization)

Let's see the following code to illustrate the cases in which the code is duplicated in different modules:

The Info interface is implemented in the same way by two different classes, ScatteringA and ScatteringB. Therefore, this is a useless duplication of code.

```
public interface Info {

    public String getName();
    public Date getCreationDate();
}


public class ScatteringA implements Info{

    public ScatteringA(String name, String author){
        creation = new Date();
        this.name = name;
        this.autor = author;
    }

    public ScatteringA(Date creation, String name, String author){
        this.creation = creation;
        this.name = name;
        this.autor = author;
    }

    public Date getCreationDate() {
        return (Date)creation.clone();
    }

    public String getName() {
        return name;
    }
```

```
    public String getAutor() {
          return autor;
    }

    private Date creation;
    private String name;
    private String autor;
}


public class ScatteringB implements Info{

    public ScatteringB(String name, String address){
          creation = new Date();
          this.name = name;
          this.address = address;
    }

    public ScatteringB(Date creation, String name, String address){
          this.creation = creation;
          this.name = name;
          this.address = address;
    }

    public Date getCreationDate() {
          return (Date)creation.clone();
    }

    public String getName() {
          return name;
    }

    public String getAddress() {
          return address;
    }

    private Date creation;
    private String name;
    private String address;
}
```

Code tangling

Code tangling occurs when a module has to manage several concerns at the same time such as logging, exception handling, security, caching, and more or when a module has elements of the implementation of other concerns inside.

In order to show what we mean by code tangling, let's look at the following code:

```
public class TanglingListUserController extends MultiActionController{

    public ModelAndView list(HttpServletRequest req,
                HttpServletResponse res) throws Exception {

        //logging
        log(req);

        // authorization
        if(req.isUserInRole("admin")){

            String username = req.getRemoteUser();

            List users ;

            //exception handling
            try {
                    //cache with authorization
                    users = cache.get(Integer.valueOf(
conf.getValue("numberOfUsers")), username);

            } catch (Exception e) {
                    users = usersManager.getUsers();
            }

            return new ModelAndView("usersTemplate", "users",
users);
        }else{

            return new ModelAndView("notAllowed");
        }
    }

    private void log(HttpServletRequest req) {
        StringBuilder sb = new StringBuilder("remoteAddress:");
        sb.append(req.getRemoteAddr());
        sb.append("username:");
        sb.append(req.getRemoteUser());
        log.fine(sb.toString());
    }

    ...
}
```

In this Spring MultiActionController, we can see how many features are managed: logging, authorisation, exception management, and caching.

In spite of dealing with just the presentation of a list of users, this controller has to do many things, and the consequence is that other concerns are heavier in its implementation. That is code tangling.

The AOP solution

We have seen that with an object-oriented system, code tangling and code scattering can occur. This can cause the system to have duplicate code and functionalities not being clear and plain. Evident problems with the implementation of further requirements arise, with modules strongly coupled in the implementation.

In the previous situations, the object-oriented system can't be of any help because the following effects occur:

- **Difficult evolution**: A module's implementation is coupled to other functionalities.
- **Poor quality**: In the `TanglingListUserController` example, if a problem arises, it's not even clear what the module's main functionality is.
- **Code not reusable**: If the implementation involves several concerns, it won't be suitable for other scenarios.
- **Productivity**: Scattered implementations move the problem's main focus to the periphery where the implementations are.
- **Traceability**: Code scattering functionality is implemented at several points. To have a hold on it, you need to check all the modules in which the implementation is spread.

Aspect-oriented programming allows:

- The modularization of crosscutting concerns by its constructs
- The uncoupling of the modules
- Using aspects, the removal of dependence of a crosscutting concern from the modules that use it

Now let's see practically what AOP provides to overcome the gaps in object-oriented programming highlighted so far in the book, and what are its main concepts.

Let's see who are the main actors that enable the aspect-oriented programming, implement the crosscutting concerns in the aspects, and define with other actors the points and the classes on which these crosscutting concerns are applied.

In the following figure, we see the normal interactions between objects:

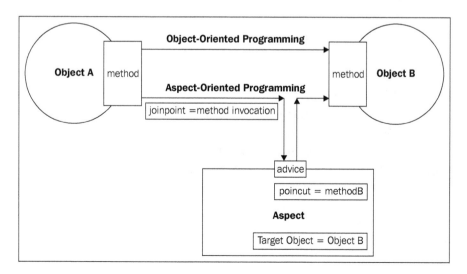

In object-oriented programming, classes cooperate by calling mutually public methods and exchanging messages.

Crosscutting concerns are placed in the implementations of the classes A, B, and C, and this leads to the problems previously explained such as code tangling, code scattering, and so on.

The following figure conceptually compares the execution flow of the invocation of a method in the case of OOP and AOP:

In the case of object-oriented programming, where the crosscutting concerns are included into the classes' implementations, Object A in its method A invokes method B on Object B. This is, apart from exceptions, the normal flow of messages' exchange between two objects that interact. The cross interactions are called back and used just in these two methods because there isn't any other way to act.

In the flow with aspect-oriented programming, the crosscutting functionalities are extracted from the object-oriented implementations and applied as advices where they are actually useful. This is because they are applied on the flow where they really have to be carried out, that is by the pointcuts and on the target object.

The whole of the advice, the pointcut, the target object, and the joinpoint, make an aspect.

Now let's introduce the AOP terms denoting the components that take part in the implementation, which are partially pictured in the previous figure.

- **Aspect**: Corresponds to the class in object-oriented programming. It's the crosscutting functionality.
- **Joinpoint**: This is the application point of the aspect. It is a point of the execution of a program such as the invocation of a constructor or the execution of a method or the management of an exception (WHEN).
- **Advice**: This is the action an aspect performs at a certain joinpoint.
- Advices can be "around", "before", and "after".
- **Pointcut**: This is the expression for the joinpoint's selection, for instance a method's execution with a certain signature (WHERE).
- **Introduction**: This is the declaration of methods or additional fields on the object to which the aspect will be applied. It allows the introduction of new interfaces and implementations on the objects.
- **Target object**: This is the module (Object) to which the aspect will be applied.
- **Weaving**: This is the linking action between the aspect and the objects to which advices must be applied.

  This action may be performed at the editing phase using an AspectJ compiler, or at runtime.

  If a runtime action is carried out, an AOP Proxy is used to implement the contracts that the aspect has to respect.

Types of advice:

- **Before advice**: This is an advice that executes before a joinpoint, but which does not have the ability to prevent execution flow proceeding to the joinpoint.

- **After returning advice**: An advice to be executed after a joinpoint completes normally.

- **Throws advice**: This is an advice to be executed if a method exits by throwing an exception.

- **After (finally) advice**: This advice is to be executed regardless of the means by which a joinpoint exits.

- **Around advice**: This advice can perform custom behavior before and after the method invocation. It is also responsible for choosing whether to proceed to the joinpoint, or to cut short the advised method execution by returning its own return value or throwing an exception.

In the case of Aspect-Oriented Programming in the earlier image, taking into account that the joinpoint is the invocation of methods and that the joinpoint is the method called **methodB**, the aspect executes the crosscutting concern included into the advice when **methodB** is invoked on the target, **Object B**. This kind of interception before **methodB** is that of a Before Advice.

What Spring provides in terms of AOP

The main aim of Spring AOP is to allow the realization of JEE functionalities in the simplest manner and without being intrusive. With this aim, it allows the use of a subset of AOP functionalities in a simple and intuitive way (introduced since version 1.x, and in version 2.x with new integrations with AspectJ).

In order to achieve this aim, since version 1.x, Spring has implemented the specifications of the AOP alliance. This is a joint effort between representatives of many open-source AOP projects, including Rod Johnson of Spring, to define a standard set of interfaces for AOP implementations.

In Spring AOP, an aspect is represented by an instance of a class that implements the Advisor interface. There are two subinterfaces of `Advisor`: `IntroductionAdvisor` and `PointcutAdvisor`. The `PointcutAdvisor` interface is implemented by all Advisors that use pointcuts to control the applicability of advice to joinpoints.

In Spring, introductions are treated as special kinds of advice. Using the `IntroductionAdvisor` interface, you can control those classes to which an introduction applies.

The core of Spring AOP is based around proxies. There are two ways of using proxies: programmatic modality and declarative modality.

The former consists of using a ProxyFactory to create a proxy of the class on which you want to apply an aspect. After creating the proxy, you use the ProxyFactory to weave all the aspects you want to use on the object.

The ProxyFactory class controls the weaving and proxy creation process in Spring.

Using the ProxyFactory class, you control which aspects you want to weave into the proxy. You can weave only an aspect, that is, advice combined with a pointcut.

However, in some cases you want an advice to apply to the invocation of all methods in a class, not just a selection. For this reason, the ProxyFactory class provides the addAdvice() method. Internally, addAdvice() wraps the advice you pass it in an instance of DefaultPointcutAdvisor, and configures it with a pointcut that includes all methods by default.

Programmatic way

This is an example of class that implements the MethodBeforeAdvice to perform a crosscutting functionality before the method of the target class.

Before advice

Before advice is performed before the invocation of the method.

Let us see an example that shows the usage of before advice, with a class that implements the MethodBeforeAdvice, and has a main method for testing.

```
package org.springaop.chapter.one;
import java.lang.reflect.Method;

import org.springaop.target.Hello;
import org.springframework.aop.MethodBeforeAdvice;
import org.springframework.aop.framework.ProxyFactory;

public class BeforeAdvice implements MethodBeforeAdvice{

    public static void main(String[] args) {

            //target class
            Hello target = new Hello();

            // create the proxy
            ProxyFactory pf = new ProxyFactory();
```

```
        // add advice
        pf.addAdvice(new BeforeAdvice());

        // setTarget
        pf.setTarget(target);

        Hello proxy = (Hello) pf.getProxy();
        proxy.greeting();
    }

    public void before(Method method, Object[] args, Object target)
                throws Throwable {

        System.out.println("Good morning");
    }
}

public class Hello {

    public void greeting(){
        System.out.println("reader");
    }
}
```

The result will be:

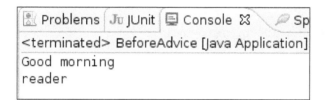

After returning advice

After returning advice is performed after the invocation of the method.

```
package org.springaop.chapter.one;
import java.lang.reflect.Method;

import org.springaop.target.Hello;
import org.springframework.aop.AfterReturningAdvice;
import org.springframework.aop.framework.ProxyFactory;

public class AfterRetuningAdvice implements AfterReturningAdvice {

    public static void main(String[] args) {
```

```
        // target class
        Hello target = new Hello();

        // create the proxy
        ProxyFactory pf = new ProxyFactory();

        // add advice
        pf.addAdvice(new AfterRetuningAdvice());

        // setTarget
        pf.setTarget(target);

        Hello proxy = (Hello) pf.getProxy();
        proxy.greeting();
    }


    public void afterReturning(Object returnValue, Method method,
                Object[] args, Object target) throws Throwable {

        System.out.println(",this is a afterReturningAdvice
message");
    }

}

public class Hello {

    public void greeting(){
        System.out.println("reader");
    }
}
```

The result will be:

Around advice

This is the `Hello` target class on which we want to apply an around advice. It is called before the method and controls its invocation.

```
public class Hello {

    public void greeting(){
            System.out.println("reader");
    }
}
```

This is the advice that must be applied around the performed method; as we can see that the invocation of the method occurs with `invocation.proceed`.

```
package org.springaop.chapter.one;

import org.aopalliance.intercept.MethodInterceptor;
import org.aopalliance.intercept.MethodInvocation;

public class MethodDecorator implements MethodInterceptor{

    public Object invoke(MethodInvocation invocation) throws Throwable
{
            System.out.print("Hello ");
        Object retVal = invocation.proceed();
        System.out.println("this is aop !");
        return retVal;

    }
}
```

This is the class where, through the `ProxyFactory`, we give the advice to apply. But, in the case of the `MethodDecorator`, it is an around advice.

```
package org.springaop.chapter.one;

import org.springaop.target.Hello;
import org.springframework.aop.framework.ProxyFactory;

public class AroundAdvice {

    public static void main(String[] args) {

            //target class
            Hello target = new Hello();

            // create the proxy
            ProxyFactory pf = new ProxyFactory();

            // add advice
```

```
        pf.addAdvice(new MethodDecorator());

        // setTarget
        pf.setTarget(target);

        Hello proxy = (Hello) pf.getProxy();
        proxy.greeting();
    }
}
```

The result will be:

After throwing advice

This advice is performed only if the method on which the advice is applied throws an exception.

This is a class that intentionally throws an exception in every method; the exceptions are of different types.

```
package org.springaop.target;

public class ExceptionTarget {

    public void errorMethod() throws Exception {
        throw new Exception("Fake exception");
    }

    public void otherErrorMethod() throws IllegalArgumentException {
        throw new NullPointerException("Other Fake exception");
    }

}
```

This is the code to try it:

```
package org.springaop.chapter.one;

import java.lang.reflect.Method;

import org.springaop.target.ExceptionTarget;
import org.springframework.aop.ThrowsAdvice;
```

```java
import org.springframework.aop.framework.ProxyFactory;

public class ThrowsAdviceClass implements ThrowsAdvice {

    public static void main(String[] args) {
            //target class
            ExceptionTarget errorBean = new ExceptionTarget();

            // create the proxy
            ProxyFactory pf = new ProxyFactory();

            // add advice
            pf.addAdvice(new ThrowsAdviceClass());

            // setTarget
            pf.setTarget(errorBean);

            ExceptionTarget proxy = (ExceptionTarget) pf.getProxy();

            try {
                    proxy.errorMethod();
            } catch (Exception ignored) {

            }

            try {
                    proxy.otherErrorMethod();
            } catch (Exception ignored) {

            }
    }

    public void afterThrowing(Exception ex) throws Throwable {
            System.out.println("+++");
            System.out.println("Exception Capture:"+ex.getClass().
getName());
            System.out.println("+++\n");
    }

    public void afterThrowing(Method method, Object[] args,
Object target, NullPointerException ex) throws Throwable {
            System.out.println("+++");
            System.out.println("NullPointerException Capture: "+ex.
getClass().getName());
            System.out.println("Method: " + method.getName());
            System.out.println("+++\n");
    }
}
```

The result will be:

```
 Problems  Ju JUnit  Console ⌗    Spring Explorer  Spring AOP Event Trace                      ⬛  ✖  ✖
<terminated> ThrowsAdviceExample [Java Application] /usr/local/jdk1.6.0_07/bin/java (Sep 13, 2008 2:22:25 PM)
+++
Exception Capture:java.lang.Exception
+++

+++
NullPointerException Capture: java.lang.NullPointerException
Method: otherErrorMethod
```

The old Spring XML way

Here we will see how to use the examples described previously, configuring the classes as Spring beans declared in XML file and using a `ProxyFactoryBean`.

```xml
<bean id="helloMatch" class="org.springframework.aop.framework.
ProxyFactoryBean">
        <property name="target">
                <bean class="org.springaop.Hello"/>
        </property>
        <property name="interceptorNames">
                <list>
                        <idref bean="helloBeforeAdvice"/>
                        <idref bean="helloAfterRetuningAdvicee"/>
                </list>
        </property>
</bean>

    <bean id="helloBeforeAdvice" class="org.springaop.advice.
BeforeAdvice"/>

    <bean id="helloAfterRetuningAdvice" class="org.springaop.advice.
AfterRetuningAdvice"/>
```

In the configuration of the example, we can see how a `helloMatch` is defined, which is in fact a `ProxyFactoryBean` that puts together the target object on which the crosscutting concern has to be applied, and the list of advice that contains the crosscutting functionalities. In this case, two of the advices are used in the programmatic modality and are applied at the target object as a reference in the list of interceptors that can be applied on the object.

It is an implementation of Spring `FactoryBean` that allows you to specify a bean to target and provides a set of advice and advisors for that bean that are eventually merged into an AOP proxy. Because you can use both advisor and advice with the `ProxyFactoryBean`, you can configure not only the advice declaratively, but the pointcuts as well.

In both modalities Spring uses internally two sorts of proxy: JDK proxy or CGLIB proxy.

The concept of an Advisor principally concerns Spring 1.x. We will see later how it can benefit by the syntax of the pointcuts of AspectJ.

From the 2.x version onwards, there is a closer integration or configuration based on AspectJ and its syntax, either through annotations or through schema-based configuration. In any case, it's always possible to use AOP in the classic way as in the 1.x version.

Spring is first of all an `IoC` Container, and so it allows using the components that implement the AOP as a simple bean, assembling them and obtaining the result of the AOP weaver through Proxy classes, as we previously described.

Instead, AspectJ provides a static implementation of AOP that is produced at compile time. Spring provides a dynamic implementation of AOP, as it is implemented through the creation and the use of proxy classes that permit the implementation of a chain of interceptors.

Obviously, a static implementation provides better performance, but requires greater knowledge and a compiler, whereas the dynamic implementation is easier to use and more accessible. It can be disabled from configuration and never requires anything different from the usual Java compiler.

Spring permits only method execution to be used as a joinpoint. So we can't use with Spring AOP all the features of AOP, but we can do so with AspectJ called by Spring. For example, we must use the support of AspectJ if we want to use as a joinpoint:

- The invocations of constructors
- Access to the domains of objects with the setter and getter
- The initialization of an object
- The initialization of an object with a calling `super()`
- The execution inside a class with `this()`
- The calling of a method

Therefore, the aspect can be normal Java classes with the annotation `@Aspect`, or configured using configuration XML.

The advices are seen as interceptors that maintain a chain of interceptors around the joinpoint.

Pointcuts are performed according to the matching of the AspectJ pointcut expression language, or according to regular expressions following the rules present since Spring 1.x.

This introduction clearly shows that Spring has a simplified pattern of the whole set of AOP features so that AOP can be used with no special editing and alterations to the bytecode. This would be necessary together with the use of AspectJ, if we wanted all the features of AOP as we will see in the rest of this book.

AOP with IoC in Spring 2.5

Now we will see what Spring 2.5 offers compared to the 1.x version.

AspectJ annotations

Now let's see some introductory examples of using the syntax of AspectJ with annotations; the purpose is to have the same sorts of advice that we saw in the programmatic examples.

```
<beans xmlns="http://www.springframework.org/schema/beans"
xmlns:xsi="http://www.w3.org/2001/XMLSchema-instance"
xmlns:aop="http://www.springframework.org/schema/aop"
xmlns:p="http://www.springframework.org/schema/p"
xsi:schemaLocation="http://www.springframework.org/schema/beans
http://www.springframework.org/schema/beans/spring-beans-2.5.xsd
http://www.springframework.org/schema/aop
http://www.springframework.org/schema/aop/spring-aop-2.5.xsd">

    <aop:aspectj-autoproxy/>
    ...
</beans>
```

In the configuration, if we use a tag `<aop:aspectj-autoproxy/>`, Spring prepares autoproxy for the classic mode that uses AspectJ annotations and we define two beans to check the annotations' behavior.

This is the body of the Target Class that we will use in the examples.

```
public class Hello {

    public void greeting(){
            System.out.println(label);
    }

    private String label = "reader";
```

```java
    public void setLabel(String label) {
        this.label = label;
    }
}
```

Before advice

Now we see how to use before advice with the annotations.

```java
package org.springaop.chapter.one.annotation.before;

import org.aspectj.lang.annotation.Aspect;
import org.aspectj.lang.annotation.Before;

@Aspect
public class BeforeAspect {

    @Before("execution(* greeting(..))")
    public void beforeGreeting() {

        System.out.println("Good morning ");
    }
}
```

```xml
<beans xmlns="http://www.springframework.org/schema/beans"
xmlns:xsi="http://www.w3.org/2001/XMLSchema-instance"
xmlns:aop="http://www.springframework.org/schema/aop"
xmlns:p="http://www.springframework.org/schema/p"
xsi:schemaLocation="http://www.springframework.org/schema/beans
http://www.springframework.org/schema/beans/spring-beans-2.5.xsd
http://www.springframework.org/schema/aop
http://www.springframework.org/schema/aop/spring-aop-2.5.xsd">

    <aop:aspectj-autoproxy/>

    <bean id="hello" class="org.springaop.target.Hello" p:
label="writer"/>

    <bean id="before" class="org.springaop.chapter.one.annotation.
before.BeforeAspect"/>

</beans>
```

Result:

```
Problems  JUnit  Console  Spring Explorer  Spring AOP Event Trace
<terminated> Test (1) [Java Application] /usr/local/jdk1.6.0_07/bin/java (Sep 13, 2008 12:47:30 PM)
Sep 13, 2008 12:47:31 PM org.springframework.context.support.AbstractApplicationContext prepareRefresh
INFO: Refreshing org.springframework.context.support.ClassPathXmlApplicationContext@100ab23: display name [o
Sep 13, 2008 12:47:32 PM org.springframework.beans.factory.xml.XmlBeanDefinitionReader loadBeanDefinitions
INFO: Loading XML bean definitions from class path resource [org/springaop/chapter/one/schema/before/applica
Sep 13, 2008 12:47:32 PM org.springframework.context.support.AbstractApplicationContext obtainFreshBeanFacto
INFO: Bean factory for application context [org.springframework.context.support.ClassPathXmlApplicationConte
Sep 13, 2008 12:47:32 PM org.springframework.beans.factory.support.DefaultListableBeanFactory preInstantiate
INFO: Pre-instantiating singletons in org.springframework.beans.factory.support.DefaultListableBeanFactory@3
Good morning
writer
```

After returning advice

The following code explains how to use after returning advice with the annotations:

```
package org.springaop.chapter.one.annotation.after.returning;

import org.aspectj.lang.annotation.AfterReturning;
import org.aspectj.lang.annotation.Aspect;

@Aspect
public class AfterReturningAspect {

    @AfterReturning("execution(* greeting(..))")
    public void afterGreeting() {

        System.out.println("this is a aop !");
    }

}

<beans xmlns="http://www.springframework.org/schema/beans"
xmlns:xsi="http://www.w3.org/2001/XMLSchema-instance"
xmlns:aop="http://www.springframework.org/schema/aop"
xmlns:p="http://www.springframework.org/schema/p"
xsi:schemaLocation="http://www.springframework.org/schema/beans
http://www.springframework.org/schema/beans/spring-beans-2.5.xsd
http://www.springframework.org/schema/aop
http://www.springframework.org/schema/aop/spring-aop-2.5.xsd">

    <aop:aspectj-autoproxy/>

    <bean id="hello" class="org.springaop.target.Hello" p:
label="writer"/>

    <bean id="afterReturning" class="org.springaop.chapter.one.
annotation.after.returning.AfterReturningAspect"/>

</beans>
```

Result:

```
Problems  JUnit  Console ☒    Spring Explorer  Spring AOP Event Trace                    ▣  ✖  ✖
<terminated> Test (2) [Java Application] /usr/local/jdk1.6.0_07/bin/java (Sep 13, 2008 12:48:04 PM)
Sep 13, 2008 12:48:04 PM org.springframework.context.support.AbstractApplicationContext prepareRefresh
INFO: Refreshing org.springframework.context.support.ClassPathXmlApplicationContext@100ab23: display name [o
Sep 13, 2008 12:48:04 PM org.springframework.beans.factory.xml.XmlBeanDefinitionReader loadBeanDefinitions
INFO: Loading XML bean definitions from class path resource [org/springaop/chapter/one/schema/after/returnin
Sep 13, 2008 12:48:05 PM org.springframework.context.support.AbstractApplicationContext obtainFreshBeanFacto
INFO: Bean factory for application context [org.springframework.context.support.ClassPathXmlApplicationConte
Sep 13, 2008 12:48:05 PM org.springframework.beans.factory.support.DefaultListableBeanFactory preInstantiate
INFO: Pre-instantiating singletons in org.springframework.beans.factory.support.DefaultListableBeanFactory@4
writer
this is a aop !
```

Around advice

Now we see how to use around advice with the annotations.

```
package org.springaop.chapter.one.annotation.around;

import org.aspectj.lang.ProceedingJoinPoint;
import org.aspectj.lang.annotation.Around;
import org.aspectj.lang.annotation.Aspect;

@Aspect
public class AroundAspect {

    @Around("execution(* greeting(..))")
    public Object aroundGreeting(ProceedingJoinPoint pjp) throws
Throwable {

        System.out.print("Hello ");
        try {
            return pjp.proceed();
        } finally {
            System.out.println("this is around aop !");
        }

    }
}

<beans xmlns="http://www.springframework.org/schema/beans"
xmlns:xsi="http://www.w3.org/2001/XMLSchema-instance"
xmlns:aop="http://www.springframework.org/schema/aop"
xmlns:p="http://www.springframework.org/schema/p"
xsi:schemaLocation="http://www.springframework.org/schema/beans
http://www.springframework.org/schema/beans/spring-beans-2.5.xsd
http://www.springframework.org/schema/aop
http://www.springframework.org/schema/aop/spring-aop-2.5.xsd">

    <aop:aspectj-autoproxy/>

    <bean id="hello" class="org.springaop.target.Hello" p:
label="writer"/>

    <bean id="around" class="org.springaop.chapter.one.annotation.
around.AroundAspect"/>

</beans>
```

Result:

```
 Problems  Ju JUnit   Console ⊠     Spring Explorer   Spring AOP Event Trace          ▦  ✖  ⚒
<terminated> Test (3) [Java Application] /usr/local/jdk1.6.0_07/bin/java (Sep 13, 2008 12:48:42 PM)
Sep 13, 2008 12:48:42 PM org.springframework.context.support.AbstractApplicationContext prepareRefresh
INFO: Refreshing org.springframework.context.support.ClassPathXmlApplicationContext@503429: display name [or
Sep 13, 2008 12:48:42 PM org.springframework.beans.factory.xml.XmlBeanDefinitionReader loadBeanDefinitions
INFO: Loading XML bean definitions from class path resource [org/springaop/chapter/one/schema/around/applica
Sep 13, 2008 12:48:43 PM org.springframework.context.support.AbstractApplicationContext obtainFreshBeanFacto
INFO: Bean factory for application context [org.springframework.context.support.ClassPathXmlApplicationConte
Sep 13, 2008 12:48:43 PM org.springframework.beans.factory.support.DefaultListableBeanFactory preInstantiate
INFO: Pre-instantiating singletons in org.springframework.beans.factory.support.DefaultListableBeanFactory@1
Hello writer
this is around aop !
```

After (finally) advice

The following code explains how to use `after (finally) advice` with the annotations:

```
package org.springaop.chapter.one.annotation.afterfinally;

import org.aspectj.lang.annotation.After;
import org.aspectj.lang.annotation.Aspect;

@Aspect
public class AfterFinallyAspect {

    @After("execution(* greeting(..))")
    public void afterGreeting() {

            System.out.println("this is afterAspect !");
    }
}

<beans xmlns="http://www.springframework.org/schema/beans"
xmlns:xsi="http://www.w3.org/2001/XMLSchema-instance"
xmlns:aop="http://www.springframework.org/schema/aop"
xmlns:p="http://www.springframework.org/schema/p"
xsi:schemaLocation="http://www.springframework.org/schema/beans
http://www.springframework.org/schema/beans/spring-beans-2.5.xsd
http://www.springframework.org/schema/aop
http://www.springframework.org/schema/aop/spring-aop-2.5.xsd">

    <aop:aspectj-autoproxy/>

    <bean id="hello" class="org.springaop.target.Hello" p:
label="writer"/>

    <bean id="afterFinally" class="org.springaop.chapter.one.
annotation.afterfinally.AfterFinallyAspect"/>

</beans>
```

Result:

```
Problems  JuJUnit  Console  ⊠    Spring Explorer  Spring AOP Event Trace                    ▦  ✕  ✕
<terminated> Test (4) [Java Application] /usr/local/jdk1.6.0_07/bin/java (Sep 13, 2008 12:49:07 PM)
Sep 13, 2008 12:49:07 PM org.springframework.context.support.AbstractApplicationContext prepareRefresh
INFO: Refreshing org.springframework.context.support.ClassPathXmlApplicationContext@100ab23: display name [
Sep 13, 2008 12:49:07 PM org.springframework.beans.factory.xml.XmlBeanDefinitionReader loadBeanDefinitions
INFO: Loading XML bean definitions from class path resource [org/springaop/chapter/one/schema/after/applicat
Sep 13, 2008 12:49:08 PM org.springframework.context.support.AbstractApplicationContext obtainFreshBeanFacto
INFO: Bean factory for application context [org.springframework.context.support.ClassPathXmlApplicationConte
Sep 13, 2008 12:49:08 PM org.springframework.beans.factory.support.DefaultListableBeanFactory preInstantiate
INFO: Pre-instantiating singletons in org.springframework.beans.factory.support.DefaultListableBeanFactory@c
writer
this is afterAspect !
```

After throwing advice

For the after throwing advice example, we're going to use a target class different from Hello, in order to be able to trigger exceptions deliberately.

This is the body of the exception target:

```
package org.springaop.target;

public class ExceptionTarget {

    public void errorMethod() throws Exception {
        throw new Exception("Fake exception");
    }

    public void otherErrorMethod() throws IllegalArgumentException {
        throw new NullPointerException("Other Fake exception");
    }
}
```

Example after throwing:

```
package org.springaop.chapter.one.annotation.throwsadvice;

import org.aspectj.lang.annotation.AfterThrowing;
import org.aspectj.lang.annotation.Aspect;

@Aspect
public class AfterThrowingAspect {

    @AfterThrowing("execution(* errorMethod(..))")
    public void afterGreeting() {

            System.out.println("+++");
            System.out.println("Exception !");
            System.out.println("+++");
    }
}
```

This is the body of the ExceptionTest class:

```
package org.springaop.chapter.one.annotation.throwsadvice;

import org.springaop.target.ExceptionTarget;
import org.springframework.context.ApplicationContext;
import org.springframework.context.support.
ClassPathXmlApplicationContext;

public class ExceptionTest {

    public static void main(String[] args) {

        String[] paths = {"org/springaop/conf/applicationContext.
xml"};
        ApplicationContext ctx = new ClassPathXmlApplicationContext(
paths);

        ExceptionTarget exceptiontarget = (ExceptionTarget)ctx.getBe
an("exceptionTarget");
        try {
            exceptiontarget.errorMethod();
        } catch (Exception ignored) {

        }
    }
}

<beans xmlns="http://www.springframework.org/schema/beans"
xmlns:xsi="http://www.w3.org/2001/XMLSchema-instance"
xmlns:aop="http://www.springframework.org/schema/aop"
xmlns:p="http://www.springframework.org/schema/p"
xsi:schemaLocation="http://www.springframework.org/schema/beans
http://www.springframework.org/schema/beans/spring-beans-2.5.xsd
http://www.springframework.org/schema/aop
http://www.springframework.org/schema/aop/spring-aop-2.5.xsd">

    <aop:aspectj-autoproxy/>

    <bean id="exceptionTarget" class="org.springaop.target.
ExceptionTarget"/>

    <bean id="throws" class="org.springaop.chapter.one.annotation.
throwsadvice.AfterThrowingAspect"/>

</beans>
```

The result will be:

```
Problems  JUnit  Console ⚛  Spring Explorer  Spring AOP Event Trace        ▣  ✕  ✕
<terminated> TestException [Java Application] /usr/local/jdk1.6.0_07/bin/java (Sep 13, 2008 12:55:05 PM)
Sep 13, 2008 12:55:05 PM org.springframework.context.support.AbstractApplicationContext prepareRefresh
INFO: Refreshing org.springframework.context.support.ClassPathXmlApplicationContext@100ab23: display name [
Sep 13, 2008 12:55:05 PM org.springframework.beans.factory.xml.XmlBeanDefinitionReader loadBeanDefinitions
INFO: Loading XML bean definitions from class path resource [org/springaop/chapter/one/schema/throwsadvice/
Sep 13, 2008 12:55:06 PM org.springframework.context.support.AbstractApplicationContext obtainFreshBeanFact
INFO: Bean factory for application context [org.springframework.context.support.ClassPathXmlApplicationConte
Sep 13, 2008 12:55:06 PM org.springframework.beans.factory.support.DefaultListableBeanFactory preInstantiate
INFO: Pre-instantiating singletons in org.springframework.beans.factory.support.DefaultListableBeanFactory@1
+++
Exception !
+++
```

Schema-based configuration

Now let's see some introductory examples for schema-based configuration, using the code of the classes of the examples used with the annotations, and with the same output results.

Before advice

The following before advice example example explains how to use the before advice with XML Schema configuration:

```
package org.springaop.aspects.schema;

public class SpringAopAspectBeforeExample {

    public void beforeGreeting() {

        System.out.println("Good morning ");
    }
}


<beans xmlns="http://www.springframework.org/schema/beans"
    xmlns:xsi="http://www.w3.org/2001/XMLSchema-instance" xmlns:
p="http://www.springframework.org/schema/p"
    xmlns:aop="http://www.springframework.org/schema/aop"
    xsi:schemaLocation="http://www.springframework.org/schema/beans
http://www.springframework.org/schema/beans/spring-beans-2.5.xsd
http://www.springframework.org/schema/aop
http://www.springframework.org/schema/aop/spring-aop.xsd">

    <aop:config>
        <aop:aspect ref="before">
```

```
        <aop:before method="beforeGreeting" pointcut="execution(*
greeting(..))" />
        </aop:aspect>
    </aop:config>

    <bean id="hello" class="org.springaop.target.Hello" p:
label="writer" />

    <bean id="before" class="org.springaop.aspects.schema.
SpringAopAspectBeforeExample" />

</beans>
```

After advice

The following after advice example explains how to use the after advice with XML Schema configuration:

```
<beans xmlns="http://www.springframework.org/schema/beans"
xmlns:xsi="http://www.w3.org/2001/XMLSchema-instance"
xmlns:p="http://www.springframework.org/schema/p"
xmlns:aop="http://www.springframework.org/schema/aop"
xsi:schemaLocation="http://www.springframework.org/schema/beans
http://www.springframework.org/schema/beans/spring-beans-2.5.xsd
http://www.springframework.org/schema/aop
http://www.springframework.org/schema/aop/spring-aop.xsd">

    <bean id="hello" class="org.springaop.target.Hello" p:
label="writer" />

    <aop:config>
        <aop:aspect ref="after">
            <aop:after method="afterGreeting" pointcut="execution(*
greeting(..))" />
        </aop:aspect>
    </aop:config>

    <bean id="after" class="org.springaop.aspects.schema.
SpringAopAspectAfterExample" />

</beans>


package org.springaop.aspects.schema;

public class SpringAopAspectAfterExample {

    public void afterGreeting() {

            System.out.println("this is afterAspect !");
    }
}
```

After returning advice

The following after returning advice example explains how to use the after returning advice with XML Schema configuration:

```
<beans xmlns="http://www.springframework.org/schema/beans"
xmlns:xsi="http://www.w3.org/2001/XMLSchema-instance"
xmlns:p="http://www.springframework.org/schema/p"
xmlns:aop="http://www.springframework.org/schema/aop"
xsi:schemaLocation="http://www.springframework.org/schema/beans
http://www.springframework.org/schema/beans/spring-beans-2.5.xsd
http://www.springframework.org/schema/aop
http://www.springframework.org/schema/aop/spring-aop.xsd">

    <bean id="hello" class="org.springaop.target.Hello" p:
label="writer"/>

    <aop:config>
        <aop:aspect ref="afterReturning">
            <aop:after-returning method="afterGreeting"
pointcut="execution(* greeting(..))" />
        </aop:aspect>
    </aop:config>

    <bean id="afterReturning" class="org.springaop.aspects.schema.
SpringAopAspectAfterReturningExample"/>

</beans>


package org.springaop.aspects.schema;

public class SpringAopAspectAfterReturningExample {

    public void afterGreeting() {

        System.out.println("this is a aop !");
    }
}
```

After throwing advice

The following after throwing advice example explains how to use the after throwing advice with XML Schema configuration:

```
<beans xmlns="http://www.springframework.org/schema/beans"
xmlns:xsi="http://www.w3.org/2001/XMLSchema-instance"
xmlns:aop="http://www.springframework.org/schema/aop"
xsi:schemaLocation="http://www.springframework.org/schema/beans
http://www.springframework.org/schema/beans/spring-beans-2.5.xsd
http://www.springframework.org/schema/aop
http://www.springframework.org/schema/aop/spring-aop.xsd">
```

```xml
        <bean id="exceptionTarget" class="org.springaop.chapter.one.
schema.throwsadvice.ExceptionTarget" />

    <aop:config>
        <aop:aspect ref="afterThrowing">
            <aop:after-throwing method="afterErrorMethod"
                pointcut="execution(* errorMethod(..)) throws
Exception" />
        </aop:aspect>
    </aop:config>

    <bean id="afterThrowing"
        class="org.springaop.aspects.schema.
SpringAopAspectAfterThrowingExample" />

</beans>
```

Target Class:

```java
package org.springaop.target;

public class ExceptionTarget {

    public void errorMethod() throws Exception {
        throw new Exception("Fake exception");
    }

    public void otherErrorMethod() throws NullPointerException {
        throw new NullPointerException("Other Fake exception");
    }

}
```

Aspect:
```java
package org.springaop.aspects.schema;

public class SpringAopAspectAfterThrowingExample {

    public void afterErrorMethod() {

            System.out.println("+++");
            System.out.println("Exception !");
            System.out.println("+++\n");
    }
}
```

Around advice

The following around advice example explains how to use the around advice with XML Schema configuration:

```xml
<beans xmlns="http://www.springframework.org/schema/beans"
xmlns:xsi="http://www.w3.org/2001/XMLSchema-instance"
xmlns:p="http://www.springframework.org/schema/p"
xmlns:aop="http://www.springframework.org/schema/aop"
xsi:schemaLocation="http://www.springframework.org/schema/beans
http://www.springframework.org/schema/beans/spring-beans-2.5.xsd
http://www.springframework.org/schema/aop
http://www.springframework.org/schema/aop/spring-aop.xsd">

    <bean id="hello" class="org.springaop.target.Hello" p:
label="writer" />

    <aop:config>
        <aop:aspect ref="around">
            <aop:around method="aroundGreeting" pointcut="execution(*
greeting(..))" />
        </aop:aspect>
    </aop:config>

    <bean id="around"
        class="org.springaop.aspects.schema.
SpringAopExampleAroundExample" />

</beans>


package org.springaop.aspects.schema;

public class SpringAopExampleAroundExample {
    public Object aroundGreeting(ProceedingJoinPoint pjp) throws
Throwable {

        System.out.print("Hello ");
        try {
            return pjp.proceed();
        } finally {
            System.out.println("this is around aop !");
        }
    }
}
```

Summary

This chapter has explained the gaps in object-oriented programming and the support offered by aspect-oriented programming to fill these gaps, especially in the implementation phase.

The AOP concepts and terms have been introduced, showing conceptually how and where they act, which of them Spring supports, and how it does so.

These concepts have then been used in short and simple introductory practical examples in order to show Spring AOP functionalities both in a programmatic and declarative manner in version 1.x, and in version 2.5, with annotations and in a declarative manner with schema-based configuration.

In the next chapters we will look into these topics in detail.

2
Spring AOP Components

This chapter gives an overview of Spring AOP and its components.

A brief outline of the topics covered in this chapter is as follows:

- Spring AOP foundations
- Spring AOP components
- Spring AOP classic XML configuration, inherited from 1.x versions

Aspect

An Aspect represents the functional unit of aspect-oriented programming.

From version 1.x, an aspect was realized as a class that implemented the **advisor** interface. An advisor is a class that combines advice and pointcuts, as we will see in Chapter 3.

Since version 2.x, with the annotations of AspectJ, an aspect is a Java class with the `@Aspect` annotation.

Pointcut

A pointcut is an expression for the selection of joinpoints. It can be a collection of joinpoints used to define an advice that has to be executed. By defining pointcuts you can have control of the objects composing the application, at the points where the advices are applied.

As Spring defines method invocation joinpoints, all the methods that can be invoked on a class will be joinpoints.

These are some examples of pointcuts:

- Methods starting with a certain prefix (such as, `getter` and `setter`)
- Methods with a particular package (such as `org.springaop.domain.*`)
- Methods that return a certain kind of output (such as `public MyClass get*(...)`)
- Any combination of the previous three examples

Pointcut and its components

A pointcut is the composition of a `ClassFilter` and a `MethodMatcher`. A `ClassFilter` narrows the matching of a pointcut or introduction to a given set of target classes, while a `MethodMatcher` checks whether the target method is eligible for advice.

```
public interface Pointcut {
    public ClassFilter getClassFilter ();
    public MethodMatcher getMethodMatcher();
}
```

The `getClassFilter` method is called first, to check if it can be applied to the class used.

The `ClassFilter` interface that filters the classes is composed in this way:

```
public interface ClassFilter {
    public boolean matches(Class clazz);
    public static final ClassFilter TRUE = TrueClassFilter.INSTANCE;
}
```

Using the constant `ClassFilter` TRUE, we obtain a match for all classes.

In its implementation, it will return a Boolean value according to whether or not the input parameter belongs to the wanted type.

Then, the `getMethodMatcher` method of the `Pointcut` interface is called. The `MethodMatcher` interface is composed in this way:

```
public interface MethodMatcher {
    boolean matches(Method m, Class targetClass);
    boolean isRuntime();
    boolean matches(Method m, Class targetClass, Object[] args);
}
```

The first method that's called is `isRuntime()`. It tells Spring whether the `MethodMatcher` is static or dynamic:

1   If the result is false, it's a static `MethodMatcher` and Spring calls the method `matches(Method, Class)` once for every method on the target class, caching the return value for subsequent invocations.

2   If the result is true, it's a dynamic `MethodMatcher`. Spring does a static check calling `matches(Method m, Class targetClass)` the first time to check the applicability. If the result is true, for every invocation the `matches(Method m, Class targetClass, Object[] args)` is called.

In this way, the checkup is done only the first time, and the subsequent times the cached value is recovered. From this, we understand that unless we need the flexibility of having a dynamic `MethodMatcher`, it's better to use the static one.

Spring provides pointcuts that are ready to use, so normally, there's no need to implement your pointcut. Pointcuts that are ready to use provided by Spring are:

1.   `NameMatchMethodPointcut`

2.   `RegexpMethodPointcut`

3.   `StaticMethodMatcherPointcut`

4.   `DynamicMethodMatcherPointcut`

NameMatchMethodPointcut

Using the `NameMatchMethodPointcut` method, you can create a pointcut that performs simple matching against a list of method names. This class is used for the programmatic creation of proxies, and for configurations in the Spring factory with Setter Injection.

The full qualified name of the `NameMAtchMethodPointcut` class is:

    org.springframework.aop.support.NameMatchMethodPointcut

The following methods are available:

1.   `NameMatchMethodPointcut addMethodName(String methodName)`

2.   `void setMappedName(String methodName)`

3.   `void setMappedNames(String methodName)`

The two setter methods are used for Setter Injection. The `addMethodName` method is used for the addition in a simple way of the names of the necessary methods. To allow calling `addMethodName` several times to add all the required method names, `this` is returned.

```
Pointcut pc = new
NameMatchMethodPointcut().addMethodName("setStartDate").addMethodName(
"setEndDate");
```

Let us see an example that explains the usage of `NameMatchMethodPointcut`.

The target class on which the advice is applied is shown as follows:

```
package org.springaop.chapter.two.pointcut;

public class NameMethodTargetExample {
    public void printName(){
        System.out.println("Max");
    }
    public void printAction(){
        System.out.println("runs");
    }
    public void printSpot(){
        System.out.println("in Poetto beach");
    }
}
```

The advice that contains the logic to be executed:

```
package org.springaop.chapter.two.pointcut;

import org.aopalliance.intercept.MethodInterceptor;
import org.aopalliance.intercept.MethodInvocation;

public class AdviceExample implements MethodInterceptor {
    public Object invoke(MethodInvocation invocation) throws Throwable
{
        System.out.println("Invoking " + invocation.getMethod().
getName());
        Object retVal = invocation.proceed();
        System.out.println("Job Done");
        return retVal;
    }
}
```

The test class:

```
package org.springaop.chapter.two.pointcut;

import org.springframework.aop.Advisor;
import org.springframework.aop.framework.ProxyFactory;
import org.springframework.aop.support.DefaultPointcutAdvisor;
import org.springframework.aop.support.NameMatchMethodPointcut;

public class NameMethodMatcherExample {

    public static void main(String[] args) {
        NameMethodTargetExample target = new
NameMethodTargetExample();
        NameMatchMethodPointcut pc = new NameMatchMethodPointcut();
        pc.addMethodName("printSpot");
        pc.addMethodName("printAction");
        Advisor advisor = new DefaultPointcutAdvisor(pc, new
AdviceExample());
        ProxyFactory pf = new ProxyFactory();
        pf.setTarget(target);
        pf.addAdvisor(advisor);
        NameMethodTargetExample proxy = (NameMethodTargetExample)pf.
getProxy();
        proxy.printName();
        proxy.printAction();
        proxy.printSpot();
    }
}
```

The result will be:

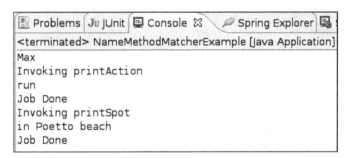

Let's try to see what happened. We defined a target class, an *around advice* that prints, before the invocation, the name of the invoked method. Subsequently, the method invokes on the target class, and after the invocation it prints **Job Done**.

To test NameMethodMatcher, we'll write the NameMethodMatcherExample class with a main method, then add to NameMatchMethodPointcut only two of the three methods that could be matched by the pointcut.

Then we'll create an advisor that binds pointcut and advice, create a new `ProxyFactory` to which we will set advisor and target object, and then invoke methods.

The result is that only the two added methods (`printAction()` and `printSpot()`) are intercepted by the pointcut, whereas `printName()` is not intercepted.

RegexpMethodPointcut

To allow pointcuts in a more generic modality than the mere declaration of names, it's possible to use regular expressions.

For this purpose in Spring 1.x, Jakarta ORO (Perl5 regexp) is being used. If we want to use JDK 1.3; otherwise, we can use the regular expression provided by `java.util.regex` if running on JDK 1.4

The full qualified name is:

```
org.springframework.aop.support.JdkRegexpMethodPointcut
```

The `JdkRexepMethodPointcut` allows you to define pointcuts using JDK 1.4 regular expression support.

```
org.springframework.aop.support.Perl5RegexpMethodPointcut
```

The `Perl5RegexpMethodPointcut` allows you to define pointcuts using Perl 5 regular expression syntax.

For their configuration, we use a single pattern or a list of patterns:

1   `patterns`: Array of regular expressions for methods that the pointcut will match

2   `pattern`: Convenient String property when you have just a single pattern and don't need an array

In Spring 2.5, we have only the `JdkRegexpMethodPointcut`, for JDK 1.4 or higher.

```
<bean id="settersAndHumorousPointcut"
  class="org.springframework.aop.support.JdkRegexpMethodPointcut">
    <property name="patterns">
            <list>
                    <value>.*get.*</value>
                    <value>.*humorous</value>
            </list>
    </property>
</bean>
```

If we use Spring 2.5 or 3.x and a JDK previous to 1.4, Jakarta ORO is used in the background, configuring an advisor in this way:

```
<bean id="settersAndHumorousAdvisor"
    class="org.springframework.aop.support.
RegexpMethodPointcutAdvisor">
    <property name="advice">
        <ref local="beanNameOfAopAllianceInterceptor"/>
    </property>
    <property name="patterns">
        <list>
            <value>.*set.*</value>
            <value>.*humorous</value>
        </list>
    </property>
</bean>
```

An example of `RegexpMethodPointcut` use follows:

The target class on which to apply the advice:

```
package org.springaop.chapter.two.pointcut;

public class RegExpTargetExample {

    public void printName(){
        System.out.println("Max");
    }

    public void printAction(){
        System.out.println("swims");
    }

    public void printSpot(){
        System.out.println("in Poetto beach");
    }

}
```

The advice that contains the logic to be executed:

```
package org.springaop.chapter.two.pointcut;

import org.aopalliance.intercept.MethodInterceptor;
import org.aopalliance.intercept.MethodInvocation;

public class AdviceExample implements MethodInterceptor {

    public Object invoke(MethodInvocation invocation) throws Throwable
    {
```

```
        System.out.println("Invoking " + invocation.getMethod().
getName());
        Object retVal = invocation.proceed();
        System.out.println("Job Done");
        return retVal;
    }
}
```

The test class:

```
package org.springaop.chapter.two.pointcut;

import org.springframework.aop.Advisor;
import org.springframework.aop.framework.ProxyFactory;
import org.springframework.aop.support.DefaultPointcutAdvisor;
import org.springframework.aop.support.JdkRegexpMethodPointcut;

public class RegExpMethodMatcherExample {

    public static void main(String[] args) {

        RegExpTargetExample target = new RegExpTargetExample();

        JdkRegexpMethodPointcut pc = new JdkRegexpMethodPointcut();
        String[] patterns = {".*Spot.*",".*Action.*"};
        pc.setPatterns(patterns);
        Advisor advisor = new DefaultPointcutAdvisor(pc, new
AdviceExample());

        ProxyFactory pf = new ProxyFactory();
        pf.setTarget(target);
        pf.addAdvisor(advisor);
        RegExpTargetExample proxy = (RegExpTargetExample)pf.
getProxy();

        proxy.printName();
        proxy.printAction();
        proxy.printSpot();
    }

}
```

The result will be:

```
Problems  Ju JUnit  Console  ⊠    Spring Explorer  
<terminated> RegExpMethodMatcherExample [Java Application]
Max
Invoking printAction
swim
Job Done
Invoking printSpot
in Poetto beach
Job Done
```

Let's see what we have done. We defined a target class and an *around advice* that prints, before the invocation, the name of the invoked method. Subsequently, the method invokes on the target class, and after the invocation it prints **Job Done**. To test `JdkRegexpMethodPointcut` we wrote the `RegExpMethodMatcherExample` class with a main method. We set a string array with the patterns of regular expressions to `JdkRegexpMethodPointcut`.

We created an advisor that bound pointcut and advice, created a new `ProxyFactory` to which we set the advisor and target object. Then, we invoked methods.

The result was that only methods that contain the regular expressions in their name were intercepted by the pointcut.

StaticMethodMatcherPointcut

The `StaticMethodMatcherPointcut` abstract class is intended as a base for building static pointcuts.

The full qualified name of the class is:

```
org.springframework.aop.StaticMethodMatcherPointcut
```

We can use it as an anonymous inner class implementing the body of the method matches:

```
public static Pointcut exampleStaticPointcut = new
StaticMethodMatcherPointcut() {
  public boolean matches(Method m, Class targetClass) {
        // implement custom check
  }
};
```

Or extending it and implementing its methods:

```
public class StaticPointcutFooExample extends
StaticMethodMatcherPointcut {
    public boolean matches(Method method, Class clazz) {
        return ("example".equals(method.getName()));
    }
    public ClassFilter getClassFilter() {
        return new ClassFilter() {
            public boolean matches(Class clazz) {
                return (clazz == MyTarget.class);
            }
        };
    }
}
```

This is an of example class to which apply advices:

```
package org.springaop.chapter.two.pointcut;

public class PointcutTargetExample {
    public void printName(){
        System.out.println("Max");
    }
    public void printSpot(){
        System.out.println("in Poetto beach");
    }
}
```

This is a second class of example to which apply advices:

```
package org.springaop.chapter.two.pointcut;

public class PointcutTargetExampleTwo {
    public void printAction(){
        System.out.println("swim");
    }
    public void printSpot (){
        System.out.println("on Mediterranean Sea");
    }
}
```

This is the `StaticPointcutMatcher` method. It represents the class in which we set out the matching rules on the type of class and on the method.

```
package org.springaop.chapter.two.pointcut;

import java.lang.reflect.Method;
import org.springframework.aop.ClassFilter;
import org.springframework.aop.support.StaticMethodMatcherPointcut;

public class StaticPointcutMatcher extends StaticMethodMatcherPointcut
{
    public boolean matches(Method method, Class cls) {
        return ("printSpot".equals(method.getName()));
    }

    public ClassFilter getClassFilter() {
        return new ClassFilter() {
            public boolean matches(Class cls) {
                return (cls == PointcutTargetExample.class);
            }
        };

    }
}
```

This is the advice. It represents the advice applied according to the `StaticMethodMatcher`.

```
package org.springaop.chapter.two.pointcut;

import org.aopalliance.intercept.MethodInterceptor;
import org.aopalliance.intercept.MethodInvocation;

public class AdviceExample implements MethodInterceptor {
    public Object invoke(MethodInvocation invocation) throws Throwable
{
        System.out.println("Invoking " + invocation.getMethod().
getName());
        Object retVal = invocation.proceed();
        System.out.println("Job Done");
        return retVal;
    }
}
```

This is the test class:

```java
package org.springaop.chapter.two.pointcut;

import org.aopalliance.aop.Advice;

import org.springframework.aop.Advisor;
import org.springframework.aop.Pointcut;
import org.springframework.aop.framework.ProxyFactory;
import org.springframework.aop.support.DefaultPointcutAdvisor;

public class StaticPointcutExample {

    public static void main(String[] args) {

        PointcutTargetExample one = new PointcutTargetExample();
        PointcutTargetExampleTwo two = new
PointcutTargetExampleTwo();

        PointcutTargetExample proxyOne;
        PointcutTargetExampleTwo proxyTwo;
        Pointcut pc = new StaticPointcutMatcher();
        Advice advice = new AdviceExample();
        Advisor advisor = new DefaultPointcutAdvisor(pc, advice);

        ProxyFactory pf = new ProxyFactory();
        pf.addAdvisor(advisor);
        pf.setTarget(one);
        proxyOne = (PointcutTargetExample)pf.getProxy();

        pf = new ProxyFactory();
        pf.addAdvisor(advisor);
        pf.setTarget(two);
        proxyTwo = (PointcutTargetExampleTwo)pf.getProxy();

        proxyOne.printName();
        proxyTwo.printAction();

        proxyOne.printSpot();
        proxyTwo.printSpot();
    }
}
```

The result will be:

```
Problems   Ju JUnit   Console ☒   Spring Explo

<terminated> StaticPointcutExample [Java Application]
Max
swim
Invoking printSpot
in Poetto beach
Job Done
on Mediterranean Sea
```

Let's try to see what has been done. We defined two target classes, `PointcutTargetExample` and `PointcutTargetExampleTwo` (they print some text), and a `StaticPointcutMatcher`, which is an *around advice* that prints, before the invocation, the name of the invoked method. Subsequently, the method invokes on the target class, and after the invocation it prints **Job Done**.

To test `StaticPointcutMatcher`, we wrote the `StaticPointcutExample` class with a main method.

Then we create an advisor that bound pointcut and advice, and created a new `ProxyFactory` to which we set advisor and target objects. Then, we invoked methods.

The result was that only the methods of the class that satisfied `StaticPointcutMatcher` were intercepted.

DynamicMethodMatcherPointcut

`DynamicMethodMatcherPointcut` is intended as a base class to build dynamic pointcuts.

The full qualified name is:

```
org.springframework.aop.support .DynamicMethodMatcherPointcut
```

The utilization is not so different from that of `StaticMethodMatcherPointcut` as the anonymous inner class:

```
public static Pointcut DynamicPointcutExample = new
DynamicMethodMatcherPointcut() {

  public boolean matches(Method m, Class targetClass) {
          // implement custom check
  }
  public boolean matches(Method m, Class targetClass, Object[] args) {
          // implement custom check
  }
}
```

As explained at the beginning of this chapter, the method matches with two arguments. It is called like `staticMethodMatcher`, and if it returns `true`, the matches are recalled at every invocation with three arguments.

Here is an example of its use:

This is the class to which advices are applied:

```
package org.springaop.chapter.two.pointcut;

public class DynamicPointcutTargetExample {
    public void setSpot(String spot){
        this.spot = spot;
    }

    public void printSpot(){
        System.out.println(spot);
    }

    private String spot;
}
```

As DynamicMethodMatcher, we use a class that executes the static match (matches(Method method, Class cls)) on the SetSpot method, and the dynamic one (matches(Method method, Class cls, Object[] args)) on parameters ending with "Ocean".

```
package org.springaop.chapter.two.pointcut;

import org.springframework.aop.ClassFilter;
import org.springframework.aop.support.DynamicMethodMatcherPointcut;

public class DynamicMethodMatcher extends DynamicMethodMatcherPointcut
{
    public boolean matches(Method method, Class cls) {
        System.out.println("Static check for " + method.getName());
        return ("setSpot".equals(method.getName()));
    }

    public boolean matches(Method method, Class cls, Object[] args) {
        System.out.println("Dynamic check for " + method.getName());
        String spot = ((String) args[0]);
        return spot.endsWith("Ocean");
    }

    public ClassFilter getClassFilter() {
        return new ClassFilter() {

            public boolean matches(Class cls) {
                return (cls == DynamicPointcutTargetExample.class);
            }
        };
    }

}
```

As advice we use the same class used in the `StaticMethodMatcher`'s example:

```
package org.springaop.chapter.two.pointcut;

import org.aopalliance.intercept.MethodInterceptor;
import org.aopalliance.intercept.MethodInvocation;

public class AdviceExample implements MethodInterceptor {

    public Object invoke(MethodInvocation invocation) throws Throwable
    {
        System.out.println("Invoking " + invocation.getMethod().
getName());
        Object retVal = invocation.proceed();
        System.out.println("Job Done");
        return retVal;
    }

}
```

This is the test class:

```
package org.springaop.chapter.two.pointcut;

import org.springframework.aop.Advisor;
import org.springframework.aop.framework.ProxyFactory;
import org.springframework.aop.support.DefaultPointcutAdvisor;

public class DynamicPointcutExample {

    public static void main(String[] args) {
        DynamicPointcutTargetExample target = new
DynamicPointcutTargetExample();

        Advisor advisor = new DefaultPointcutAdvisor(
                new DynamicMethodMatcher(), new AdviceExample());

        ProxyFactory pf = new ProxyFactory();
        pf.setTarget(target);
        pf.addAdvisor(advisor);
        DyinamicPointcutTargetExample proxy = (
DynamicPointcutTargetExample)pf.getProxy();

        proxy.setSpot("Pacific Ocean");
        proxy.setSpot("Mediterranean Sea");
        proxy.setSpot("Atlantic Ocean");

        proxy.printSpot();
        proxy.printSpot();
        proxy.printSpot();
    }

}
```

The result will be:

```
Problems | Ju JUnit | Console ⌧ | Spring Explorer
<terminated> DynamicPointcutExample [Java Application]
Static check for setSpot
Static check for printSpot
Static check for clone
Static check for toString
Static check for setSpot
Dynamic check for setSpot
Invoking setSpot
Job Done
Dynamic check for setSpot
Dynamic check for setSpot
Invoking setSpot
Job Done
Static check for printSpot
Atlantis Ocean
Atlantis Ocean
Atlantis Ocean
```

Let's see what has been done. We defined a target class
(DynamicPointcutTargetExample), a DynamicPointcutMatcher with the definition
of the class and of the method valid for the match, an *around advice* that prints the
name of the invoked method before the invocation. Subsequently, the method is
invoked on the target class, and after the invocation, it prints **Job Done**.

To test DynamicPointcutMatcher, we wrote the DynamicPointcutExample class
with a main method.

Then we created an advisor that bound pointcuts and advices. We also created a new
ProxyFactory to which we set advisors and target objects. Then, we invoked methods.

The result was that at the first invocation, a static check was done on methods called
from the proxy (the first four static checks). Then only when the static check was
satisfied, the dynamic check was called to verify if we should apply advice.

Operations on Pointcut

The Pointcut class exposes two methods for the union and intersection of pointcuts.

```
public static Pointcut union (Pointcut a, Pointcut b)
public static Pointcut intersection (Pointcut a, Pointcut b)
```

The union of two pointcuts is the pointcut matching any method matched by either pointcut (Boolean OR). The intersection matches only methods matched by both pointcuts (Boolean AND).

Pointcuts can be composed using the static methods in the `org.springframework.aop.support.Pointcuts` (union and intersection) class, or using the `ComposablePointcut` class in the same package.

ComposablePointcut

The `ComposablePointcut` class is used to compose two or more pointcuts together with operations such as `union()` and `intersection()`.

The full qualified name of the class is:

```
org.springframework.aop.support.ComposablePointcut
```

By default, `ComposablePointcut` is created with a `ClassFilter` that matches all the classes and a `MethodMatcher` that matches all the methods.

We can supply our own initial `ClassFilter` and `MethodMatcher` if we like:

```
ComposablePointcut(ClassFilter classFilter,
MethodMatcher methodMatcher)
```

The `union()` and `intersection()` methods are both overloaded to accept `ClassFilter` and `MethodMatcher` arguments.

Invoking the `union()` method, the `MethodMatcher` of `ComposablePointcut` is replaced with a `UnionMethodMatcher` that uses the current `MethodMatcher` of the `ComposablePointcut` and the `MethodMatcher` passed to the `union()` method as arguments.

The `UnionMethodMatcher` method then returns `true` for a match if either of its wrapped `MethodMatchers` returns `true`.

This way it is possible to invoke the `union()` method as many times as we want, with each call creating a new `UnionMethodMatcher` that wraps the current `MethodMatcher` with the `MethodMatcher` passed to `union()`.

Internally, the `intersection()` method works in a similar way to the `union ()`.

Here is the target class:

```
package org.springaop.chapter.two.pointcut;

import java.util.Date;

public class ComposableTargetExample {
```

```
    public ComposableTargetExample() {
          startDate = new Date();
    }
    public ComposableTargetExample(String description) {
          startDate = new Date();
          this.description = description;
    }
     public void setDescription(String description) {
          this.description = description;
    }
    public String getDescription() {
          return description;
    }
    public Date getStartDate() {
          return (Date) startDate.clone();
    }
    private Date startDate;
    private String description;
}
```

Here is the example class:

```
package org.springaop.chapter.two.pointcut;

import java.lang.reflect.Method;

import org.springframework.aop.Advisor;
import org.springframework.aop.ClassFilter;
import org.springframework.aop.framework.ProxyFactory;
import org.springframework.aop.support.ComposablePointcut;
import org.springframework.aop.support.DefaultPointcutAdvisor;
import org.springframework.aop.support.StaticMethodMatcher;

public class ComposablePointcutExample {

    public static void main(String[] args) {

            ComposableTargetExample target = new
ComposableTargetExample();

        ComposablePointcut pc = new ComposablePointcut(
ClassFilter.TRUE,
                new GetterMethodMatcher());

        System.out.println("Test GetterMetodMatcher :");
        ComposableTargetExample proxy = getProxy(pc, target);
        testInvoke(proxy);

        System.out.println("Test GetterMetodMatcher UNION
SetterMethodMatcher :");
        pc.union(new SetterMethodMatcher());
```

```
        proxy = getProxy(pc, target);
        testInvoke(proxy);

        System.out.println("Test (GetterMetodMatcher UNION
        SetterMethodMatcher) INTERSECT GetStartDateMethodMatcher :");
        pc.intersection(new GetStartDateMethodMatcher());
        proxy = getProxy(pc, target);
        testInvoke(proxy);
    }

    private static ComposableTargetExample getProxy(
    ComposablePointcut pc, ComposableTargetExample target) {
        Advisor advisor = new DefaultPointcutAdvisor(pc,
                new ComposableBeforeAdvice());
        ProxyFactory pf = new ProxyFactory();
        pf.setTarget(target);
        pf.addAdvisor(advisor);
        return (ComposableTargetExample) pf.getProxy();
    }

    private static void testInvoke(ComposableTargetExample proxy) {
                proxy.getStartDate();
                proxy.getDescription();
          proxy.setDescription("New Description");
    }
    private static class GetterMethodMatcher extends
StaticMethodMatcher {
        public boolean matches(Method method, Class cls) {
            return (method.getName().startsWith("get"));
        }
    }

    private static class GetStartDateMethodMatcher extends
StaticMethodMatcher {
        public boolean matches(Method method, Class cls) {
            return "getStartDate".equals(method.getName());
        }
    }
    private static class SetterMethodMatcher extends
StaticMethodMatcher {
        public boolean matches(Method method, Class cls) {
            return (method.getName().startsWith("set"));
        }

    }
}
```

The result will be:

```
Problems   Ju JUnit   Console    Spring Explorer   Spring AOP Event Trace

<terminated> ComposablePointcutExample [Java Application] /usr/local/jdk1.6.0_07/bin/java (Sep 13, 2008 5:39:03 PM)
Test GetterMetodMatcher :
ComposableBeforeAdvice
ComposableBeforeAdvice
Test GetterMetodMatcher UNION SetterMethodMatcher :
ComposableBeforeAdvice
ComposableBeforeAdvice
ComposableBeforeAdvice
Test (GetterMetodMatcher UNION SetterMethodMatcher) INTERSECT GetStartDateMethodMatcher :
ComposableBeforeAdvice
```

Let's try to see what has been done. We defined a target class
(`ComposableTargetExample`), a `ComposableBeforeAdvice` that prints
"`ComposableBeforeAdvice`".

To test `ComposablePointcut` we wrote the `ComposableTargetExample` class with a
main method.

In a `getProxy` method, we created an advisor that bound pointcuts and advices,
created a new `ProxyFactory` to which we set advisors and target objects, and
returned the target object.

In the `testInvoke` method, we invoked two `Get` methods and one `Set` method.

In the `Main` method, we created the pointcut declaring we wanted to use a
`GetterMethodMatcher`, and we called `testInvoke`. The result was the application
of the advice to two `Get` methods. Then we made a union of pointcuts that at the
beginning contained the `GetterMethodMatcher` with a `SetterMethodMatcher`,
and then we called the `testInvoke` method. The result was the application of the
advice three times.

Then we make the intersection with a `GetStartDateMethodMatcher`, and call the
`testInvoke` method. The result is the application of advice only on the method that
satisfies the intersection.

ControlFlowPointcut

The `ControlFlowPointcut` is a pointcut that matches all methods within the control
flow of another method — that is, any method that is invoked either directly or
indirectly as the result of another method being invoked.

Control flow pointcuts allow us to apply advices to an object in a selective manner
depending on the context in which it is executed.

The full qualified name of the class is:

```
org.springframework.aop.support.ControlFlowPointcut
```

However, we have to pay attention to the performance we get when using it. The Spring documentation indicates that a control flow pointcut is typically five times slower than other pointcuts on a 1.4 JVM, and ten times slower on a 1.3 JVM.

Here is the target class:

```
package org.springaop.chapter.two.pointcut;

public class ControlFlowTargetExample {

    public void greeting(){
            System.out.println("Cheers");
    }
}
```

This is the before advice:

```
package org.springaop.chapter.two.pointcut;

import java.lang.reflect.Method;
import org.springframework.aop.MethodBeforeAdvice;

public class ControlFlowBeforeAdvice implements MethodBeforeAdvice {

    public void before(Method method, Object[] args, Object target)
                throws Throwable {

            System.out.println("ControlFlow beforeAdvice ");
    }
}
```

Here is the example class:

```
package org.springaop.chapter.two.pointcut;

import org.springframework.aop.Advisor;
import org.springframework.aop.Pointcut;
import org.springframework.aop.framework.ProxyFactory;
import org.springframework.aop.support.ControlFlowPointcut;
import org.springframework.aop.support.DefaultPointcutAdvisor;

public class ControlFlowPointcutExample {

    public static void main(String[] args) {
            ControlFlowPointcutExample ex = new
ControlFlowPointcutExample();
            ex.run();
    }
```

```
        public void run() {

                ControlFlowTargetExample target = new
    ControlFlowTargetExample();
                Pointcut pc = new ControlFlowPointcut(ControlFlowPointcutE
    xample.class, "test");
                Advisor advisor = new DefaultPointcutAdvisor(pc,
                        new ControlFlowBeforeAdvice());

                ProxyFactory pf = new ProxyFactory();
                pf.setTarget(target);
                pf.addAdvisor(advisor);

                ControlFlowTargetExample proxy =
    (ControlFlowTargetExample) pf.getProxy();

                System.out.println("Trying normal invoke");
                proxy.greeting();
                System.out.println("Trying under
    ControlFlowPointcutExample.test()");
                test(proxy);
        }

        private void test(ControlFlowTargetExample bean) {
                bean.greeting();
        }

}
```

The result will be:

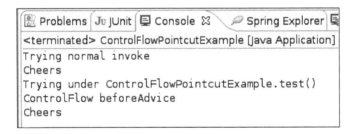

Let's see what has been done. We defined a target class
(`ControlFlowTargetExample`), a `ControlFlowBeforeAdvice` that
prints **ControlFlow beforeAdvice**.

To test `ControlFlowPointcut`, we wrote the `ControlFlowPointcutExample` class
with a main method that only calls a run method, where we put the real test body.
We did this to show the effects of the flow of a calling of a method from a given class.

The result was that when the method was called directly by the proxy, the advice was not applied, whereas when the call came from within another object (`ControlFlowPointcutExample` in this case), the advice was applied.

Pointcut constants

For the common operations, pointcut constants are available in this package:

```
org.springframework.aop.support.Pointcuts
```

The constants are:

GETTERS is a constant Pointcut object, matching all bean property getters, in any class.

SETTERS is a constant Pointcut object matching all bean property setter in any class.

Joinpoint

A joinpoint is a well-defined point during the execution of your application. Typical examples of joinpoints include a method call, method execution, class initialization, and object instantiation. Joinpoints are a core concept of AOP and define the points in your application at which you can insert additional logic using AOP.

Spring AOP only supports one joinpoint type—method invocation. This makes Spring more accessible. But if we need to advise some code at a joinpoint other than a method invocation, we can always use Spring and AspectJ together.

Advice

An advice specifies what must be done at a joinpoint.

Spring uses a chain of interceptors to wrap the invocation of the method and apply to it the advices contained into this chain. As said before, Spring is consistent with the specifications of the AOP Alliance, but provides a slightly different programming model.

The AOP Alliance defines the `MethodInterceptor` interface:

```
public interface org.aopalliance.intercept.MethodInterceptor extends
Interceptor {
        Object invoke(MethodInvocation invocation) throws Throwable;
}
```

By implementing this interface and using the `invocation.proceed()` method, it is possible to build a chain of interceptors with the same behavior as filter servlets. In the following figure, we can see this behavior:

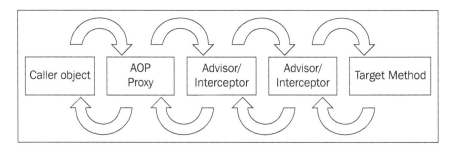

Spring, on the other hand, provides prepared advices that extend the `org.aopalliance.aop.Advice` interface.

In the following figure, we can see a diagram of the hierarchy of advices:

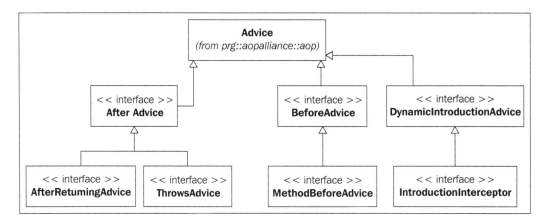

Advices have been presented with some examples in Chapter 1, but now we will see them in greater detail.

Let's say that as good practice you have to choose the advice that best meets your requirements.

Before advice

Before advice interposes actions before the joinpoint. Spring provides the `org.springframework.aop.BeforeAdvice` interface, and in order to use it we have to implement an interface that extends it and has the following signature:

```
public interface MethodBeforeAdvice extends BeforeAdvice {

    void before(Method m, Object[] args, Object target) throws
Throwable;
}
```

Our implementation will then be called before the jointpoint. We will put the logic we want to execute into the body of the `before` method. This type of advice is particularly appropriate for pre-test (before) operations.

```
package org.springaop.chapter.two.advice;

import java.lang.reflect.Method;
import java.util.logging.Logger;

import org.springframework.aop.MethodBeforeAdvice;

public class BeforeAdvice implements MethodBeforeAdvice {

    public void before(Method m, Object[] args, Object target) {
        logger.fine(traceInvocation(m, args, target));
        //do something
    }
    private String traceInvocation(Method m, Object[] args, Object
target) {
    StringBuilder sb = new StringBuilder("Invoked method :").append(m.
getName());
        sb.append("with args :").append(args);
        sb.append("on object :").append(target);
        return sb.toString();
    }
}
```

After returning advice

This executes logic after the method executed at the joinpoint gives back control to the calling method in a normal way, that is, without throwing any exception.

Spring provides the `org.springframework.aop.AfterAdvice` interface, whose extension must be implemented. Its signature is:

```
public interface org.springframework.aop.AfterReturningAdvice extends
Advice {

    void afterReturning(Object returnValue, Method m,
            Object[] args, Object target)
            throws Throwable;
}
```

This advice can't modify the value returned to the target caller.

Example:

```
package org.springaop.chapter.two.advice;

import java.lang.reflect.Method;
import java.util.logging.Logger;

import org.springframework.aop.AfterReturningAdvice;

public class AfterAdvice implements AfterReturningAdvice {

    public void afterReturning(Object returnValue, Method m, Object[] args,
                        Object target) {
        logger.fine(traceResultInvocation(m, args,
target,returnValue));
    }

    private String traceResultInvocation(Method m, Object[] args,
Object target,Object returnValue) {
        StringBuilder sb = new StringBuilder("Invoked method :").
append(m.getName());
        sb.append("with args :").append(args);
        sb.append("on object :").append(target);
        sb.append("return value :").append(returnValue);
        return sb.toString();
    }
}
```

After throwing advice

This advice is called after an exception has been thrown. It's therefore suitable for tracing and possibly correcting or signalling actions after an exception of a particular kind.

The `org.springframework.aop.ThrowsAdvice` interface is a Tag Interface.

There are no methods, as methods are invoked by reflection. Implementing classes must implement methods of the form:

```
void afterThrowing([Method, args, target], ThrowableSubclass);
```

This means, as explained in the reference documentation, it can be a method in one of the following forms:

```
public void afterThrowing(Exception ex);
public void afterThrowing(RemoteException);
public void afterThrowing(Method method, Object[] args, Object target,
Exception ex);
public void afterThrowing(Method method, Object[] args, Object target,
ServletException ex);
```

All the parameters (excluding the exception) are used to have further information, but in fact are optional.

Example:

```
package org.springaop.chapter.two.advice;

import java.lang.reflect.Method;
import java.util.logging.Logger;

import org.springframework.aop.ThrowsAdvice;

public class RuntimeExceptionAdvice implements ThrowsAdvice {
    public void afterThrowing(Method m, Object[] args, Object target,
                RuntimeException ex) {

        logger.fine(traceExceptionContext(m, args, target, ex));

    }

    private String traceExceptionContext(Method m, Object[] args,
Object target, RuntimeException ex) {
        StringBuilder sb = new StringBuilder(«Exception on method
:»).append(m.getName());
        sb.append(«with args :»).append(args);
        sb.append(«on object :»).append(target);
        sb.append(«exception msg :»).append(ex.getMessage());
        return sb.toString();
    }
}
```

Advisor

The advisor isn't a concept from AOP in general, but is specific to Spring AOP.

The advisor links together pointcuts and advice. So it contains both the action to be executed (defined in the advice) and the point where it is to be executed (defined in the pointcut). The advisor's role is to decouple pointcuts and advice, in order to reuse them independently from each other.

The Advisor interface allows support for different types of advice, such as before and after advice, which need not be implemented using interception.

```
public interface Advisor {
        Advice getAdvice ();
        boolean perInstance();
}
```

In the following figure, we can see the diagram of the hierarchy of advisors:

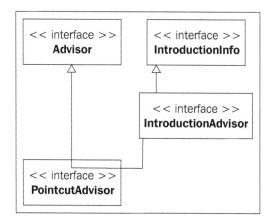

When we call addAdvice() on a ProxyFactory:

```
pf.addAdvice(new AfterAdviceExample());
```

the addAdvice delegates to addAdvisor() behind the scenes, creating an instance of DefaultPointcutAdvisor and configuring it with a pointcut that points to all methods.

The addAdvisor creates a DefaultPointcutAdvisor, and it applies a pointcut that targets all the methods. This is the default behavior when Spring uses the canonical instance Pointcut.TRUE.

The most common implementation to use is provided by Spring:

```
org.springframework.aop.support.DefaultPointcutAdvisor
```

It can be used in a programmatic way:

```
Advisor advisorExample = new DefaultPointcutAdvisor(pointcutExample,
adviceExample);
```

or in a declarative way:

```
<bean name ="advisorExample"
class="org.springframework.aop.support.DefaultPointcutAdvisor">
    <property name="pointcut"><ref local="pointcutExample" />
</property>
    <property name="advice"><ref local="adviceExample" /></property>
</bean>
```

In the earlier section (with various `MethodMatchers`), we have seen the use of advisors in programmatic way.

Introductions

Introductions are a very strong component of the Spring AOP. They permit us to dynamically introduce new one-object functionalities as the implementation of interfaces on existing objects:

- To create a *mixin*, adding to the state held in the object. This is probably the most important use.

- To expose additional states associated with a special TargetSource. This is used within Spring, for example, with scripting support.

- To expose an object or object graph in a different way — for example, making an object graph implement the XML DOM interfaces.

Introductions are often mixins that allow one to obtain the effects of multiple inheritance in Java.

To allow the implementation of interfaces at runtime rather than more simply at compile time makes sense in cases where the crosscutting functionalities don't allow us to easily choose the way at compile time.

In the documentation of Spring 1.x, we had introductions, object locking, and modification detection as examples of use.

In the case of object locking, to lock an object's internal state we should implement the `Lockable` interface. All the objects that we want to have the functionalities should implement it, duplicating in this way the implementation in all the objects. Otherwise, we should create a base class that contains the implementation, but the classes that would modify its state should anyway do a state check.

In this situation, we can centralize the implementation on introductions, and have classes at runtime that implement the `Lockable` interface. This interface becomes an instance of `Lockable`.

The implementation can be controlled by the introduction. In Spring AOP it extends `MethodInterceptor`, and thus can intercept the calls before the exception is thrown if the object is "locked".

This example shows how introductions are suitable to be used in declarative services.

As we have mentioned, for Spring an introduction is a special type of `AroundAdvice`. But we have to be careful because it is applied at the level of Class, and pointcuts can't be used: This is because an introduction adds the implementation of an interface, whereas pointcuts choose which method to apply to the advice.

Spring simplifies the use by providing `DelegatingIntroductionInterceptor`, an implementation of the `IntroductionInterceptor` interface, which has to be extended where we have to implement the interfaces that we want to introduce. Then, to add the introduction, we use a special Advisor — the `IntroductionAdvisor`, of which the implementation `DefaultIntroductionAdvisor` is used.

We have to pay attention to the fact that whereas a normal advice can be applied to any object since it has a **per-class lifecycle**, an introduction has a **per-instance lifecycle**. So we must have a different instance for each advised object, and the `ProxyFactory.addAdvice()` method mustn't be called because it would throw an exception.

The interface of `introductionAdvisor` is as follows:

```
public interface IntroductionAdvisor extends Advisor, IntroductionInfo
{
    ClassFilter getClassFilter();
    void validateInterfaces() throws IllegalArgumentException;
}
```

`ClassFilter` is useful to show the classes on which it must be used.

The `ValidateInterfaces` method is used internally to determine whether one of introduced interface can be implemented or not.

The implementation of `IntroductionAdvisor` has to implement this as well:

```
public interface IntroductionInfo {
    Class[] getInterfaces();
}
```

Here is an example:

We want to manage to call sets on Object domains just once, and just if the variables are null, because they haven't been valorised through the default constructor `DomainObjectTarget()`:

```java
package org.springaop.chapter.two.introduction;

public class DomainObjectTarget {

    public DomainObjectTarget(){}

    public DomainObjectTarget(String description, Integer id){
            this.description = description;
            this.id = id;
    }
    public String getDescription() {
            return description;
    }
    public void setDescription(String description) {
            this.description = description;
    }
    public Integer getId() {
            return id;
    }
    public void setId(Integer id) {
            this.id = id;
    }
    public boolean isNew(){
            return null == description && null == id;
    }
    private String description;
    private Integer id = null;
}
```

This is the interface to be applied:

```java
package org.springaop.chapter.two.introduction;

public interface IsModifiable {

    public boolean isModifiable();
}
```

Here is the advisor:

```
package org.springaop.chapter.two.introduction;

public class IsModifiableAdvisor extends DefaultIntroductionAdvisor {

    public IsModifiableAdvisor(){
            super(new IsModifiableMixin());
    }
}
```

Here is the mixin class:

```
package org.springaop.chapter.two.introduction;

import java.lang.reflect.Method;
import java.util.HashMap;
import java.util.Map;

import org.aopalliance.intercept.MethodInvocation;
import org.springframework.aop.support.
DelegatingIntroductionInterceptor;

public class IsModifiableMixin extends
DelegatingIntroductionInterceptor
        implements IsModifiable {

    public boolean isModifiable() {
        return isModifiable;
    }

    public Object invoke(MethodInvocation invocation) throws Throwable
{

        Authentication auth = SecurityContextHolder.getContext().
getAuthentication();

        if (isModifiable) {
            StringBuilder sb = new StringBuilder();
            if ((invocation.getMethod().getName().startsWith(«set»))
&& (invocation.getArguments().length == 1)) {

                Method getter = getGetter(invocation.getMethod());
                sb.append(auth == null ? «Anonymous» : auth.getName())
                    .append(« has try to modify the object state,
method:»)
                    .append(getter.getName()).append(« and
arguments:»).append(invocation.getArguments()[0]);

                if (getter != null) {
                    Object value = getter.invoke(invocation.getThis(),
null);
```

```
                            if (value == null) {
                                isModifiable = false;
                            }
                        }
                    }
                    logger.debug(sb.toString());
                }
                return super.invoke(invocation);
            }
            private Method getGetter(Method setter) {
                Method getter = (Method) setterMethodCache.get(setter);
                if (getter != null) {
                    return getter;
                }
                String getterName = setter.getName().replaceFirst(«set»,
        «get»);
                try {
                    getter = setter.getDeclaringClass().getMethod(getterName,
        null);
                    synchronized (setterMethodCache) {
                        setterMethodCache.put(setter, getter);
                    }
                    return getter;
                } catch (NoSuchMethodException ex) {
                    return null;
                }
            }
            private boolean isModifiable = true;
            private Map setterMethodCache = new HashMap();
            private Logger logger = Logger.getLogger(IsModifiableMixin.class);
        }
```

Here is the test class:

```
    package org.springaop.chapter.two.introduction;

    import org.springframework.aop.IntroductionAdvisor;
    import org.springframework.aop.framework.ProxyFactory;

    public class IntroductionTest {

        public static void main(String[] args) {

            DomainObjectTarget target = new DomainObjectTarget();
```

```
        IntroductionAdvisor advisor = new IsModifiableAdvisor();
        ProxyFactory pf = new ProxyFactory();
        pf.setTarget(target);
        pf.addAdvisor(advisor);
        pf.setOptimize(true);
        DomainObjectTarget proxy = (DomainObjectTarget)pf.getProxy();
        IsModifiable proxyInterface = (IsModifiable)proxy;
        System.out.println("Is TargetBean?: " + (proxy instanceof
DomainObjectTarget));
        System.out.println("Is IsModifiable?: " + (proxy instanceof
IsModifiable));
        System.out.println("Has been modified?: " + proxyInterface.
isModifiable());
        proxy.setDescription("One for the money");
        System.out.println("Has been modified?: " + proxyInterface.
isModifiable());
        proxy.setDescription("Two for the show");
        System.out.println("Has been modified?: " + proxyInterface.
isModifiable());
    }
}
```

The result will be:

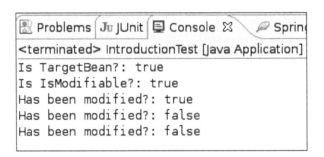

In this example of introductions, we test how they allow us to apply the IsModifiable interface on the DomainObjectTarget object, providing an implementation contained in the IsModifiableMixin class.

The example follows the usual steps to bind target and advisor, which in this case has the main role because it instantiates IsModifiableMixin, which implements introduction.

Summary

The aim of this chapter was to show the basic components of Spring AOP, pointcut, joinpoint, advice, advisor, and introduction.

Each one realizes a component of the AOP functions, using joinpoints that are the invocations of methods and advisors, specific to Spring.

This chapter describes advices: the results obtained and the most appropriate application scenarios, and introductions, which are one of the most powerful components because they allow the application the implementation of interfaces to any object. In this chapter we saw one example for each of the advices. We will look at the same components in Chapter 4, but using AspectJ to allow a much easier and shorter configuration both through annotations and using XML Schema.

3
Spring AOP Proxies

In this chapter, we will discuss how to get started with Spring AOP proxies.

Some of the topics discussed in this chapter are:

- JDK and CGLIB proxy
- Creating proxy programmatically
- ProxyFactoryBean
- Autoproxies
- Target sources

Proxy

It is proxies that realize AOP in Spring and allow the application of crosscutting functionalities. We will see the application of proxies both in the classic version of Spring, and with the support of AspectJ with annotations and XML Schema. We will also see the possible matching of configuration to adapt proxies to our demands, and use their advanced features.

Proxy is a structural design pattern that is a part of the 23 design patterns of the **GoF (Gang of Four)** composed by Erich Gamma, Richard Helm, Ralph Johnson, and John Vlissides.

The idea put into practice by Proxy is to wrap an object and intercept all the calls made to it and take its place, so that the calling object has the feeling of interacting with the object rather than the proxy.

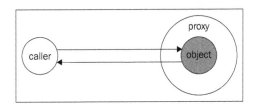

Since a proxy intercepts all the calls to the object, it can also decide to call some other application logic before making a call to the object, or to execute some application logic before giving back the object's answer, or it can even not send the call to the object. Given these features, the proxy is the ideal point to introduce and execute chains of actions to be performed before or after the calls to the object.

In our case, the chains of actions are the crosscutting concerns to be applied to specific joinpoints. To realize this structural behavior pattern of Proxy, we have two choices: implementing it or using appropriate classes provided by JDK 1.3 and upwards.

The only constraint is that the object must implement one or more interface, and that only the methods present in the interface(s) must be intercepted.

Another way is to use the CGLIB library (CGLIB is a powerful high-performance code generation library), which doesn't require implementation of an interface.

JDK proxy

To realize a dynamic proxy with JDK, we need to implement the interface that manages invocations.

```
package java.lang.reflect;

public interface InvocationHandler {

public Object invoke(Object proxy, Method method, Object[] args)
throws Throwable;
}
```

The method to implement receives the proxy object, the invoked method, and the input parameters of the target method. An implementation would be made like this:

```
package org.springaop.chapter.three.handler;

import java.lang.reflect.InvocationHandler;
import java.lang.reflect.Method;
import java.lang.reflect.Proxy;

public class FooInvocationHandler implements InvocationHandler {

    public FooInvocationHandler(Object target) {
            this.target = target;
    }

    public Object invoke(Object proxy, Method method, Object[] args)
                throws Throwable {
```

```
        System.out.println("remove before fly :-)");

        Object result = method.invoke(target, args);

        System.out.println(result+", mmh it's not rocket science ");
        return result;
    }

    public static Object createProxy(Object target) {
        return Proxy.newProxyInstance(
                    target.getClass().getClassLoader(),
                    target.getClass().getInterfaces(),
                    new FooInvocationHandler(target));
    }

    private Object target;

}
```

The constructor receives the target object on which the invocation will be made.

The `invoke` method performs the invocation of the method on the target object (second argument) using an array of parameters (third argument). The proxy (first argument) is not needed in this case. The `createProxy` method creates a new proxy, initializing it with the classloader and interfaces of the target class.

The handler would be used in this way:

```
package org.springaop.chapter.three.handler;

public static void main(String[] args) {
        Info info = new DefaultInfo();

        Info information = (Info) FooInvocationHandler.
createProxy(info);
        information.isJmxEnabled();
}
```

The result will be:

```
Problems  Ju JUnit  Console ⊠   Spring
<terminated> Test (5) [Java Application] /usr/local
remove before fly :-)
false
  mmh it's not rocket science
```

CGLIB proxy

In the beginning, the use of the CGLIB library was introduced in Spring 1.1 because JDK 1.3 proxies weren't really efficient. With versions 1.4 and following, they have been improved. However, even with JDK 1.5, CGLIB proxies are still three times faster.

Despite all this, we have to notice that JDK proxies need an interface to do their job, and only the methods declared in the interface can be used by the proxy. But this is not always possible, particularly when the code we deal with is written by others.

In this case, it's better to use CGLIB proxies that don't require the presence of interfaces to implement. CGLIB proxies generate the bytecode for the new class on the fly for each proxy, reusing in those cases that were already created. This allows some optimizations.

But we have to be clear that to use CGLIB proxies, we need to have the CGLIB JAR. Whereas with JDK, any JAR is required. Moreover, if we deal with final methods, we cannot do the override, and so we can apply any advice.

The creation of CGLIB proxies is completely transparent for Spring users, since it's provided as one of the two implementations of the class used with Spring — the ProxyFactory and JDK proxy.

Creating proxies programmatically

In some situations it could be necessary to create proxies programmatically (for example in test classes), in the classic manner or with classes annotated with "@Aspect".

ClassicProxy

To see a proxy in action, we will use as example class a class that implements a Command Pattern. A Command Pattern is used when a client class doesn't know the details about an implementation of the called class that executes some logic.

```
package org.springaop.chapter.three.proxy;

public interface Command {

    public void execute();
}
```

We define an interface that implements the Command Pattern
(http://en.wikipedia.org/wiki/Command_pattern).

```
package org.springaop.chapter.three.proxy;

public class CommandImpl implements Command{

    public void execute(){
            System.out.println(label);
    }

    private final String label = "Goooo !";
}
```

We create a class that implements the interface.

```
package org.springaop.chapter.three.proxy;

public class BeforeAdviceProxyExample implements MethodBeforeAdvice{

    public void before(Method arg0, Object[] arg1, Object arg2)
                throws Throwable {

        System.out.println("I'm a proxied invocation");

    }

}
```

We create a `MethodBeforeAdvice` to execute before the execute method.

```
package org.springaop.chapter.three.proxy;

public class ProxyFactoryExample {

    public static void main(String[] args) {
        //target class
            Command target = new CommandImpl();

        // create the proxy
        ProxyFactory pf = new ProxyFactory();

        //add interface
        pf.addInterface(Command.class);

        // add pointcut
    NameMatchMethodPointcut pc = new NameMatchMethodPointcut();

    pc.addMethodName("execute");

        // add advisor
        Advisor advisor = new DefaultPointcutAdvisor(pc, new
BeforeAdviceProxyExample());
```

```
                    pf.addAdvisor(advisor);

                    // setTarget
                    pf.setTarget(target);

                    Command proxy = (Command) pf.getProxy();
                    proxy.execute();
        }
    }
```

In the test class we instantiate the target class `CommandImpl`, create the `ProxyFactory`, to which we add the interface on which the proxy (Command class) has to operate. We create the pointcut to which we append the names of the methods to intercept.

Then we create the advisor, passing the pointcut and the `BeforeAdviceExample`. We add the advisor and the target to the `ProxyFactory`. Finally, we retrieve the proxy class that is seen as the Command interface and invoke the method on the proxy.

The result will be:

```
 Problems  Ju JUnit  Console    Spring Explorer
<terminated> ProxyFactoryExample [Java Application] /usr/
I'm a proxied invocation
Goooo !
```

With the instruction `pf.setExposeProxy(true)`, we could have at our disposal the proxy as `ThreadLocal` to retrieve it with the class `AopContext`; by default it is false to improve performance.

Usually, it is used if a class on which an advice is applied has to call another method on itself, advised too. (If it uses this, the invocation will not be advised.)

AspectJProxy

It is also possible to programmatically create AspectJ aspects using the `@Aspect` annotation.

The class `org.springframework.aop.aspectj.annotation.AspectJProxyFactory` can be used to create a proxy for a target object that is advised by one or more AspectJ aspects.

```
package org.springaop.chapter.three.proxy;

import org.aspectj.lang.annotation.Aspect;
import org.aspectj.lang.annotation.Before;
import org.aspectj.lang.annotation.Pointcut;
import org.springframework.aop.aspectj.annotation.AspectJProxyFactory;

@Aspect
public class BeforeAspectJProxyExample {

    @Pointcut("execution(* org.springaop.chapter.three.proxy.
CommandImpl.execute(..))")
    void beforeExecute(){}

    @Before("beforeExecute()")
    public void before() {
        System.out.println("I'm a AspectJ proxied invocation");
    }

    public static void main(String[] args) {
        Command target = new CommandImpl();
        AspectJProxyFactory factory = new AspectJProxyFactory(target
);
        factory.addAspect(BeforeAspectJProxyExample.class);
        Command proxy = factory.getProxy();
        proxy.execute();
    }
}
```

The annotation @Aspect marks a class as an aspect.

The annotation @Pointcut marks the method beforeExecute() as a pointcut that can be used as parameter in the annotation @Before.

These annotations enable the crosscutting functionality in this class, instead of in the programmatic way that we saw in the previous chapters.

ProxyFactoryBean

As we've previously seen, we have at our disposal two kinds of proxies: the ones provided by JDK, which we can also write as seen in the previous section, and those provided by the CGLIB, which work in a transparent manner.

In everyday use, we don't directly use either of the two implementations. We rather rely on a factory that provides the proxy class ready for use. This allows us to focus our attention and development on crosscutting concerns to apply through the proxy, rather than focus on the proxy.

To make our job easier Spring provides the class `org.springframework.aop.config.ProxyFactoryBean`, and we mostly use it in a declarative way by doing the "dirty work" that we have seen. It is necessary to create and use proxies in a programmatic way. `ProxyFactoryBean` is a central component in Spring AOP because if proxies act as links among advices, targets, joinpoints, and advisors, the `ProxyFactoryBean` performs its tasks in a declarative manner rather than by code in a programmatic manner.

As a factory bean, it creates beans of the required type by introducing a layer of indirection and allowing the creation of different types of objects. The intrinsic advantage that it brings is the use of IoC to use AOP and its components.

The interface of the `ProxyFactoryBean` is as follows:

- `setTarget`: Specify the target object you want to proxy.
- `setProxyTargetClass`: The default behavior is the following:
  - If an interface is available, it's used as a JDK proxy.
  - If an interface is not available, it's used as a CGLIB proxy.
  - If we set the value to true, it's used as a CGLIB proxy.
- `setOptimize`: If a CGLIB proxy is used, this instruction tells the proxy to apply some aggressive optimizations. It doesn't have any effect if the proxy is a JDK proxy.
- `setFrozen`: The default value is false. If a proxy configuration is `frozen`, then changes to the configuration are no longer allowed. This is useful as a slight optimization, and is also useful for those cases where you don't want callers to be able to manipulate the proxy (via the `Advised` interface), after the proxy has been created.
- `setExposeProxy`: If a target needs to obtain the proxy and the `exposeProxy` property is set to true, the target can use the `AopContext.currentProxy()`. The `proxy` is exposed in a `ThreadLocal` so that it can be accessed by the target.
- `setAopProxyFactory`: The implementation of `AopProxyFactory` offers a way of customizing whether to use dynamic proxies, CGLIB, or any other proxy strategy.

Parameters that can be passed to the `ProxyFactoryBean`'s constructor:

- `proxyInterfaces`: These are an array of String interface names. If they aren't supplied, a CGLIB proxy for the target class will be used.

- `interceptorNames`: These are a string array of `Advisor`, interceptor, or other advice names to apply. Ordering is significant, on a first-come-first-served basis. That is to say, the first interceptor in the list will be the first to be able to intercept the invocation. The names are bean names in the current factory, including those from the ancestor factories. You can't mention bean references here since doing so would result in the `ProxyFactoryBean` ignoring the singleton setting of the advice. You can append an interceptor name with an asterisk (*). This will result in the application of all advisor beans with names starting with the part before the asterisk to be applied.

- `singleton`: If true, a singleton pattern is applied (the factory creates a single instance of the object and returns it at every `getObject()` invocation). The default value is `true`. If you want to use stateful advice, use prototype advices along with a singleton value of `false`.

ProxyFactoryBean and proxies

Now we will see the strategy with which the `ProxyFactoryBean` chooses whether to use a JDK proxy or a CGLIB proxy, and the manner in which it autonomously gets the presence of interfaces.

Scenarios:

- If the target class doesn't implement interfaces, a CGLIB proxy is created. In this case, we simply have to indicate the list of interceptors to introduce as `interceptorNames`. If the target class implements one or more interfaces, the creation of the type of proxy depends on the configuration in detail.

- If the property `proxyTargetClass` of the `ProxyFactoryBean` is true, a CGLIB proxy is created even if the property `proxyInterfaces` is set with one or more interfaces.

- If the property feature `proxyTargetClass` isn't set and the feature `proxyInterfaces` is set with one or more interfaces, a JDK proxy that implements these interfaces declared in `proxyInterfaces` is created.

- If the property `proxyInterfaces` is not set, but the target class actually implements one or more interfaces, the `ProxyFactoryBean` detects the fact that the object implements interfaces and creates a JDK proxy. Unfortunately, with this self-discovery, the proxy implements all the interfaces of the class — not only those we wish and that are indicated with the feature `proxyInterfaces` — if the class implements several interfaces.

ProxyFactoryBean in action

After having seen the main features and strategies on the type of proxy created, we are going to see how the `ProxyFactoryBean` must be configured in XML.

In this example we have three "anemic" objects — User, Command, and PersonUser. The User implementation has two interfaces, while the Command implementation has only one, and the PersonUser doesn't implement any interface at all. We will see how to configure the bean factory with some lists of interceptors, and how to choose which interfaces must be considered by the proxy.

The interfaces:

```
package org.springaop.chapter.three.domain;

public interface User {

    public String getName();
    public String getSurname();
}

package org.springaop.chapter.three.domain;

public interface Address {

    public String getAddress();
    public String getNation();
    public String getState();

}

package org.springaop.chapter.three.domain;

public interface Command {

    public Object execute();
}
```

The following class implements the User and Address interfaces:

```
package org.springaop.chapter.three.domain;

public class UserImpl implements User, Address {

    public String getAddress() {
        return address;
    }
    public String getNation() {
        return nation;
    }
    public String getState() {
```

```
                    return state;
        }
    public String getName() {
            return name;
        }
    public String getSurname() {
            return surname;
        }
    public void setAddress(String address) {
            this.address = address;
        }
    public void setNation(String nation) {
            this.nation = nation;
        }
    public void setState(String state) {
            this.state = state;
        }
    public void setName(String name) {
            this.name = name;
        }
    public void setSurname(String surname) {
            this.surname = surname;
        }
    private String address, nation, state, name, surname;
}
```

The following class contains implementation of the method `execute`, which performs the print of a point on a new line in the output on console and file:

```
package org.springaop.chapter.three.domain;

public class CommandImpl implements Command {

    public Object execute() {
            for (int x = 0; x < 1000; x++) {
                    action();
            }
            return null;
    }

    private void action() {
            System.out.println("\n .");
    }
}
```

The following class `PersonUser` doesn't implement any interface:

```
package org.springaop.chapter.three.domain;

public class PersonUser {

    public String getName(){
            return user.getName();
    }

    public String getSurname(){
            return user.getSurname();
    }

    public void setUser(User user) {
            this.user = user;
    }

    private User user;
}
```

After the three principal classes, we see the interceptors used in the example.

In the following code, we have the interceptor `MethodLoggerInterceptor` that logs the executions of methods and writes to files through `log4j`, which is an appropriate library for logging.

The method `invoke` receives the `MethodInvocation` that contains all runtime information about invocation.

```
package org.springaop.chapter.three;

import org.aopalliance.intercept.MethodInterceptor;
import org.aopalliance.intercept.MethodInvocation;
import org.apache.log4j.Logger;
import org.springaop.chapter.three.util.Constants;

public class MethodLoggerInterceptor implements MethodInterceptor {

    public Object invoke(MethodInvocation invocation) throws Throwable
{
            Logger log = Logger.getLogger(Constants.LOG_NAME);
            StringBuilder sb = new StringBuilder();
            sb.append("\n Method:").append(invocation.getMethod())
                    .append("\n on class:").append(invocation.
getClass()).append(  "\n with arguments:").append(invocation.
getArguments());
            log.info(sb.toString());
```

```
            Object retVal = invocation.proceed();
            log.info("\n return value:" + retVal);
            return retVal;
    }
}
```

The `TimeExecutionInterceptor` class measures the time before and after the method's invocation. It uses the class `StopWatch`, which is a class of Spring, to measure the milliseconds used for the execution of the method invoked from the interceptor's interior.

It performs a dump of the invocation, recording through `log4j` the invoked method, the class on which it was invoked, the input arguments, and the return value.

```
package org.springaop.chapter.three;

import java.lang.reflect.Method;

import org.aopalliance.intercept.MethodInterceptor;
import org.aopalliance.intercept.MethodInvocation;
import org.apache.log4j.Logger;
import org.springaop.chapter.three.util.Constants;
import org.springframework.util.StopWatch;

public class TimeExecutionInterceptor implements MethodInterceptor{

  public Object invoke(MethodInvocation invocation) throws Throwable{
        long timeBeforeMethodExecution = 0;
        long timeAfterMethodExecution = 0;

        Logger log = Logger.getLogger(Constants.LOG_NAME);

        // Spring util class
        StopWatch sw = new StopWatch();

        log.info(new StringBuilder("\n Time before execution:")
                    .append(timeBeforeMethodExecution));

        sw.start(invocation.getMethod().getName());

        Object returnValue = invocation.proceed();

        sw.stop();

        timeAfterMethodExecution = System.currentTimeMillis();
        log.info(new StringBuilder("\n Time after execution:")
        .append((timeAfterMethodExecution -
        timeBeforeMethodExecution)).append(" ms").append(
        "\n result:").append(returnValue));
```

```
            dumpInfo(invocation, sw.getTotalTimeMillis(), log);

            return returnValue;
    }

    private void dumpInfo(MethodInvocation invocation, long ms, Logger
log) {

            Method m = invocation.getMethod();
            Object[] args = invocation.getArguments();

            log.info(new StringBuilder("\n Method :").append(m.
getName()).append(
                            "\n On object type: :").append(
                            invocation.getThis().getClass().getName()).
append(
                            (" \n With arguments : \n")));

            for (int x = 0; x < args.length; x++) {
                    log.info(new StringBuilder("      >
").append(args[x]));
            }
            log.info(new StringBuilder(" \n Time of execution:
").append(ms)
                            .append(" ms"));
    }
}
```

The following class does not differ in its functionality from the
MethodLoggerInterceptor. But in the configuration, it will be used with pointcut
and advisor to show how an advisor can be put in the list of interceptorNames.

```
package org.springaop.chapter.three;

import org.aopalliance.intercept.MethodInterceptor;
import org.aopalliance.intercept.MethodInvocation;

public class ConsoleAdvice implements MethodInterceptor {

    public Object invoke(MethodInvocation invocation) throws Throwable
{

            StringBuilder sb = new StringBuilder();
            sb.append("ConsoleAdvice");

            sb.append("\n Method:").append(invocation.getMethod())
                            .append("\n on class:").append(invocation.
getClass()).append("\n with arguments:").append(invocation.
getArguments());
```

```
            System.out.println(sb.toString());

            Object retVal = invocation.proceed();

            System.out.println("\n return value:" + retVal);

            System.out.println();
            return retVal;
        }
    }
```

Now, we see the configuration Spring file that contains the configuration of the previous classes.

```
<beans xmlns="http://www.springframework.org/schema/beans"
xmlns:xsi="http://www.w3.org/2001/XMLSchema-instance"
xsi:schemaLocation="http://www.springframework.org/schema/beans
http://www.springframework.org/schema/beans/spring-beans-2.5.xsd">
    <bean id="userTarget" class="org.springaop.chapter.three.domain.
UserImpl">
        <property name="name" value="james"/>
        <property name="surname" value="bond"/>
    </bean>
    <bean id="personUserTarget" class="org.springaop.chapter.three.
domain.PersonUser">
        <property name="user" ref="userTarget"/>
    </bean>
    <bean id="commandTarget" class="org.springaop.chapter.three.
domain.CommandImpl"/>

    <bean id="methodLoggerInterceptor" class="org.springaop.chapter.
three.MethodLoggerInterceptor"/>
    <bean id="timeExecutionInterceptor" class="org.springaop.chapter.
three.TimeExecutionInterceptor"/>
    <bean id="consoleAdvice" class="org.springaop.chapter.three.
ConsoleAdvice"/>
    <!-- Advisor -->
    <bean id="consoleAdvisor" class="org.springframework.aop.support.
DefaultPointcutAdvisor">
        <property name="pointcut" ref="methodNamePointcut"/>
        <property name="advice" ref="consoleAdvice"/>
    </bean>
    <!-- Pointcut -->
    <bean id="methodNamePointcut" class="org.springframework.aop.
support.NameMatchMethodPointcut">
        <property name="mappedName" value="execute"/>
    </bean>
```

```
      <bean id="user" class="org.springframework.aop.framework.
ProxyFactoryBean">
            <property name="proxyInterfaces" value="org.springaop.chapter.
three.domain.User"/>
            <property name="target"><ref local="userTarget"/></property>
            <property name="interceptorNames">
                <list>
                    <value>methodLoggerInterceptor</value>
                </list>
            </property>
      </bean>

      <bean id="personUser" class="org.springframework.aop.framework.
ProxyFactoryBean">
            <property name="proxyTargetClass" value="true"/>
            <property name="target">
                <bean class="org.springaop.chapter.three.domain.
PersonUser">
                    <property name="user">
                        <bean class="org.springaop.chapter.three.domain.
UserImpl">
                            <property name="name" value="jack"/>
                            <property name="surname" value="folla"/>
                        </bean>
                    </property>
                </bean>
            </property>
            <property name="interceptorNames">
                <list>
                    <value>methodLoggerInterceptor</value>
                </list>
            </property>
      </bean>

      <bean id="command" class="org.springframework.aop.framework.
ProxyFactoryBean">
            <property name="proxyInterfaces" value="org.springaop.chapter.
three.domain.Command"/>
            <property name="target"><ref local="commandTarget"/></
property>
            <property name="interceptorNames">
                <list>
                    <value>timeExecutionInterceptor</value>
                    <value>consoleAdvisor</value>
                </list>
            </property>
      </bean>
</beans>
```

In the configuration files, the beans `UserTarget`, `PersonUserTarget`, and `CommandTarget` describe the three normal classes. The beans `methodLoggerInterceptor`, `timeExecutionInterceptor`, and `consoleAdvice` describe the three interceptors that contain the logic to be executed.

The bean `consoleAdvisor` exists to put together (that is the purpose of an advisor) the pointcut `methodNamePointcut` and advice `consoleAdvice`. The bean `methodNamePointcut` contains the name of the method (`execute`) to intercept.

The bean `user` contains the fully qualified name of the interfaces, the reference to the bean that implements the interface (`userTarget`), and the list of interceptors to apply (only `methodLoggerInterceptor`).

The bean `personUser` defines inline the target bean (which doesn't implement any interface), and the list of interceptors to apply (only `methodLoggerInterceptor`).

The bean `command` contains the fully qualified name of the interfaces, the reference to the bean that implements the interface (`commandTarget`), and the list of interceptors (`timeExecutionInterceptor` and `consoleAdvisor`).

The following configuration contains the configuration of `log4j` to write to the console and log files in the file system.

```
# Global logging configuration
log4j.rootLogger=INFO, stdout, logfile_application

# Console output...
log4j.logger.org.springaop= INFO, logfile_application, stdout

#SPRING
log4j.logger.org.springframework =INFO, logfile_spring

log4j.appender.stdout=org.apache.log4j.ConsoleAppender
log4j.appender.stdout.layout=org.apache.log4j.PatternLayout
log4j.appender.stdout.layout.ConversionPattern=%5p [%t] - %m%n

log4j.appender.logfile_application=org.apache.log4j.
DailyRollingFileAppender
log4j.appender.logfile_application.file=/tmp/logs/apringaop.log
# change the path on windows
log4j.appender.logfile_application.layout=org.apache.log4j.
PatternLayout
log4j.appender.logfile_application.layout.ConversionPattern=%5p [%t]
- %m%n
log4j.appender.logfile_application.DatePattern='.'yyyy-MM-dd

log4j.appender.logfile_spring=org.apache.log4j.
DailyRollingFileAppender
```

```
log4j.appender.logfile_spring.file=/tmp/logs/springaop.log
# change the path on windows

log4j.appender.logfile_spring.layout=org.apache.log4j.PatternLayout
log4j.appender.logfile_spring.layout.ConversionPattern=%5p [%t] - %m%n
log4j.appender.logfile_spring.DatePattern='.'yyyy-MM-dd

# log4j debug
log4j.debug=false
```

Test class:

```
package org.springaop.chapter.three;

import org.springaop.proxies.proxyfactorybean.domain.Command;
import org.springaop.proxies.proxyfactorybean.domain.PersonUser;
import org.springaop.proxies.proxyfactorybean.domain.User;
import org.springframework.context.ApplicationContext;
import org.springframework.context.support.
ClassPathXmlApplicationContext;

public class ProxyFactoryBeanTest {

    public static void main(String[] args) {

        String[] paths = {"org/springaop/chapter/three/
applicationContext.xml"};
        ApplicationContext ctx = new ClassPathXmlApplicationContext(
paths);

        User user = (User)ctx.getBean("user");
        user.getName();

        Command command = (Command)ctx.getBean("command");
        command.execute();

        PersonUser person = (PersonUser)ctx.getBean("personUser");
        person.getName();

    }
}
```

In the test class, first of all we load Spring's `ApplicationContext` with the beans'
definitions. Once we've loaded them we do the lookup of three beans, `user`,
`command`, and `personUser`.

The proxy returns the bean `user` from the target class `UserImpl`, which implements
two interfaces, of which we want the proxy to use just one. To this bean the
`ProxyFactoryBean` applies the `methodLoggerInterceptor`, which logs class,
method, and arguments on the method on which the methods defined in the `User`
interface are invoked.

The bean `command` is what the proxy returns from the target class `CommandImpl`, which implements just one interface. To this bean, it applies the `timeExecutionInterceptor` that logs the time needed for method's invocations.

Bean `personUser` is the bean the proxy returns from the target class `PersonUser`, which doesn't implement any interface. To this the `ProxyFactoryBean` applies the `methodLoggerInterceptor`. It logs class, method, and arguments to the method on which methods defined on the `PersonUser` class are invoked.

Output:

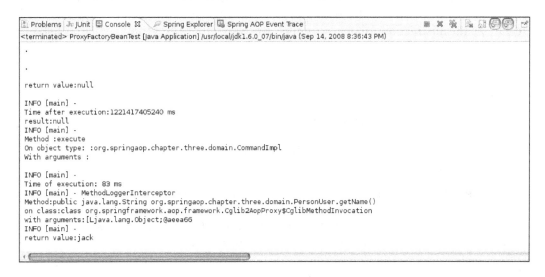

We can organize interceptors so that we don't need to list them all, for example by giving a prefix to names of the interceptors—for example `profile`; we can use it in the `interceptorsName` list with `profile*`.

```
<beans xmlns="http://www.springframework.org/schema/beans"
xmlns:xsi="http://www.w3.org/2001/XMLSchema-instance"
xsi:schemaLocation="http://www.springframework.org/schema/beans
http://www.springframework.org/schema/beans/spring-beans-2.5.xsd">
...
<bean id="profileMethodLoggerInterceptor"
    class="org.springaop.chapter.three.MethodLoggerInterceptor"/>
<bean id="profileTimeExecutionInterceptor"
    class="org.springaop.chapter.three.TimeExecutionInterceptor"/>
<bean id="command"
    class="org.springframework.aop.framework.ProxyFactoryBean">
    <property name="proxyInterfaces" value="org.springaop.chapter.
three.domain.Command"/>
        <property name="target"><ref local="commandTarget"/></
property>
        <property name="interceptorNames">
            <list>
                <value>profile*</value>
            </list>
        </property>
</bean>
...
</beans>
```

In order to simplify the XML necessary for the configuration, we might as well define an abstract template, for example to define the list of interceptors list, and declare as the abstract template's parent all the beans that need that particular list of interceptors list.

The possibility to define a bean `abstract` and use it as a completion of other beans is available in any Spring configuration.

A bean can be a `parent` of just one bean.

Let's see a configuration's example with a bean `abstract`, and a bean that is a parent of the abstract one.

```
<beans xmlns="http://www.springframework.org/schema/beans"
xmlns:xsi="http://www.w3.org/2001/XMLSchema-instance"
xsi:schemaLocation="http://www.springframework.org/schema/beans
http://www.springframework.org/schema/beans/spring-beans-2.5.xsd">
    ...
    <bean id="user" class="org.springframework.aop.framework.
ProxyFactoryBean" parent="profileInterceptorTemplate">
```

```
    <property name="proxyInterfaces" value="org.springaop.chapter.
three.domain"/>
    <property name="target"><ref local="userTarget"/></property>
</bean>
...

    <bean id="profileInterceptorTemplate" abstract="true">
        <property name="interceptorNames">
            <list>
                    <value>methodLoggerInterceptor</value>
<value>timeExecutionInterceptor</value>
<value>memoryJVMInterceptor</value>
            </list>
        </property>
    </bean>
...
</beans>
```

Advised objects

In the examples used in this chapter, we have seen the different proxies available. It's significant to note that Spring even allows the manipulation of proxies, with the `org.springframework.aop.framework.Advised` interface that is implemented by proxies. The default operations exposed by this interface can be can be done on an existing proxy.

An exception is constituted by the introductions (`introduction advisor`), which can't be applied on the already created proxy. (If necessary, a new proxy instance is requested.)

```
Advisor[] getAdvisors();
```

This returns the advisor's array contained in the proxy.

```
void addAdvice(Advice advice) throws AopConfigException;
```

This allows the addition of an advice.

```
void addAdvice(int pos, Advice advice) throws AopConfigException;
```

This adds an advice at the specified position (the order reflects the order of application to the target object).

```
void addAdvisor(Advisor advisor) throws AopConfigException;
```

This adds an advisor. If that's an interceptor, it is wrapped in a
DefaultPointcutAdvisor, which uses a pointcut that always returns
true, and as an interceptor it returns the passed argument.

```
void addAdvisor(int pos, Advisor advisor) throws AopConfigException;
```

This adds an advisor at the defined position. If that's an interceptor it is wrapped in a
DefaultPointcutAdvisor, which uses a pointcut that always returns true, and
as an interceptor returns the passed argument.

```
int indexOf(Advisor advisor);
```

This returns the index where the advisor is:

```
boolean removeAdvisor(Advisor advisor) throws AopConfigException;
```

This removes an advisor.

```
void removeAdvisor(int index) throws AopConfigException;
```

This removes the advisor at the specified position.

```
boolean replaceAdvisor(Advisor a, Advisor b) throws
AopConfigException;
```

This replaces an advisor with another one.

```
boolean isFrozen();
```

This signals if it's in the frozen state (already explained in the chapter).

Now let's see an example.

```
package org.springaop.chapter.three;

import org.springaop.proxies.proxyfactorybean.domain.Command;
import org.springframework.aop.Advisor;
import org.springframework.aop.framework.Advised;
import org.springframework.context.ApplicationContext;
import org.springframework.context.support.
ClassPathXmlApplicationContext;

public class TestClass {

    public static void main(String[] args) {

            String[] paths = {"org/springaop/chapter/three/
applicationContext.xml"};
            ApplicationContext ctx = new ClassPathXmlApplicationContext(
paths);
```

```
        Command command = (Command)ctx.getBean("command");

        Advisor consoleAdvisor = (Advisor)ctx.getBean(
        "consoleAdvisor");

        Advised advised = (Advised) command;

        System.out.println("Is Frozen ?:"+advised.isFrozen());
        System.out.println("Advisors size:"+advised.getAdvisors().
        length);
        System.out.println("IndexOf consoleAdvisor :"
        +advised.indexOf(consoleAdvisor));

    }
}
```

This test class shows how the `advised` interface's method can be called on a proxy. First of all, a bean (`command`) that we know is behind a proxy is retrieved.

Another bean is retrieved because it's known to be an advisor containing pointcut and advice. After that, we obtain pieces of information from `command` through the `advised` interface.

We could even add other advisors at runtime in particular positions by calling the `addAdvisor` methods on the advised object, and specifying the positions where we want to add them.

```
applicationContext.xml:

<beans xmlns="http://www.springframework.org/schema/beans"
xmlns:xsi="http://www.w3.org/2001/XMLSchema-instance"
xsi:schemaLocation="http://www.springframework.org/schema/beans
http://www.springframework.org/schema/beans/spring-beans-2.5.xsd">
...
<bean id="commandTarget"
    class="org.springaop.chapter.three.domain.CommandImpl"/>
...
<bean id="consoleAdvice"
    class="org.springaop.chapter.three.ConsoleAdvice"/>
<!-- Advisor -->
<bean id="consoleAdvisor" class="org.springframework.aop.support.
DefaultPointcutAdvisor">
        <property name="pointcut" ref="methodNamePointcut"/>
        <property name="advice" ref="consoleAdvice"/>
    </bean>
<!-- Pointcut -->
<bean id="methodNamePointcut"
    class="org.springframework.aop.support.NameMatchMethodPointcut">
    <property name="mappedName" value="execute"/>
```

```
        </bean>
        ...
        <bean id="command"
             class="org.springframework.aop.framework.ProxyFactoryBean">
               <property name="proxyInterfaces"
                  value="org.springaop.proxies.proxyfactorybean.domain.
Command"/>
               <property name="target"><ref local="commandTarget"/>
        </property>
               <property name="interceptorNames">
                  <list>
                     <value>timeExecutionInterceptor</value>
                     <value>consoleAdvisor</value>
                  </list>
               </property>
        </bean>

        </beans>
```

Output:

If we don't want changes to be allowed anymore, we have to set the proxy property setFrozen as true; after that, any attempt to add or remove advices would cause an AopConfigException.

The adoption of freezing the proxy state is advisable. For example, when you're already managing an aspect concerning security, removing any type of advice or interceptor would mean revoking the authorization rules.

Autoproxy

Spring also allows us to use "autoproxy" bean definitions, which can automatically proxy selected bean definitions.

Autoproxy with classic Spring

In the section about `ProxyFactoryBean`, we saw how to use AOP in the classic way. But it's clear that writing seperately for each bean on which we want to apply an advisor is not a pleasant thing to see, especially if they are many. So let's consider it as a practicable way only if the beans to be configured in that modality are few.

On the other hand, if the beans to which we have to apply AOP are many, in order to avoid finding ourselves with very long configuration files, we adopt another tactic: We use the auto proxy creator system, which allows us to automatically create proxies for the beans and avoid using `ProxyFactoryBean`.

There are two classes made available by Spring to allow the autoproxy creator: `BeanNameAutoProxyCreator` and `DefaultAdvisorAutoProxyCreator`.

BeanNameAutoProxyCreator

`BeanNameAutoProxyCreator` just has a list of beans names to which proxies can be created automatically.

The way in which the autoproxy is created is really simple. It implements the `BeanPostProcessor` interface, which in its implementation replaces the bean (target) with a proxy.

Example:

This is the interface describing an animal.

```
package org.springaop.chapter.three.autoproxy.domain;

public interface Animal {

    public Integer getNumberPaws();
    public Boolean hasTail();
    public boolean hasFur();
    public Boolean hasHotBlood();

}
```

The interface `Bird` extends `Animal`.

```
package org.springaop.chapter.three.autoproxy.domain;

public interface Bird extends Animal{

    public Boolean hasBeak();
    public Boolean hasFeathers();

}
```

The class that implements the `Animal` interface to describe `Cat`:

```
package org.springaop.chapter.three.autoproxy.domain;

public class Cat implements Animal{

    public boolean hasFur() {
        return true;
    }

    public Integer getNumberPaws() {
        return 4;
    }

    public Boolean hasTail() {
        return true;
    }

    public Boolean hasHotBlood() {
        return true;
    }

    public void setSpecies(String species) {
        this.species = species;
    }

    public String getSpecies() {
        return species;
    }

    public String getColour() {
        return colour;
    }

    public void setColour(String colour) {
        this.colour = colour;
    }

    private String species, colour;
}
```

The class that implements `Animal` and `Bird` to describe a `Seabird`:

```
package org.springaop.chapter.three.autoproxy.domain;

public class Seabird implements Animal,Bird{

    public Integer getNumberPaws() {
        return 2;
    }
```

```
    public Boolean hasTail() {
        return false;
    }

    public Boolean hasBeak() {
        return true;
    }

    public Boolean hasFeathers() {
        return true;
    }

    public boolean hasFur() {
        return false;
    }

    public Boolean hasHotBlood() {
        return false;
    }

    public String getName() {
        return name;
    }

    public void setName(String name) {
        this.name = name;
    }

    private String name;
}
```

`AnimalAdvice` containing just the log with the target class, the invoked method, and the result:

```
package org.springaop.chapter.three.autoproxy;

import org.aopalliance.intercept.MethodInterceptor;
import org.aopalliance.intercept.MethodInvocation;

public class AnimalAdvice implements MethodInterceptor {

    public Object invoke(MethodInvocation invocation) throws Throwable
    {
        Logger log = Logger.getLogger(Constants.LOG_NAME);
        StringBuilder sb = new StringBuilder();
        sb.append("Target Class:").append(invocation.getThis()).
append("\n").append(
                        invocation.getMethod()).append("\n");

        Object retVal = invocation.proceed();
```

```
            sb.append(" return value:").append(retVal).append("\n");
            log.info(sb.toString());
            return retVal;
    }
}
```

The configuration file `applicationContext.xml`:

```xml
<beans xmlns="http://www.springframework.org/schema/beans"
xmlns:xsi="http://www.w3.org/2001/XMLSchema-instance"
xsi:schemaLocation="http://www.springframework.org/schema/beans
http://www.springframework.org/schema/beans/spring-beans-2.5.xsd">

    <bean id="tiger" class="org.springaop.chapter.three.autoproxy.
domain.Cat">
        <property name="species" value="tiger"/>
        <property name="colour" value="tear stripes"/>
</bean>

    <bean id="albatross" class="org.springaop.chapter.three.autoproxy.
domain.Seabird">
     <property name="name" value="albatross"/>
</bean>

    <!-- Pointcut -->
    <bean id="methodNamePointcut" class="org.springframework.aop.
support.NameMatchMethodPointcut">
        <property name="mappedNames">
            <list>
                    <value>has*</value>
                    <value>get*</value>
            </list>
        </property>
    </bean>

    <!-- Advices -->
    <bean id="animalAdvice" class="org.springaop.chapter.three.
autoproxy.AnimalAdvice"/>

    <!-- Advisor -->
    <bean id="animalAdvisor" class="org.springframework.aop.support.
DefaultPointcutAdvisor">
        <property name="pointcut" ref="methodNamePointcut"/>
        <property name="advice" ref="animalAdvice"/>
    </bean>
```

```
        <bean id="autoProxyCreator" class="org.springframework.aop.
framework.autoproxy.BeanNameAutoProxyCreator">
                <property name="proxyTargetClass" value="true"/>
                <property name="beanNames">
                        <list>
                                <value>tiger</value>
                                <value>albatross</value>
                        </list>
                </property>
                        <property name="interceptorNames">
                                <list>
                                        <value>animalAdvisor</value>
                                </list>
                        </property>
                </bean>

        </beans>
```

Application context contains two beans, `tiger` and `albatross`. The `methodNamePointcut` acts on the methods starting with `has` and `get`.

The `animalAdvice` (around `advice`) contains the logic to be executed, the animal advisor that links the `animalAdvice` to the `methodNamePointcut`, and the `autoProxyCreator`, where we declare just the beans' names and the list of interceptors' names.

```
    package org.springaop.chapter.three.autoproxy;

    public class AutoProxyTest {

        public static void main(String[] args) {

                String[] paths = { "org/springaop/chapter/three/
autoautoproxy/applicationContext.xml" };

                ApplicationContext ctx = new ClassPathXmlApplicationContext(
paths);

                Cat tiger = (Cat)ctx.getBean("tiger");
                tiger.hasHotBlood();

                Bird albatross = (Bird)ctx.getBean("albatross");
                albatros.hasBeak();
        }
    }
```

The test class invokes two methods on the beans `tiger` and `albatross`.

Output:

```
Problems  Ju JUnit  Console ⊠    Spring Explorer  Spring AOP Event Trace          ■ ✖
<terminated> AutoProxyTest [Java Application] /usr/local/jdk1.6.0_07/bin/java (Sep 14, 2008 1:14:17 AM)
 INFO [main] - Refreshing org.springframework.context.support.ClassPathXmlApplicationContext@872380: dis
 INFO [main] - Loading XML bean definitions from class path resource [org/springaop/chapter/three/autopr
 INFO [main] - Bean factory for application context [org.springframework.context.support.ClassPathXmlApp
 INFO [main] - Pre-instantiating singletons in org.springframework.beans.factory.support.DefaultListable
 INFO [main] - Target Class:org.springaop.chapter.three.autoproxy.domain.Cat@f18e8e
public java.lang.Boolean org.springaop.chapter.three.autoproxy.domain.Cat.hasHotBlood()
 return value:true

 INFO [main] - Target Class:org.springaop.chapter.three.autoproxy.domain.Cat@f18e8e
public java.lang.Integer org.springaop.chapter.three.autoproxy.domain.Cat.getNumberPaws()
 return value:4

tiger.hasHotBlood():true
tiger.getNumberPaws():4

 INFO [main] - Target Class:org.springaop.chapter.three.autoproxy.domain.Seabird@14b5f4a
public java.lang.Boolean org.springaop.chapter.three.autoproxy.domain.Seabird.hasBeak()
 return value:true

 INFO [main] - Target Class:org.springaop.chapter.three.autoproxy.domain.Seabird@14b5f4a
public java.lang.Integer org.springaop.chapter.three.autoproxy.domain.Seabird.getNumberPaws()
 return value:2

albatross.hasBeak():true
albatross.getNumberPaws():2
```

DefaultAdvisorAutoProxyCreator

With `BeanNameAutoProxyCreator`, we've seen that the configuration file's length has reduced; but we can do better.

Using the previous example, we modify only the configuration file.

```
<beans xmlns="http://www.springframework.org/schema/beans"
xmlns:xsi="http://www.w3.org/2001/XMLSchema-instance"
xsi:schemaLocation="http://www.springframework.org/schema/beans
http://www.springframework.org/schema/beans/spring-beans-2.5.xsd">

    <bean id="tiger" class="org.springaop.proxies.autoproxy.domain.
Cat">
            <property name="species" value="tiger"/>
            <property name="colour" value="tear stripes"/>
    </bean>

    <bean id="albatross" class="org.springaop.chapter.three.autoproxy.
domain.Seabird">
     <property name="name" value="albatross"/>
    </bean>
```

```xml
    <!-- Pointcut -->
    <bean id="methodNamePointcut" class="org.springframework.aop.
support.NameMatchMethodPointcut">
        <property name="mappedNames">
            <list>
                <value>has*</value>
                <value>get*</value>
            </list>
        </property>
    </bean>

    <!-- Advices -->
    <bean id="animalAdvice" class="org.springaop.chapter.three.
autoproxy.AnimalAdvice"/>

    <!-- Advisor -->
    <bean id="animalAdvisor" class="org.springframework.aop.support.
DefaultPointcutAdvisor">
        <property name="pointcut" ref="methodNamePointcut"/>
        <property name="advice" ref="animalAdvice"/>
    </bean>

    <bean class="org.springframework.aop.framework.autoproxy.
DefaultAdvisorAutoProxyCreator" >
        <property name="proxyTargetClass" value="true"/>
    </bean>

</beans>
```

With `DefaultAdvisorAutoProxyCreator`, we don't need to define anything, apart from declaring it. This is because it applies the proxies' creation for the classes concerned in the advisors' application through pointcuts. It's important to have advisors, and not any other type of interceptor, because the operation is based on advisors.

The result of the advices' application is the same as you can see from the output:

```
Problems  JUnit  Console ⊠    Spring Explorer  Spring AOP Event Trace              ⊠
<terminated> AutoProxyTest (1) [Java Application] /usr/local/jdk1.6.0_07/bin/java (Sep 14, 2008 1:13:45 AM)
 INFO [main] - Refreshing org.springframework.context.support.ClassPathXmlApplicationContext@872380: dis
 INFO [main] - Loading XML bean definitions from class path resource [org/springaop/chapter/three/autopr
 INFO [main] - Bean factory for application context [org.springframework.context.support.ClassPathXmlApp
 INFO [main] - Pre-instantiating singletons in org.springframework.beans.factory.support.DefaultListable
 INFO [main] - Target Class:org.springaop.chapter.three.autoproxy.domain.Cat@f18e8e
public java.lang.Boolean org.springaop.chapter.three.autoproxy.domain.Cat.hasHotBlood()
 return value:true

 INFO [main] - Target Class:org.springaop.chapter.three.autoproxy.domain.Cat@f18e8e
public java.lang.Integer org.springaop.chapter.three.autoproxy.domain.Cat.getNumberPaws()
 return value:4

tiger.hasHotBlood():true
tiger.getNumberPaws():4

 INFO [main] - Target Class:org.springaop.chapter.three.autoproxy.domain.Seabird@14b5f4a
public java.lang.Boolean org.springaop.chapter.three.autoproxy.domain.Seabird.hasBeak()
 return value:true

 INFO [main] - Target Class:org.springaop.chapter.three.autoproxy.domain.Seabird@14b5f4a
public java.lang.Integer org.springaop.chapter.three.autoproxy.domain.Seabird.getNumberPaws()
 return value:2

albatross.hasBeak():true
albatross.getNumberPaws():2
```

AbstractAdvisorAutoProxyCreator

If you want to create your own `AutoproxyCreator`, you can employ
the `DefaultAdvisorAutoProxyCreator` superclass, which is the
`AbstractAdvisorAutoProxyCreator`, just by extending it.

AutoProxyCreator with metadata

This autoproxy option concerns the possibility of employing annotations in the
classes, for example to define transactions.

In order to be able to employ this type of configuration, we have to use
`DefaultAdvisorAutoProxyCreator`, a `CommonsAttributes` bean that interprets
source-level metadata, and another bean that employs those attributes.

In order to employ the `CommosAttributes` bean, we must have in the classpath the
Jakarta library Commons Attributes (`http://commons.apache.org/attributes`).

```
<beans xmlns="http://www.springframework.org/schema/beans"
xmlns:xsi="http://www.w3.org/2001/XMLSchema-instance"
xsi:schemaLocation="http://www.springframework.org/schema/beans
http://www.springframework.org/schema/beans/spring-beans-2.5.xsd">
```

...

```
<bean id="autoProxyCreator" class="org.springframework.aop.framework.
autoproxy.DefaultAdvisorAutoProxyCreator"/>

    <bean id="advisor" class="org.springframework.transaction.
interceptor.TransactionAttributeSourceAdvisor">
        <property name="transactionInterceptor" ref="transactionInte
rceptor" />
    </bean>

    <bean id="transactionInterceptor" class="org.springframework.
transaction.interceptor.TransactionInterceptor">
        <property name="transactionManager" ref="transactionManager"
/>
        <property name="transactionAttributeSource">
            <bean class="org.springframework.transaction.
interceptor.AttributesTransactionAttributeSource">
                <property name="attributes"
ref="metadataAttributes" />
            </bean>
        </property>
    </bean>

    <bean id="metadataAttributes" class="org.springframework.metadata.
commons.CommonsAttributes" />

    <bean name="transactionManager" class="org.springframework.jdbc.
datasource.DataSourceTransactionManager">
        <property name="dataSource" ref="datasource"/>
    </bean>

</beans>
```

The `autoProxyCreator` bean creates proxies according to what advisors in the application context indicate to it, or the advices to apply and the pointcuts at which apply them.

In the example case, it is composed by a `transactionInterceptor`, the rules of which are defined into classes through annotations. In order to interpret these annotations, which are the bean's `attributes` property, it uses the `metadataAttributes` bean, which is of the type `CommonsAttributes`.

This type of configuration used mostly to be employed before JDK 1.5, and it requires a particular compilation task.

With the use of JDK 1.5 or upward, configuration doesn't require the use of the bean `CommonsAttributes` to interpret annotations.

```
<beans xmlns="http://www.springframework.org/schema/beans"
xmlns:xsi="http://www.w3.org/2001/XMLSchema-instance"
xsi:schemaLocation="http://www.springframework.org/schema/beans
http://www.springframework.org/schema/beans/spring-beans-2.5.xsd">
    <bean class="org.springframework.aop.framework.autoproxy.
DefaultAdvisorAutoProxyCreator"/>
    <bean class="org.springframework.transaction.interceptor.
TransactionAttributeSourceAdvisor">
        <property name="transactionInterceptor" ref="transactionInte
rceptor"/>
    </bean>
    <bean id="transactionInterceptor" class="org.springframework.
transaction.interceptor.TransactionInterceptor">
        <property name="transactionManager" ref="
transactionManager"/>
            <property name="transactionAttributeSource">
                <bean class="org.springframework.transaction.
annotation.AnnotationTransactionAttributeSource"/>
            </property>
    </bean>
    <bean name="transactionManager" class="org.springframework.jdbc.
datasource.DataSourceTransactionManager">
        <property name="dataSource" ref="datasource"/>
    </bean>
</beans>
```

Autoproxy with AspectJ

We have seen how autoproxy is used with the classic configuration of Spring. Now we're going to see a short introduction on proxies with AspectJ. We will have a full overview of their use in the chapter *AspectJ support*.

The use of AspectJ can be connected to two typologies: through code annotations or through XML Schema. Here are the rules that define which beans are excluded from the autoproxy:

- Proxy is not applied to beans that implement the interfaces `BeanPostProcessor` or `BeanFactoryPostProcessor`.

    The class `AnnotationAwareAspectJAutoProxyCreator` implements the interface `BeanPostProcessor`, which allows the class to modify the life cycle of beans on which a proxy must be created and applied.

- Classes with annotations @AspectJ and classes that implement or extend any other AOP component are excluded from the autoproxy. This is because they aren't target classes, and they perform tasks in Spring AOP infrastructure.

Apart from the beans that belong to these two cases, the others can be subject to proxy auto-creation. This is so if they are subject to aspects and advisors with the matching rules defined in pointcuts that are defined in the applicationContext.

Autoproxy with annotation

If we use annotations, we will tell Spring that proxies must be created according to them:

```
<beans xmlns="http://www.springframework.org/schema/beans"
xmlns:xsi="http://www.w3.org/2001/XMLSchema-instance"
xsi:schemaLocation="http://www.springframework.org/schema/beans
http://www.springframework.org/schema/beans/spring-beans-2.5.xsd">

    <bean class="org.springframework.aop.aspectj.annotation.
AnnotationAwareAspectJAutoProxyCreator"/>

    ...
</beans>
```

AnnotationAwareAspectJAutoProxyCreator must be declared only one time. It's used by Spring to configure all the classes that have the annotation @Aspect, in order to create the proxy for the annotated class and return it for the execution of advices when a pointcut is matched.

Autoproxy with XML Schema

If we want automatic generation of proxies, we will use the tag <aop:aspectj-autoproxy/> through the AOP namespaces. This tag too must be used one time. But in case of error, beans' proxies will be created only once, whereas if we declare AnnotationAwareAspectJAutoProxyCreator at several points in beans, we'll have the proxies created several times. The effect is anyway identical to the use of the bean AnnotationAwareAspectJAutoProxyCreator.

```
<?xml version="1.0" encoding="UTF-8"?>
<beans xmlns="http://www.springframework.org/schema/beans"
xmlns:xsi="http://www.w3.org/2001/XMLSchema-instance"
xmlns:aop="http://www.springframework.org/schema/aop"
xsi:schemaLocation="http://www.springframework.org/schema/beans
http://www.springframework.org/schema/beans/spring-beans-2.5.xsd
http://www.springframework.org/schema/aop
```

```
http://www.springframework.org/schema/aop/spring-aop-2.5.xsd">
...
    <aop:aspectj-autoproxy/>
    ...
</beans>
```

If we want to force the use of CGLIB proxies, we will modify the tag `aspectj-autoproxy` in this way:

```
<?xml version="1.0" encoding="UTF-8"?>
<beans xmlns="http://www.springframework.org/schema/beans"
xmlns:xsi="http://www.w3.org/2001/XMLSchema-instance"
xmlns:aop="http://www.springframework.org/schema/aop"
xsi:schemaLocation="http://www.springframework.org/schema/beans
http://www.springframework.org/schema/beans/spring-beans-2.5.xsd
http://www.springframework.org/schema/aop
http://www.springframework.org/schema/aop/spring-aop-2.5.xsd">

    <aop:aspectj-autoproxy proxy-target-class="true"/>
...
</beans>
```

Target sources

Until now, we have used the word "target" to define the object that receives the calls from a caller object, where a proxy was interposed to add logic contained in advices.

In this interposition mechanism, Spring puts at our disposal the interface `org.springframework.aop.TargetSource`, which returns the `object target`.

```
public interface TargetSource {

Class getTargetClass();

boolean isStatic();

Object getTarget() throws Exception;

void releaseTarget(Object target) throws Exception;
}
```

This interface is interesting as it permits target pooling and hot swapping.

Without specifying the `targetSource`, the default implementation that wraps the local object is returned and also the target is returned for all the following invocations.

Hot swappable target sources

The target source `org.springframework.aop.target.HotSwappableTargetSource` allows a proxy's target object to be replaced in a `ThreadSafe` way with immediate effect, and the caller doesn't lose the reference.

To make the change, the method `swap()` is called.

Example interface:

```
package org.springaop.chapter.three.autoproxy.domain;

public interface Animal {

    public Integer getNumberPaws();
}
```

Implementing class:

```
package org.springaop.chapter.three.autoproxy.domain;

public class AnimalImpl implements Animal{

    public Integer getNumberPaws() {
            return paws;
    }

    public void setPaws(Integer paws) {
            this.paws = paws;
    }

    private Integer paws;
}
```

`ApplicationContext.xml`, which contains three `AnimalImpl`, one swappable bean, and one `ProxyFactoryBean`:

```
<beans xmlns="http://www.springframework.org/schema/beans"
xmlns:xsi="http://www.w3.org/2001/XMLSchema-instance"
xsi:schemaLocation="http://www.springframework.org/schema/beans
http://www.springframework.org/schema/beans/spring-beans-2.5.xsd">

    <bean id="animal1" class="org.springaop.chapter.three.autoproxy.
domain.AnimalImpl">
      <property name="paws" value="2" />
</bean>
```

```xml
<bean id="animal2" class="org.springaop.chapter.three.autoproxy.
domain.AnimalImpl">
    <property name="paws" value="4" />
</bean>

<bean id="animal3" class="org.springaop.chapter.three.autoproxy.
domain.AnimalImpl">
    <property name="paws" value="1000" />
</bean>
    <bean id="swapper" class="org.springframework.aop.target.
HotSwappableTargetSource">
        <constructor-arg><ref local="animal1"/></constructor-arg>
    </bean>

    <bean id="swappable" class="org.springframework.aop.framework.
ProxyFactoryBean">
        <property name="targetSource"><ref local="swapper"/></
property>
    </bean>

</beans>
```

The test class:

```java
package org.springaop.chapter.three.targetsource.swap;

import org.springaop.targetsources.domain.Animal;
import org.springframework.aop.target.HotSwappableTargetSource;
import org.springframework.context.ApplicationContext;
import org.springframework.context.support.
ClassPathXmlApplicationContext;

public class SwappableTargetSourceTest {

    public static void main(String[] args) {

        String[] paths = { "org/springaop/chapter/three/
targetsource/swap/applicationContext.xml" };
        ApplicationContext ctx = new ClassPathXmlApplicationContext(
paths);

        Animal target1 = (Animal) ctx.getBean("animal1");
        Animal target2 = (Animal) ctx.getBean("animal2");
        Animal target3 = (Animal) ctx.getBean("animal3");

        Animal proxied = (Animal) ctx.getBean("swappable");

        System.out.println(proxied.getNumberPaws());

        HotSwappableTargetSource swapper =
(HotSwappableTargetSource)
```

```
            ctx.getBean("swapper");

            Object old = swapper.swap(target2);

            System.out.println(proxied.getNumberPaws());

            Object oldTwo = swapper.swap(target3);

            System.out.println(proxied.getNumberPaws());
        }
    }
```

Output:

```
Problems  Ju JUnit  Console ⊠   Spring Explorer  Spring AOP Event Trace
<terminated> SwappableTargetSourceTest [Java Application] /usr/local/jdk1.6.0_07/bin/j
 INFO [main] - Refreshing org.springframework.context.support.ClassPat
 INFO [main] - Loading XML bean definitions from class path resource [
 INFO [main] - Bean factory for application context [org.springframewc
 INFO [main] - Pre-instantiating singletons in org.springframework.bea
2
4
1000
```

Pooling target sources

The target source `org.springframework.aop.target.CommonsPoolTargetSource` works with Jakarta Library's Commons pool that must be in the classpath, and provides a behavior where the objects are part of a pool and one of these objects is provided to the caller. But the target object must be `prototype`, and this is because the `PoolingTargetSource` creates a new instance of the target object every time it's necessary.

If we need it, we can have information about the pool and can tell Spring to cast the pool objects with `org.springframework.aop.target.PoolingConfig`.

Example:

```
<beans xmlns="http://www.springframework.org/schema/beans"
xmlns:xsi="http://www.w3.org/2001/XMLSchema-instance"
xsi:schemaLocation="http://www.springframework.org/schema/beans
http://www.springframework.org/schema/beans/spring-beans-2.5.xsd">

<bean id="animalTarget" class="org.springaop.chapter.three.autoproxy.
domain.AnimalImpl" scope="prototype">
    <property name="paws" value="2" />
</bean>
```

```
    <bean id="poolTargetSource" class="org.springframework.aop.target.
CommonsPoolTargetSource">
        <property name="targetBeanName" value="animalTarget"/>
        <property name="maxSize" value="14"/>
    </bean>

    <bean id="animal" class="org.springframework.aop.framework.
ProxyFactoryBean">
        <property name="targetSource" ref="poolTargetSource"/>
    </bean>
...
</beans>
```

Prototype target sources

With this targetSource, a new instance of the target class is provided at every invocation. We have to consider the fact that if the creation of new objects is not wasteful, then the wiring of every object in the applicationContext could be wasteful.

Unless we have particular needs, this type of targetSource is inadvisable.

```
<beans xmlns="http://www.springframework.org/schema/beans"
xmlns:xsi="http://www.w3.org/2001/XMLSchema-instance"
xsi:schemaLocation="http://www.springframework.org/schema/beans
http://www.springframework.org/schema/beans/spring-beans-2.5.xsd">

<bean id="animalTargetObject" class="org.springaop.chapter.three.
autoproxy.domain.AnimalImpl" scope="prototype" >
    <property name="paws" value="4"/>
</bean>

    <bean id="animalObject" class="org.springframework.aop.framework.
ProxyFactoryBean">
        <property name="targetSource" ref="prototypeAnimalTargetSour
ce"/>
    </bean>

    <bean id="prototypeAnimalTargetSource" class="org.springframework.
aop.target.PrototypeTargetSource">
        <property name="targetBeanName" ref="animalTarget"/>
    </bean>
...
</beans>
```

ThreadLocal target source

A `ThreadLocal` target source is indicated when we need to have an object for each request (that is, per thread). The concept of a `ThreadLocal` provides a JDK-wide facility to transparently store resources alongside a thread.

With this type of `targetSource` we have to pay attention to problems that can arise, such as memory leaks. It would be appropriate to wrap the `ThreadLocal` and never use it directly, and to set and remove resources properly from the thread. Spring provides support for the `ThreadLocal`, and its use should be favored.

```
<beans xmlns="http://www.springframework.org/schema/beans"
xmlns:xsi="http://www.w3.org/2001/XMLSchema-instance"
xsi:schemaLocation="http://www.springframework.org/schema/beans
http://www.springframework.org/schema/beans/spring-beans-2.5.xsd">
    ...

    <bean id="animalTargetThreadObject" class="org.springaop.chapter.
three.autoproxy.domain.AnimalImpl" scope="prototype">
        <property name="paws" value="4"/>
</bean>

    <bean id="threadlocalTargetSource" class="org.springframework.aop.
target.ThreadLocalTargetSource">
        <property name="targetBeanName" value="animalTargetThreadObj
ect"/>
    </bean>
...

</beans>
```

Summary

In this chapter we have seen the important role of proxies on which all Spring AOP is based. We have seen how to use proxies in a programmatic way and with several implementations (JDK and CGLIB). We have seen how `ProxyFactoryBean` simplifies and masks the work of proxies' creation and preparation. Then we saw how to reduce the configuration with the features provided by Spring for the automatic creation of beans with three types of autoproxy. Towards the end of the chapter we glanced at how Spring allows us to act on advised objects and target sources, to enable us to do advanced operations in our code.

4
AspectJ Support

In this chapter, we will see how AspectJ facilitates Spring AOP. We will particularly focus on syntax for pointcuts and the possibility of using IoC on domain objects: either the definition is applied to the hierarchies of objects (context bindings), or pointcuts are applied on the names of Spring beans. We will see how aspects are set up in complex contexts to avoid conflicts, and which advanced functionalities are allowed (annotations on annotations). The possibility of using AspectJ syntax means that we can define the rules on which aspects can be applied through pointcuts in a better way. There are two modalities to use AspectJ's features with Spring: by means of annotations and XML configuration.

AspectJ annotations

The annotations introduced in Java 5 allow us to add features in a very simple way.

In our context, they allow us to define aspects and other AOP components already seen in this book, by means of annotations.

The power of this functionality lies in allowing the definition of aspect, pointcut, and advice directly on Java classes with features provided by AspectJ. One doesn't have to put up with inconveniences such as the alteration of bytecode required by a solution based only on AspectJ.

To put the AOP components together, a proxy is created (autoproxy) on the beans on which annotations have been defined.

In SpringAOP, an aspect can't be a target of another aspect.

Annotation:

To use AspectJ as shown below, there must be the two JARs in the classpath: `aspectjweaver.jar` and `aspectjrt.jar`.

They are available in the `lib/aspectj` folder in the distribution Spring-with-dependencies, or in the `lib` folder of the installation of AspectJ (1.5.x or upwards).

Aspect

An aspect is a normal Java class with the annotation `@Aspect`, and also a Spring bean.

```
import org.aspectj.lang.annotation.Aspect;

@Aspect
public class AspectJAnnotatedExample {
...
}
```

Like any other class, it can have methods and fields, and can contain pointcuts, advices, and introductions.

To tell Spring that it must create autoproxies for the classes that are noted in the configuration, we have to write:

```
<?xml version="1.0" encoding="UTF-8"?>
<beans xmlns="http://www.springframework.org/schema/beans"
xmlns:xsi="http://www.w3.org/2001/XMLSchema-instance"
xsi:schemaLocation="http://www.springframework.org/schema/beans
http://www.springframework.org/schema/beans/spring-beans-2.5.xsd">

<bean class="org.springframework.aop.aspectj.annotation.
AnnotationAwareAspectJAutoProxyCreator"/>
...
</beans>
```

If we want to use AOP namespaces, we have to write:

```
<?xml version="1.0" encoding="UTF-8"?>
<beans xmlns="http://www.springframework.org/schema/beans"
xmlns:xsi="http://www.w3.org/2001/XMLSchema-instance"
xmlns:aop="http://www.springframework.org/schema/aop"
xsi:schemaLocation="http://www.springframework.org/schema/beans
http://www.springframework.org/schema/beans/spring-beans-2.5.xsd
```

```
http://www.springframework.org/schema/aop
http://www.springframework.org/schema/aop/spring-aop-2.5.xsd">

<aop:aspectj-autoproxy/>

</beans>
```

Pointcut

In the previous chapters, we said that Spring AOP uses the execution of the methods on Spring beans as a pointcut.

The declaration of a pointcut is composed of two parts: a signature with parameters, and the expression that determines exactly the method execution that must be intercepted by the pointcut.

By annotating methods, it's possible to indicate at which points of the execution flow (in the Aspect class) the advices must be applied with their additional logic.

```
package org.springaop.chapter.four.pointcut;

import org.aspectj.lang.annotation.Aspect;
import org.aspectj.lang.annotation.Before;

@Aspect
public class AspectJAnnotatedExample {

    ...

    @Before("execution(* insert(..))")
    public void fooMethod(){

    }
    ...
}
```

As I have said several times, Spring AOP provides fewer pointcuts compared to AspectJ in order to simplify the use of Aspect-Oriented Programming. The expressions that can be defined in methods that function as advice, as in the case of the **before** method in the example, are the expressions to designate pointcuts. They are indicated as **Pointcut Designators (PCD)**.

With Spring AOP, PCD that acts with the execution of methods as joinpoints are available. They are:

* execution
* within
* this

- target
- args
- @target
- @args
- @within
- @annotation
- bean

Moreover, we have the possibility of indicating a Spring bean that acts at instance level, and is available only with Spring AOP and not with AspectJ.

target and args are more commonly used in the binding form. @target, @within, @annotation and @args can also be used in the binding form.

We will explain the binding form later in this chapter.

The wildcard characters that can be used in the definition of pointcut designators are:

*, && (AND), || (OR), ! (negated), and +, which indicates the hierarchy of the object to which it is applied.

Let's see the role of each PCD.

execution

This PCD is used to define the execution of methods as joinpoints. This is the main pointcut designator used.

within

This limits the matching of joinpoints to the execution from within some types of classes.

this

This limits matching to joinpoints where the bean reference (Spring AOP proxy) is an instance of the given type.

target

This limits matching to joinpoints where the target object (application object being proxied) is an instance of the given type.

args

This limits matching to joinpoints (the execution of methods when using Spring AOP) where the arguments are instances of the given types.

@target

This limits matching to joinpoints where the class of the executing object has an annotation of the given type.

@args

This limits matching to joinpoints where the runtime type of the actual arguments passed has annotations of the given type(s).

@ within

This limits matching to joinpoints within types that have the given annotation (the execution of methods declared in types with the given annotation when using Spring AOP).

@ annotation

This limits matching to joinpoints where the subject of the joinpoint has the given annotation.

bean

The form to define the execution of a bean is `bean(idOrNameOfBean)`. This pointcut designator acts only at instance level, rather than at type level, since Spring 2.5.

This pointcut is only supported in XML-based Spring AOP configurations, and not in AspectJ annotations.

The following of AspectJ's PCD are not available in Spring: their use causes an `IllegalArgumentException`:

- `call`
- `get`
- `set`
- `preinitialization`
- `staticinitialization`

- initialization
- handler
- adviceexecution
- withincode
- cflow
- cflowbelow
- if
- @this
- @withincode

The advantage of defining a poincut rather than the type of advice in methods' annotation is having the possibility of reusing pointcuts in the aspects and combining them to compose more complex rules.

 If the pointcut used in the aspect is not located in the same class, you have to include the package name also.

Now let's declare them:

```
package org.springaop.chapter.four.pointcut;

import org.aspectj.lang.annotation.Aspect;
import org.aspectj.lang.annotation.Pointcut;

@Aspect
public class ApplicationPointcutsAspect {

    @Pointcut("execution (public * *(..))")
    public void allPublicMethod(){}

    @Pointcut("within(org.springaop.web..*)")
    public void inWebLayer(){}

    @Pointcut("within(org.springaop.service..*)")
    public void inServiceLayer(){}

    @Pointcut("within(org.springaop.dao..*)")
    public void inResourceLayer(){}

    @Pointcut("inWebLayer() && inServiceLayer() && inResourceLayer()
")
    public void inAllLayers(){}
}
```

The @Pointcut must be declared within a class annotated with @Aspect.

In the method allPublicMethod, the matching is declared on the execution of public methods.

Its body is empty. This method is in fact not called, but is used just to define a pointcut.

Once pointcuts have been defined, it is possible to use them in the annotations with advices.

```
package org.springaop.chapter.four.pointcut;

import org.aspectj.lang.annotation.Aspect;
import org.aspectj.lang.annotation.Before;

@Aspect
public class FooAspect {

    @Before ("org.springaop.chapter.four.pointcut.
ApplicationPointcutsAspect.inResourceLayer()")
    public void beforeFooMethods(){
        //do something
    }

}
```

In class FooAspect, a pointcut defined in class ApplicationPointcutsAspect was used with a before advice.

Let's see the formal syntax of a pointcut execution as an example:

```
execution(modifiers-pattern? ret-type-pattern declaring-type-pattern?
name-pattern(param-pattern) throws-pattern?
```

All the fields apart from ret-type-pattern, that is the return-type pattern, name-pattern (method name), and param-pattern (name and type of parameters) are optional (indicated with the "?")

Usable patterns include the wildcard characters as well.

The asterisk (*) indicates any type, and can be used as a wildcard even in a fully qualified type name.

Empty brackets () indicate a method without parameters, whereas brackets containing two dots (..) indicate any number of parameters (even no parameters).

An asterisk between brackets (*) means just a parameter of any type.

Let's see some examples.

```
execution(public * *(..))
```

In this case, the `modifiers-pattern` is `public`, and therefore it refers to public methods.

The "*" (asterisk) means "any value": applied to the method's return type and name (`declaring-type-pattern`) it matches with a public method with any return type and with any name. For the `name-pattern` there is an *, which matches a method with any name, and the (`param-pattern`) is (..) so any number of parameters is allowed.

In this example, this pointcut designator will match any public method in any package.

```
execution(* set*(..))
```

This pointcut intercepts the execution of any type of method (`public`, `protected`), whose name starts with "set" and accepts any number and type of parameters.

```
execution(* org.springaop.service.Example.*(..))
```

This pointcut intercepts the execution of methods with any visibility (`public`, `protected`, `private`, `default`) that are contained in the `Example` class in the `org.springaop.service` package and accept any type and number of parameters.

```
execution(* org.springaop.service.*.*(..))
```

This pointcut intercepts the execution of methods with any visibility (`public`, `protected`) and name that are contained in the package `org.springaop.service` and accept any type and number of parameters.

```
execution(* org.springaop.service..*.*(..))
```

This pointcut intercepts the execution of methods with any visibility (`public`, `protected`, `private`, `default`) and name that are contained in the package `org.springaop.service` or in its subpackages and accept any type and number of parameters.

```
within(org.springaop.service..*)
```

This pointcut intercepts the execution of any method into the package or subpackages of `org.springaop.service`.

```
within(org.springaop.service.*)
```

This pointcut intercepts the execution of any method into the package
`org.springaop.service`.

Pointcuts equivalent:
```
execution(*org.springaop.service.ExampleService.*(..))
within(org.springaop.service.ExampleService)
```

```
this(org.springaop.service.ExampleService)
```

This pointcut intercepts any method where the proxy implements the
`ExampleService` interface.

```
target(org.springaop.service.ExampleService)
```

This pointcut intercepts the execution of any method where the target object
implements the `ExampleService` interface.

```
args(java.lang.String)
```

This pointcut intercepts the execution of any method where at runtime a parameter
is String type.

```
args(*, java.lang.String)
```

This pointcut intercepts the execution of any method where at runtime the first
parameter is of any type, and the second parameter is String type.

The difference between

```
args(java.lang.String)
```

and

```
execution(* *(java.lang.String))
```

is that in the first case we consider the String type argument a runtime,
whereas the second one is String type in the method's declaration.

```
@target(org.springframework.transaction.annotation.Transactional)
```

This pointcut intercepts the execution of any method where the target object has the
`@Transactional` annotation.

```
@args(org.company.Classified)
```

This pointcut intercepts the execution of any method where, at runtime, a parameter has the `@Classified` annotation.

```
bean(magicbox.ehCache)
```

This pointcut intercepts any joinpoint on the bean called `magicbox.ehCache`.

```
bean(magicbox.*)
```

This pointcut intercepts any joinpoint on the beans with a name starting with `magicbox`.

```
execution(public * *(..)) throws java.lang.IOException
```

This pointcut intercepts the execution of public methods with any name, which return anything, accept any number and type of parameters, and have `throws java.lang.IOException` in the declaration.

```
within(org.company.domain.Example+)
```

This pointcut intercepts methods coming from examples or classes belonging to its own hierarchy, that is, of the same type.

After looking at these short introductory examples, we can logically collect the types of pointcut designators on the strength of general groupings.

- Selection on methods' names
- Selection on types of argument
- Selection on types of return
- Selection on declared exceptions
- Selection on hierarchy
- Selection on annotations

Selection on methods' names

Using wildcards, it is possible to compose pointcuts using the names of methods.

```
@Aspect
public class ApplicationPointcutsAspect {
...
@Pointcut("execution(* swim*(..)) || execution(* play*(..)) ||
execution(* run(..))")
    public void goodTimesOnTheBeach() {}
...
}
```

In this case, we are joining with logical OR the executions of methods whose name starts with `swim`, `play`, or `run`. The result is that the advice intercepts the execution of each of the three methods.

Selection on types of argument

We can compose several pointcuts using the arguments of the declarations of methods (opposite to `args`, which uses the values of arguments at runtime).

Let's see some pointcuts with names that explain their function:

```
package org.springaop.chapter.four.pointcut;
...
@Aspect
public class ApplicationPointcutsAspect {
...

    @Pointcut("execution(* *())")
    public void allMethodsWithoutArguments() {}

    @Pointcut("execution(* *(..))")
    public void allMethodsWithOneOrMoreArgumentRegarlessOfType() {}

    @Pointcut("execution(* *(java.lang.Integer, java.lang.String))")
    public void allMethodsWithTwoArgumentFirstIntegerSecondString() {}

    @Pointcut("execution(* *(java.lang.Integer,..))")
    public void
allMethodsWithFirstArgumentOfTypeIntegerAndZeroOrMoreOtherArguments()
{}

    @Pointcut("execution(* *(*,java.lang.Integer,..))")
    public void
allMethodsWithSecondArgumentOfTypeIntegerAndZeroOrMoreOtherArguments
() {}

    @Pointcut("args(java.util.Hashtable)")
    public void allMethodsWithHashtableInsteadOfMap() {}
...
}
```

Selection on type of return

Let's see some pointcuts with names that explain their functions:

```
package org.springaop.chapter.four.pointcut;

@Aspect
public class ApplicationPointcutsAspect {
...
        @Pointcut("execution (* get*(..))")
        public void methodsWithAllReturnType() {}

        @Pointcut("execution (java.lang.Integer get*(..))")
        public void getterMethodsWithIntegerReturnType() {}

        @Pointcut("execution (void set*(..))")
        public void setterMethods() {}
...
}
```

Selection on declared exceptions

Declared exceptions are supposed to be CheckedException.

Let's see some pointcuts with names that explain their function:

```
package org.springaop.chapter.four.pointcut;

@Aspect
public class ApplicationPointcutsAspect {
...
    @Pointcut("execution (* *(..) throws java.lang.IOException)")
    public void methodsThatThrowsIoExceptions() {}

@Pointcut("execution (* *(..) throws  java.lang.
IllegalThreadStateException)")
public void  methodsThatThrowsIllegalThreadStateException() {}
...
}
```

Selection on hierarchy

In this case, it is necessary to select the classes of a hierarchy (subtype pattern).

```
execution(* com.company.Product+.*(..))
```

or:

```
within(com.company.Product+)
```

Selection on annotations

Let's define an annotation:

```
package org.springaop.chapter.four.pointcut.annotation;

import java.lang.annotation.Retention;
import java.lang.annotation.RetentionPolicy;

@Retention(RetentionPolicy.RUNTIME)
public @interface SensitiveOperation {

}
```

Then we can use it:

```
package org.springaop.chapter.four.pointcut.annotation;

public class OnLineBanking {

    @SensitiveOperation
    public boolean addMoney(Integer amount){
        ...
    }
}
package org.springaop.chapter.four.pointcut;

@Aspect
public class ApplicationPointcutsAspect {
...
    @Pointcut("@annotation (org.springaop.chapter.four.pointcut.
annotation.SensitiveOperation)")
    public void methodsWithSensitiveOperationAnnotation(){}
...
}
```

It is now possible to use it in an advice like this:

```
@Before("org.springaop.chapter.four.pointcut.
ApplicationPointcutsAspect.methodsWithSensitiveOperationAnnotation
()")
public void methodsWithSensitiveOperationAnnotation() {}
```

or:

```
@Pointcut("@within(org.springaop.chapter.four.pointcut.annotation.
SensitiveOperation)")
public void methodsWithSensitiveOperationAnnotation() {}
```

Binding advice arguments

We can add arguments to advice methods and bind any argument value, exception, return value, or annotation.

JoinPoint

Advices can use a joinpoint implementation that contains information about the entering arguments (`getArgs()`), about the method on which the advice must be applied (`being advised`) (`getSignature()`), about the proxy object (`getThis()`), or about the target object (`getTarget()`). In around advices, the joinpoint's implementation is the `ProceedingJoinPoint`.

 In advices, `JoinPoint` (if present) must be the first argument passed.

Binding arguments

While using joinpoints, it may be necessary to read and to use arguments' methods with before advices, above all in order to limit the matching of methods that can be invoked simply with the execution.

Arguments can be obtained through `JoinPoint`, recovering them from the array of objects that is passed, and casting it.

```
@Before("execution(* set*(..))")
public void foo(JoinPoint jp){
        Object[] args = jp.getArgs();
}
```

or even defining `args` on the static match that is made with the execution.

In this way, Spring AOP binds a method's parameters, which must match.

```
@Before("execution(* set*(..)) && args(param,..)")
public void foo(String param){
    . . .
}
```

Parameters' binding in invocations is based on names contained in joinpoints, but not with reflection. SpringAOP uses the following strategy.

If the arguments' names are present, they are used:

```
@Before("execution(* set*(..) && args(name, surname))")
public void foo(String name, String surname){
    //do something
}
```

If `JoinPoint` is present too, both of them are used. But it's convenient to use `JoinPoint` if there is no other information available.

If there aren't arguments' names, Spring AOP recovers the information from the debug information, that can have been set at the time of compilation if the flag (`'-g: vars'`) has been set.

If the latter has NOT been set, Spring tries to deduce the binding matching variable with the parameter. If there were ambiguities that Spring could not resolve, an `AmbiguousBindingException` would be thrown.

If none of the previous points work, an `IllegalArgumentException` will be thrown.

 When declaring an independent pointcut that exposes parameters, you have to include it in the argument list of the pointcut method as well.

Binding of return values

Binding of return values can be useful with `AfterReturning` advices; you can assign a name to the return value (with `returning`) that is the name of the argument to be used in the advice.

```
@AfterReturning(value = "execution(com.company.service.*Service
get(..))", returning = "output")
public void interceptOutputParam(String output) {
    ...
}
```

Exception binding

Exception binding is used with an `AfterThrowing` advice; the `throwing` property specifies the argument name to be used in the advice.

```
@AfterThrowing(value = "execution(* startMatch(..) throws java.lang.
IOException)", throwing = "ioex")
public void interceptIOException(IOException ioex) {
    ..
}
```

Annotation binding

Annotations that compose the compiled class can be used to bind information they contain. Two cases are possible: annotation on methods or on classes.

If we define an annotation that has a value, this value can be bound.

```
package org.springaop.chapter.four.pointcut.annotation;

import java.lang.annotation.Retention;
import java.lang.annotation.RetentionPolicy;

@Retention(RetentionPolicy.RUNTIME)
public @interface SensitiveOperation {

    String value() default "secret";
}
```

In this way, the value given in the annotation-sensitive operation can be bound and passed to the method on which the pointcut is defined.

```
@Pointcut("@annotation(operation)")
    public void methodsForAccounting(SensitiveOperation operation){}
```

In case of annotation on class:

```
@SensitiveOperation(value="superSecret")
public class OnLineBanking {…}
```

the pointcut uses `within`, which works in a static manner at the level of class, using information obtained from the method's signature at the time of proxy creation.

```
@Pointcut("@within(operation)")
    public void bankingMethods(SensitiveOperation operation) {}
```

Advice

An advice is the logic part that is executed when a joinpoint's matching is done.

It's simply the action at the point indicated by the joinpoint during the execution of the application.

In the previous paragraph, we saw with several examples all the ways to define a pointcut. In the first two chapters, we saw the classic part of Spring AOP present since 1.x version, where advices were defined at the level of interfaces to be implemented.

In this section, we will see how advices are defined by normal methods. The difference is in annotations that declare for which use and in which context those methods must be used inside a class. This is also annotated too so that it is treated as aspect.

Advices must always be defined with annotations within a class annotated with @Aspect. So, we will have a regular Java class with the annotation @Aspect above the definition of the class, and public methods with annotations indicated in the following list. This indicates that those methods are eligible to be used as advice and can be applied according to the rules present and points indicated in the annotation.

An aspect can contain any number of advices.

```
package org.springaop.chapter.four;

import org.aspectj.lang.annotation.Aspect;
import org.aspectj.lang.annotation.Before;

@Aspect
public class AspectAdvicesExamples {

    @Before("execution (org.springaop.service.AccessOperation.*(..))")
    public void controlAccessCheck(){
            . . .
    }
...
}
```

Advices must be defined within a class annotated with @Aspect.

As we said in earlier chapters, advices can be of different types, but in this case they are formed with the annotations:

```
@Before
@AfterReturning
@AfterThrowing
@After (After Finally)
@Around
```

Let's describe them in detail:

@Before

Before advice allows us to perform actions before the proxy does the call on the target object (thus, before the joinpoint's execution). The annotated method returns nothing, so the signature will be `public void`.

In the before annotation, we will have to indicate the pointcut that tells Spring where to apply it (bean, package class, and so on).

This advice doesn't forestall the continuation of processing, unless an exception is thrown.

```
package org.springaop.chapter.four;

@Aspect
public class AspectAdvicesExamples {

...

@Before("execution(* org.springaop.service.AccessOperation.*(..))")
    public void controlAccessCheck(){
            ...
        }

...
}
```

In this case, we are declaring that we want the content of method `ControlAccessCheck` to be executed when any method is called on the `AccessOperation` class; or, even better, using pointcut designators:

```
package org.springaop.chapter.four;

@Aspect
public class AspectAdvicesExamples {

...

@Before("execution(* org.springaop.app.services.*.*(..))")
    public void controlAccessCheck(){
            ...
        }
...
}
```

@AfterReturning

The after returning advice is executed once the method on which we are applying the advice has finished its execution normally (no exception thrown).

Even in this case, a public method must be annotated within a class that is annotated as @Aspect.

```
package org.springaop.chapter.four;

@Aspect
public class AspectAdvicesExamples {

...

    @AfterReturning("execution(* org.springaop.service.*.*(..))")
    public void logOperationCommited(){

    }
...
}
```

If we want to have the return value of the method to use in the advice, we have to bind it. So we will write :

```
package org.springaop.chapter.four;

@Aspect
public class AspectAdvicesExamples {

...

  @AfterReturning(pointcut="execution
(* org.springaop.service.*.*(..))", returning="returningValue")
    public void logOperationPerformed(Object returningValue){
        ...
    }
...
}
```

The type of value for which the bind is done is given in the advice. Putting object as the type of the return, we are sure that any type of object will fit. Naturally, it's not possible to return another object different from the one returned by the method on which the advice is applied.

@AfterThrowing

The after throwing advice is applied when a method's execution ends with the throwing of an exception.

It is defined by declaring the annotation `@AfterThrowing` on a method within a class annotated with `@Aspect`:

```
package org.springaop.chapter.four;

@Aspect
public class AspectAdvicesExamples {
...
@AfterThrowing("execution(* org.springaop.service.*.*(..))")
        public void doRecoveryActionsOnDataAccessException(){
...
}
}
```

Or using the pointcut designators, you can make the exception object available to the advice.

```
package org.springaop.chapter.four;

@Aspect
public class AspectAdvicesExamples {

...

    @AfterThrowing(pointcut="execution
(* org.springaop.service.*.*(..))", throwing="ex")
    public void doRecoveryActionsOnDataAccessException(DataAccessExce
ption ex){
...
}


}
```

As usual, the name used in the annotation's `throwing` has to be the same as the advice's parameter one.

The advice's parameter narrows down the type of exception that can be thrown.

@After

The after (finally) advice is executed after the execution of the method on which the pointcut's matching is performed. The advice is executed in any case, that is whether an exception is thrown or not.

It is defined by the annotation `@After` on a method within a class annotated with `@Aspect`.

 This advice wasn't present in Spring 1.x and in the configurations we called "classic".

```
package org.springaop.chapter.four;

@Aspect
public class AspectAdvicesExamples {

    @After("execution (* org.springaop.service.*.*(..))")
    public void releaseResource(){

    }
}
```

In this type of advice we don't have any type of specific binding, except for the one that we could have using a pointcut designator with `argNames`.

@Around

The around advice presents some peculiarities compared with the ones we've previously seen, and it is the most complicated to use as well because it wasn't designed for a specific action. Before using it, it is recommended to verify if the requirements can be satisfied by another type of advice which is less powerful than this one.

This advice has full control over the method to be called, both before and after the invocation, and it can even decide not to invoke it.

The aim with which it is most often used is sharing state in a thread-safe manner before and after the invocation of the method.

- The advice has a return value, unlike the others, which return `void`.
- The advice has as first type of parameter `org.aspectj.lang.ProceedingJoinPoint`.
- The advice declares in the signature `throws Throwable`.

```
package org.springaop.chapter.four;

@Aspect
public class AspectAdvicesExamples {

    ...

    @Around("execution(* startMatch(..))")
```

```
        public Object doTimeProfiling(ProceedingJoinPoint pjp) throws
    Throwable{
            // start stopwatch
            Object retVal = pjp.proceed();
            // stop stopwatch
            return retVal;
        }
    ...
    }
```

The first parameter has to be an object of the type `ProceedingJoinPoint`.

`ProceedingJoinPoint` contains parameters in an array of objects, the target object, the proxy object, and all the other pieces of information of the execution context.

In order to invoke the method on the target object, you need to call the method `proceed()` on `ProceedingJoinPoint` .

Depending on requirements the method `proceed()` can be invoked one or more times or not be invoked at all.

Introduction

An introduction is defined by the annotation `@DeclareParents`, and indicates that the type of class used for the matching has a new parent that will be the implementation of a new interface. Below it is used to declare the `Matter` and `GeometricForm` interfaces.

```
    package org.springaop.chapter.four.introduction;

    import org.aspectj.lang.annotation.Aspect;
    import org.aspectj.lang.annotation.DeclareParents;

    @Aspect
    public class ParallelepipedIntroduction {

        @DeclareParents(value = "org.springaop.chapter.four.introduction.
    Box",
                defaultImpl = Titanium.class)
        public Matter matter;
```

```
        @DeclareParents(value = "org.springaop.chapter.four.introduction.
Box",
                defaultImpl = Cube.class)
    public GeometricForm geometricForm;

}
```

In this way, we have a chance to define interfaces (`Matter` and `GeometricForm`) and provide implementations (`Titanium` and `Cube`) to apply them on the target classes detected by joinpoints.

The test class:

```
package org.springaop.chapter.four.introduction;

import org.springframework.context.ApplicationContext;
import org.springframework.context.support.
ClassPathXmlApplicationContext;

/* run with jvm argument: -javaagent:<path>/spring-agent.jar */
public class TestIntroduction {

    public static void main(String[] args) {
            String[] paths = {"org/springaop/chapter/four/introduction/
applicationContext.xml"};
            ApplicationContext ctx = new ClassPathXmlApplicationContext
(paths);

            Box bean = (Box)ctx.getBean("box");
            System.out.println(bean.getName());

            Matter beanMatter = (Matter) bean;
            System.out.println(beanMatter.getType());

            GeometricForm geoMetricBean = (GeometricForm) bean;
            System.out.println(geoMetricBean.getShape());
    }
}
```

The configuration in eclipse for `spring-agent.jar`:

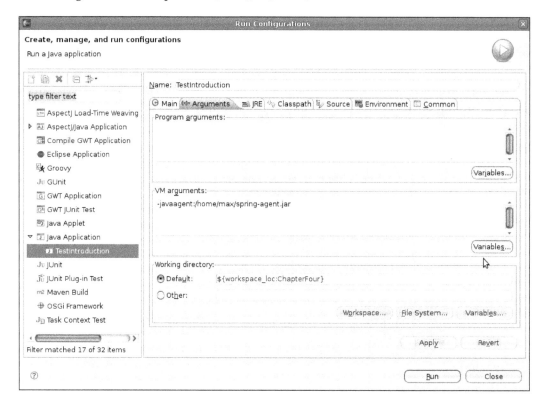

The output will be:

XML Schema-based configuration

Now we are going to see SpringAOP configuration using XML configuration.

The choice to use XML instead of annotations, beyond personal preferences, is the only practicable one in contexts where we use JDK previous to 1.5; it is the first JDK version in which annotations have been introduced.

Therefore, if you want to use Spring with JDK 1.3 or 1.4, the use of schema-based configuration is mandatory.

The only supported instantiation model for XML-defined aspects is the Singleton model.

In order to use XML tags and namespaces instead of annotations, we have to import:

```
<?xml version="1.0" encoding="UTF-8"?>
<beans xmlns="http://www.springframework.org/schema/beans"
xmlns:xsi="http://www.w3.org/2001/XMLSchema-instance"
xmlns:aop="http://www.springframework.org/schema/aop"
xsi:schemaLocation="http://www.springframework.org/schema/beans
http://www.springframework.org/schema/beans/spring-beans-2.5.xsd
http://www.springframework.org/schema/aop
http://www.springframework.org/schema/aop/spring-aop-2.5.xsd">
...
</beans>
```

While using annotations, the class annotated with @Aspect acts as a container of advices and pointcuts; with XML configuration advices and pointcuts are declared inside the tag:

```
<aop:config>
```

An aspect equivalent to a class annotated with @Aspect is indicated with:

```
<aop:aspect>
```

An advisor is configured with:

```
<aop:advisor>
```

It enables the link between an AspectJ pointcut and a classic SpringAOP advice object.

A pointcut is configured with:

```
<aop:pointcut>
```

The tag `<aop:config>` heavily uses the Spring autoproxy mechanism. Therefore, there could be some problems if Spring was configured to explicitly use per this autoproxying with the `BeanNameAutoProxyCreator`.

Aspect

An aspect in the case of XML schema configuration can be any other bean defined in the application context.

```xml
<?xml version="1.0" encoding="UTF-8"?>
<beans xmlns="http://www.springframework.org/schema/beans"
xmlns:xsi="http://www.w3.org/2001/XMLSchema-instance"
xmlns:aop="http://www.springframework.org/schema/aop"
xsi:schemaLocation="http://www.springframework.org/schema/beans
http://www.springframework.org/schema/beans/spring-beans-2.5.xsd
http://www.springframework.org/schema/aop
http://www.springframework.org/schema/aop/spring-aop-2.5.xsd">

    <aop:config>
            <aop:aspect id="myAspect" ref="exampleBean"></aop:aspect>
    </aop:config>

    <bean id="exampleBean class="org.springaop.schemabased.
ExampleBean/>

</beans>
```

Pointcut

A named pointcut can be inserted in the tag `<aop:config>`.

```xml
<?xml version="1.0" encoding="UTF-8"?>
<beans xmlns="http://www.springframework.org/schema/beans"
xmlns:xsi="http://www.w3.org/2001/XMLSchema-instance"
xmlns:aop="http://www.springframework.org/schema/aop"
xsi:schemaLocation="http://www.springframework.org/schema/beans
http://www.springframework.org/schema/beans/spring-beans-2.5.xsd
http://www.springframework.org/schema/aop
http://www.springframework.org/schema/aop/spring-aop-2.5.xsd">

    <aop:config>
            <aop:pointcut expression="execution(* org.springaop.app.
services.*.*(..))" id="pointcutServices"/>
```

```
        <aop:aspect id="myAspect" ref="exampleBean"></aop:aspect>
    </aop:config>

    <bean id="exampleBean" class="org.springaop.schemabased.
ExampleBean"/>

</beans>
```

The syntax used to define the pointcut's intervention is the same used by AspectJ.

If you use the schema-based notation on JDK 1.5 (or upward), you can refer to pointcuts defined in @Aspect annotated classes in the pointcut.

```
<?xml version="1.0" encoding="UTF-8"?>
<beans xmlns="http://www.springframework.org/schema/beans"
xmlns:xsi="http://www.w3.org/2001/XMLSchema-instance"
xmlns:aop="http://www.springframework.org/schema/aop"
xsi:schemaLocation="http://www.springframework.org/schema/beans
http://www.springframework.org/schema/beans/spring-beans-2.5.xsd
http://www.springframework.org/schema/aop
http://www.springframework.org/schema/aop/spring-aop-2.5.xsd">

    <aop:config>
            <aop:pointcut expression="org.springaop.pointcuts.
ApplicationPointcutsAspect.inServiceLayer()" id="pointcutServices"/>
            <aop:aspect id="myAspect" ref="exampleBean"></aop:aspect>
    </aop:config>

    <bean id="exampleBean" class="org.springaop.schemabased.
ExampleBean"/>

</beans>
```

A limitation of XML notation is that from XML you can refer to an annotated class, but you cannot do the other way round. That is, you can't use a pointcut in an annotation identified by its ID in the XML file.

An action you can perform is defining the pointcut directly inside the tag <aop:aspect>, with the advantage of the chance of the binding of parameters as we have seen with annotations.

```
<?xml version="1.0" encoding="UTF-8"?>
<beans xmlns="http://www.springframework.org/schema/beans"
xmlns:xsi="http://www.w3.org/2001/XMLSchema-instance"
xmlns:aop="http://www.springframework.org/schema/aop"
xsi:schemaLocation="http://www.springframework.org/schema/beans
http://www.springframework.org/schema/beans/spring-beans-2.5.xsd
http://www.springframework.org/schema/aop
http://www.springframework.org/schema/aop/spring-aop-2.5.xsd">
```

```
<bean id="exampleBean" class="org.springaop.schemabased.ExampleBean/>

<aop:config>
<aop:aspect id="myAspect" ref=exampleBean>
<aop:pointcut expression="execution(* org.springaop.pointcuts.*.*(..)
&& this(service)" id="pointcutServices"/>
<aop:before pointcut-ref="fooService" method="foo"/>
</aop:aspect>
</aop:config>

</beans>
```

Of course, the advice has to declare to receive the pieces of information from the joinpoint's context:

```
public void foo(Object fooService) {
...
}
```

In situations where more expressions must be combined, the symbols OR (||), AND (&&), and NEGATION (!) can be substituted by or, and, and not.

Advice

The advices that were used in the annotations can be used here as well.

Before advice

The function is the same as when using annotations — executing some logic before the target class.

With XML, you declare it in this manner:

```
<?xml version="1.0" encoding="UTF-8"?>
<beans xmlns="http://www.springframework.org/schema/beans"
xmlns:xsi="http://www.w3.org/2001/XMLSchema-instance"
xmlns:aop="http://www.springframework.org/schema/aop"
xsi:schemaLocation="http://www.springframework.org/schema/beans
http://www.springframework.org/schema/beans/spring-beans-2.5.xsd"
http://www.springframework.org/schema/aop
http://www.springframework.org/schema/aop/spring-aop-2.5.xsd>

<bean id="exampleBean" class="org.springaop.schemabased.ExampleBean"/>

    <aop:pointcut expression="execution(* org.springaop.
pointcuts.*.*(..) && this(service)" id="pointcutServices"/>

    <aop:config>
        <aop:aspect id="myAspect" ref="exampleBean">
            <aop:before pointcut-ref="pointcutServices"
```

```
method="foo"/>
        </aop:aspect>
    </aop:config>

</beans>
```

The pointcut's syntax declares the type, in this case `before`, of the pointcut to which we should refer for the matching rules, and the name of the method containing the advice's body, or defining inline the matching rule.

```
<?xml version="1.0" encoding="UTF-8"?>
<beans xmlns="http://www.springframework.org/schema/beans"
xmlns:xsi="http://www.w3.org/2001/XMLSchema-instance"
xmlns:aop="http://www.springframework.org/schema/aop"
xsi:schemaLocation="http://www.springframework.org/schema/beans
http://www.springframework.org/schema/beans/spring-beans-2.5.xsd
http://www.springframework.org/schema/aop
http://www.springframework.org/schema/aop/spring-aop-2.5.xsd">

    <aop:config>

        <aop:aspect id="aspect" ref="myAspect">
            <aop:before method="trace"
                pointcut="execution (* org.springaop.chapter.four.
schema.*.*(..))"
                arg-names="msg"/>
        </aop:aspect>
    </aop:config>

    <bean id="myAspect" class="org.springaop.chapter.four.schema.
MyAspect"/>

    <bean id="exampleBean" class="org.springaop.chapter.four.schema.
ExampleBean"/>

</beans>
```

After returning advice

The after returning advice's behavior is the same as when using annotations, that is, to execute some logic after the invoked method has finished its execution normally without throwing any exceptions.

The configuration declaring the advice within the `aspect` tag is:

```
<?xml version="1.0" encoding="UTF-8"?>
<beans xmlns="http://www.springframework.org/schema/beans"
xmlns:xsi="http://www.w3.org/2001/XMLSchema-instance"
xmlns:aop="http://www.springframework.org/schema/aop"
xsi:schemaLocation="http://www.springframework.org/schema/beans
http://www.springframework.org/schema/beans/spring-beans-2.5.xsd
```

```
http://www.springframework.org/schema/aop
http://www.springframework.org/schema/aop/spring-aop-2.5.xsd">

    <aop:config>
        <aop:aspect ref="myAspect">
            <aop:after-returning method="afterGreeting"
pointcut="execution(* greeting(..))" />
        </aop:aspect>
    </aop:config>

    <bean id="myAspect" class="org.springaop.chapter.four.schema.
MyAspect"/>

    <bean id="exampleBean" class="org.springaop.chapter.four.schema.
ExampleBeanImpl"/>

</beans>
```

Also in this type of advice, we can use the return value (returnValue) to pass it to the class method:

```
<?xml version="1.0" encoding="UTF-8"?>
<beans xmlns="http://www.springframework.org/schema/beans"
xmlns:xsi="http://www.w3.org/2001/XMLSchema-instance"
xmlns:aop="http://www.springframework.org/schema/aop"
xsi:schemaLocation="http://www.springframework.org/schema/beans
http://www.springframework.org/schema/beans/spring-beans-2.5.xsd
http://www.springframework.org/schema/aop
http://www.springframework.org/schema/aop/spring-aop-2.5.xsd>

<aop:config>
<aop:aspect ref="myAspect">
<aop:after-returning method="afterGreeting" pointcut="execution(*
greeting(..))" returning="returnValue"/>
</aop:aspect>
</aop:config>

    <bean id="myAspect" class="org.springaop.chapter.four.schema.
MyAspect"/>

    <bean id="exampleBean" class="org.springaop.chapter.four.schema.
ExampleBeanImpl"/>

</beans>
```

In the class that contains the method with the body of the advice to execute, we'll have a parameter with the same name of the returnValue.

```
public void fooAfterReturning(Object returnValue) {
...
}
```

After throwing advice

The after throwing advice, as specified earlier in this chapter, is executed after a method's execution throws an exception.

It is configured in this way:

```xml
<?xml version="1.0" encoding="UTF-8"?>
<beans xmlns="http://www.springframework.org/schema/beans"
xmlns:xsi="http://www.w3.org/2001/XMLSchema-instance"
xmlns:aop="http://www.springframework.org/schema/aop"
xsi:schemaLocation="http://www.springframework.org/schema/beans
http://www.springframework.org/schema/beans/spring-beans-2.5.xsd
http://www.springframework.org/schema/aop
http://www.springframework.org/schema/aop/spring-aop-2.5.xsd">

    <aop:config>
        <aop:pointcut id="fooMethod"
        expression="execution (* org.springaop.chapter.four.schema.
afterthrowing.ExceptionBean.*(..))"/>
        <aop:aspect id="aspect" ref="myAspect">
            <aop:after-throwing pointcut-ref="fooMethod" method="fooRe
coveryActions"
                throwing="nullPointerException"/>
        </aop:aspect>
    </aop:config>

    <bean id="myAspect" class="org.springaop.chapter.four.schema.
MyAspect"/>

    <bean id="exceptionBean" class="org.springaop.chapter.four.schema.
afterthrowing.ExceptionBean"/>

</beans>
```

Here it's also possible to indicate the parameter to pass, that is the exception in this case, which we call `DataAccessException`.

```xml
<?xml version="1.0" encoding="UTF-8"?>
<beans xmlns="http://www.springframework.org/schema/beans"
xmlns:xsi="http://www.w3.org/2001/XMLSchema-instance"
xmlns:aop="http://www.springframework.org/schema/aop"
xsi:schemaLocation="http://www.springframework.org/schema/beans
http://www.springframework.org/schema/beans/spring-beans-2.5.xsd
http://www.springframework.org/schema/aop
http://www.springframework.org/schema/aop/spring-aop-2.5.xsd">
    <bean id="exampleBean"    class="org.springaop.schemabased.
ExampleBean"/>

                <aop:config>
```

```
    <aop:aspect id="afterThrowingExample" ref="aBean">
        <aop:after-throwing pointcut-ref="pointcutServices" method="
fooRecoveryActions throwing=dataAccessException"/>
    </aop:aspect>
        </aop:config>
</beans>
```

In the method that contains the advice to apply, the input parameter will be:

```
public void fooRecoveryActions(DataAccessException dataAccessEx) {
...
}
```

After (finally) advice

The after (finally) advice is the advice type that is always executed, irrespective of success or failure of the joinpoint.

The configuration is the following:

```
<?xml version="1.0" encoding="UTF-8"?>
<beans xmlns="http://www.springframework.org/schema/beans"
xmlns:xsi="http://www.w3.org/2001/XMLSchema-instance"
xmlns:aop="http://www.springframework.org/schema/aop"
xsi:schemaLocation="http://www.springframework.org/schema/beans
http://www.springframework.org/schema/beans/spring-beans-2.5.xsd
http://www.springframework.org/schema/aop
http://www.springframework.org/schema/aop/spring-aop-2.5.xsd">

    <aop:config>
        <aop:aspect ref="myAspect">
            <aop:after method="afterGreeting" pointcut="execution(*
greeting(..))" />
        </aop:aspect>
    </aop:config>

    <bean id="myAspect" class="org.springaop.chapter.four.schema.
MyAspect"/>

    <bean id="exampleBean" class="org.springaop.chapter.four.schema.
ExampleBeanImpl"/>

</beans>
```

Around advice

The last advice we look at is the most powerful, but it less easy to use as well.

Let's recall that it is the most powerful one because it allows us to execute logic before and after the method's execution, and also allows us to prevent its invocation, if necessary.

In order to proceed with the invocation, it's necessary that the advice's body should call the method `proceed()` on the `ProceedingJoinPoint` that's passed as a parameter.

```xml
<?xml version="1.0" encoding="UTF-8"?>
<beans xmlns="http://www.springframework.org/schema/beans"
xmlns:xsi="http://www.w3.org/2001/XMLSchema-instance"
xmlns:aop="http://www.springframework.org/schema/aop"
xsi:schemaLocation="http://www.springframework.org/schema/beans
http://www.springframework.org/schema/beans/spring-beans-2.5.xsd
http://www.springframework.org/schema/aop
http://www.springframework.org/schema/aop/spring-aop-2.5.xsd">

    <aop:config>
        <aop:pointcut id="fooMethod"
        expression="execution (* org.springaop.chapter.four.schema.
ExampleBean.foo())"/>
        <aop:aspect id="aspect" ref="myAspect">
            <aop:around method="around" pointcut-ref="fooMethod"/>
        </aop:aspect>
    </aop:config>

    <bean id="myAspect" class="org.springaop.chapter.four.schema.
MyAspect"/>

    <bean id="exampleBean" class="org.springaop.chapter.four.schema.
ExampleBean"/>

</beans>
```

Then, in the around method it is executed like this:

```java
public Object around(ProceedingJoinPoint pjp) throws Throwable {
...
Object retVal = pjp.proceed();
...
return retVal;
}
```

As in the configuration with annotations, the first parameter has to be a `ProceedingJoinPoint` and the method has to declare `throws Throwable`.

Introduction

As I said before in this chapter, introductions allow declaring that a target object implements interfaces, providing the implementation.

To allow the building of introductions, we declare the tag `<aop:declare-parents>` within the tag `<aop:aspect>` using the same example code as for annotations:

```xml
<?xml version="1.0" encoding="UTF-8"?>
<beans xmlns="http://www.springframework.org/schema/beans"
xsi:schemaLocation="http://www.springframework.org/schema/beans
http://www.springframework.org/schema/beans/spring-beans-2.5.xsd
http://www.springframework.org/schema/aop
http://www.springframework.org/schema/aop/spring-aop-2.5.xsd">

    <aop:config>
        <aop:aspect id="introduction" ref="counterIntroduction">
            <aop:declare-parents
                types-matching=
"org.springaop.chapter.four.schema.introduction."*
                implement-interface=
"org.springaop.chapter.four.schema.introduction.CounterTracker"
                default-impl=
"org.springaop.chapter.four.schema.introduction.CounterTrackerImpl"/>
            <aop:after pointcut="execution(* org.springaop.chapter.
four.schema.introduction.*.*(..)) and this(counter)"
                method="increase" />
        </aop:aspect>
    </aop:config>

    <bean id="counterIntroduction" class="org.springaop.chapter.four.
schema.introduction.CounterIntroduction" />

    <bean id="cube" class="org.springaop.chapter.four.schema.
introduction.Cube" />

    <bean id=titanium class="org.springaop.chapter.four.schema.
introduction.Titanium" />
</beans>
```

`types-matching` is the usual pattern for matching with AspectJ. `implement-interface` indicates the interface to be implemented, and `default-impl` indicates the implementation of the interface to be used.

The class of bean `counterIntroduction` will contain the call to the method `increaseCounter`, defined in interface `CounterTracker`.

```java
public class CounterIntroduction {

    public void increase(CounterTracker counter){
            counter.increaseCounter();
    }
}
```

Advisors

As I explained, in the classic part of Spring AOP, advisors are useful for joining together the aspect and advice. They are a typical construction of Spring, not of AspectJ.

Using annotations advisors aren't present, whereas with XML schema they can be used with the tag `<aop:advisor>`. The most common use is with the advice for transactions `<tx:advice>`.

```xml
<?xml version="1.0" encoding="UTF-8"?>
<beans xmlns="http://www.springframework.org/schema/beans"
xmlns:xsi="http://www.w3.org/2001/XMLSchema-instance"
xmlns:aop="http://www.springframework.org/schema/aop"
xsi:schemaLocation="http://www.springframework.org/schema/beans
http://www.springframework.org/schema/beans/spring-beans-2.5.xsd
http://www.springframework.org/schema/aop
http://www.springframework.org/schema/aop/spring-aop-2.5.xsd">

    ...

    <aop:config>
            <aop:pointcut id="pointcutServices" expression="execution(*
org.springaop.pointcuts.*.*(..) && this(service)"/>
                    <aop:advisor pointcut-ref="pointcutServices"
order="1" advice-ref="tx-advice"/>
    </aop:config>
            <tx:advice id="tx-advice">
            <tx:attributes>
                    <tx:method name="*" propagation="REQUIRED"/>
            </tx:attributes>
    </tx:advice>
</beans>
```

Recipes

Let's see some recipes on how to use AOP with the domain object to solve the concurrency of aspects and the mixin of configurations.

Dependency injection in domain objects

Spring instantiates and configures beans contained in application context configuration files. If you use Domain-Driven Design, you can ask a bean factory to configure your domain object.

The `spring-aspects.jar` contains an annotation-driven aspect that exploits this capability to allow dependency injection of any object with `@Configurable` annotation, and with `AnnotationBeanConfigurerAspect` behind the scenes. In this way, you can apply dependency injection with objects created outside the control of any IoC container using the new operator.

An example of a domain class:

```
package org.springaop.chapter.four.configurable;

import org.springframework.beans.factory.annotation.Autowired;
import org.springframework.beans.factory.annotation.Configurable;

@Configurable()
public class User {

    public String getName(){
        return name;
    }

    @Autowired
    public void setName(String name) {
        this.name = name;
    }

    private String name;
}
```

To enable the `@Configurable` aspect, add `<context:spring-configured>` in the configuration file and configure the bean with `scope=prototype`.

```
<?xml version="1.0" encoding="UTF-8"?>
<beans xmlns="http://www.springframework.org/schema/beans"
xmlns:xsi="http://www.w3.org/2001/XMLSchema-instance"
xmlns:context=http://www.springframework.org/schema/context
xsi:schemaLocation="http://www.springframework.org/schema/beans
http://www.springframework.org/schema/beans/spring-beans-2.5.xsd
http://www.springframework.org/schema/context
http://www.springframework.org/schema/context/spring-context-2.5.xsd">

    <context:load-time-weaver />
    <context:annotation-config />

    <bean scope="prototype" class="org.springaop.chapter.four.
configurable.User">
        <property name="name" value="max"/>
    </bean>
</beans>
```

To use the Spring aspect, you have to include the `spring-aspects.jar` file (located in the `dist/weaving` directory of the Spring distribution) in your classpath.

Advice ordering

A situation that could occur in the execution of logic contained in advices is a conflict in their execution. This is because some pointcuts could be defined so that they are executed concurrently during a method's execution.

To solve this problem, we can specify a priority order of advices and aspects, implementing the interface contained in the package `org.springframework.core`.

```
public interface Ordered {
int getOrder();
}
```

These are the cases that we can have:

- The aspect classes that don't implement this interface are executed after those that implement it.
- The aspect classes that implement it are executed according to the value: the lower the value, the higher is the priority.
- Classes that have the same order are not executed in a predefined sequence; however, they are executed before any class with lower order and after those with higher order.

With annotations, we put `@Order(value)`, whereas with XML schema we use the tag `<property name="order" value="100"/>` on the bean or implement the Ordered interface.

Configuration mixin

The two types of configuration can be easily used simultaneously. They indicate to Spring to use the annotations with the autoproxying tag and the XML based scheme.

Aspect instantiation model

The default instantiation model of `Aspect` is Singleton model. Therefore, there will be a single instance of each aspect within the application context.

It is possible to define aspects with alternative lifecycles:

AspectJ's `perthis` and `pertarget` instantiation models (`percflow`, `percflowbelow`, and `pertypewithin`) are not supported in Spring 2.5.

Here is an example of a `perthis` aspect:

```
import org.aspectj.lang.annotation.Aspect;
import org.aspectj.lang.annotation.Before;

@Aspect("perthis(org.springaop.app.Manager.execute())")
public class AspectPerThis {

    @Before("execution(org.springaop.app.Manager.execute())")
    public void controlExecuteCheck(){
            //...
    }

}
```

The effect of the `perthis` is that one aspect instance will be created for each unique `Manager` object executing an `execute` method (each unique object bound to `this` at joinpoints matched by the pointcut expression).

The aspect instance is created the first time the method `execute` is invoked on the `Manager` object. The aspect goes out of scope when the `Manager` object goes out of scope.

The `pertarget` instantiation model works in exactly the same way as `perthis`, but creates one aspect instance for each unique target object at matched joinpoints.

Here is an example of a `pertarget` aspect:

```
import org.aspectj.lang.JoinPoint;
import org.aspectj.lang.annotation.Aspect;
import org.aspectj.lang.annotation.Before;

@Aspect("pertarget(@annotation(javax.annotation.security.RolesAllowed)
|| " +
        "@annotation(javax.annotation.security.PermitAll) || " +
        "@annotation(javax.annotation.security.DenyAll))")
public class AspectPerTarget {

    @Before("@annotation(javax.annotation.security.DenyAll)")
    public void deny(JoinPoint jp) throws Throwable {
            throw new SecurityException();
    }

}
```

AspectJ weaving in Spring

AspectJ is a language with a full compiler and support for weaving binary class files either offline or at runtime, as classes are loaded into the virtual machine. Let's see how we can use **load-time weaving (LTW)** with Spring.

The Spring AOP framework only supports limited types of AspectJ pointcuts (method invocation). If you want use the complete set of AspectJ pointcuts, you must use AspectJ load-time weaver to enable the AspectJ framework.

This is an example of a class with `call` pointcut:

```
package org.springaop.aspectj.aspects;

public aspect AspectJAspectExample {

    before(): call(* relax(..)) {
            System.out.println("relax() method is about to be
executed!");
    }
}
```

AspectJ load-time weaving happens when the target classes are loaded into JVM by a class loader. For a class to be woven, a special class loader is required to enhance the bytecode of the target class. The configuration of the AspectJ framework is done through a file named `aop.xml` in the `META-INF` directory in the classpath root.

```
<!DOCTYPE aspectj PUBLIC "-//AspectJ//DTD//EN" "http://www.eclipse.
org/aspectj/dtd/aspectj.dtd">
<aspectj>
    <weaver>
            <include within="org.springaop.aspectj.aspects.*" />
    </weaver>
    <aspects>
            <aspect        name="org.springaop.aspectj.aspects.
AspectJAspectExample" />
    </aspects>
</aspectj>
```

In this `AspectJ` configuration file, you have to specify the aspects and the classes into which you want your aspects woven. Here we specify weaving `AspectJAspectExample` into all the classes in the `org.springaop.aspectj.aspects` package.

Load-time weaving with Spring

You may enable Spring's support for LTW in any Java application (standalone as well as application server based) through the use of the Spring-provided instrumentation agent.

To do so, start the VM by specifying the `-javaagent:path/to/spring-agent.jar` option. But Spring offers a more simple choice. You only need to declare the empty XML element `<context:load-time-weaver>`.

```
<?xml version="1.0" encoding="UTF-8"?>
<beans xmlns="http://www.springframework.org/schema/beans"
xmlns:xsi="http://www.w3.org/2001/XMLSchema-instance"
xmlns:aop="http://www.springframework.org/schema/aop"
xmlns:context="http://www.springframework.org/schema/context"
xsi:schemaLocation="http://www.springframework.org/schema/beans
http://www.springframework.org/schema/beans/spring-beans-2.5.xsd
http://www.springframework.org/schema/aop
http://www.springframework.org/schema/aop/spring-aop-2.5.xsd
http://www.springframework.org/schema/context
http://www.springframework.org/schema/context/spring-context-2.5.xsd">

<context:load-time-weaver />
...
</beans>
```

From the command line:

```
java -javaagent:<path_on_your_machine>/spring-framework-X.X/dist/weaving/
spring-agent.jar

<package>.<yourclass>.Main
```

Load-time weaving with AspectJ

AspectJ provides a load-time weaving agent. You only need to add a VM argument to the command line. Then your classes will get woven when they are loaded into the JVM.

From the command line:

```
java -javaagent:<path_on_your_machine>/spring-framework-X.X/lib/aspectj/
aspectjweaver.jar

<package>.<yourclass>.Main
```

AOP strategy considerations

In this chapter we have seen several configuration strategies. XML, annotations, autoproxy and Load-Time Weaving. These strategies can be reduced to three approaches: Spring AOP proxy, Spring with AspectJ weaver, or simply AspectJ. Now think about the conditions that best fit the following prerequisites.

Spring AOP proxy:

- There are no domain objects with crosscutting functionality.
- Full features of AspectJ are not required.
- The IDE must support AJDT.
- You don't want to use AspectJ compiler.
- You don't want to change the deploy configuration.

Spring with AspectJ Weaver:

- Domain objects have crosscutting functionalities.
- LTW can be enabled at deploy time.
- Long load time at LTW is not an issue.

AspectJ:

- Full joinpoints are required.
- The build system can use AspectJ.
- Long compile time is not an issue.

Summary

In this chapter, we gave a general view of the integration between AspectJ and Spring using the powerful syntax of joinpont definition, both through annotations and XML configuration.

We saw how AspectJ, through annotations, makes the work of defining the application of advices easier. We have much shorter configuration files, since we don't have to configure each AOP component in the classic way.

The other option is the configuration with AspectJ through XML file, which is far simpler compared to the classic version and becomes nearly compulsory if we use a JDK previous to 1.5, which is the one that supports annotations.

In the last part, I gave some advice to solve conflicts in the priorities of execution, and about the possible uses of the different configuration methods.

5
Design with AOP

In this chapter, we're going to examine some design decisions that are important for building better applications. In these design decisions, the AOP plays a significant role because it provides smart solutions to common crosscutting problems.

We will look at the following AOP design solutions:

- Concurrency with AOP
- Transparent caching with AOP
- Security with AOP

Designing and implementing an enterprise Java application means not only dealing with the application core business and architecture, but also with some typical enterprise requirements.

We have to define how the application manages concurrency so that the application is robust and does not suffer too badly from an increase in the number of requests. We have to define the caching strategies for the application because we don't want CPU- or data-intensive operations to be executed over and over.

We have to define roles and profiles, applying security policies and restricting access to application parts, because different kinds of users will probably have different rights and permissions. All these issues require writing additional code that clutters our application business code and reduces its modularity and maintainability.

But we have a choice. We can design our enterprise Java application keeping AOP in mind. This will help us to concentrate on our actual business code, taking away all the infrastructure issues that can otherwise be expressed as crosscutting concerns.

This chapter will introduce such issues, and will show how to design and implement solutions to them with Spring 2.5 AOP support.

Concurrency with AOP

For many developers, **concurrency** remains a mystery.

Concurrency is the system's ability to act with several requests simultaneously, such a way that threads don't corrupt the state of objects when they gain access at the same time.

A number of good books have been written on this subject, such as *Concurrent Programming in Java* and *Java Concurrency in Practice*. They deserve much attention, since concurrency is an aspect that's hard to understand, and not immediately visible to developers. Problems in the area of concurrency are hard to reproduce. However, it's important to keep concurrency in mind to assure that the application is robust regardless of the number of users it will serve.

If we don't take into account concurrency and document when and how the problems of concurrency are considered, we will build an application taking some risks by supposing that the CPU will never simultaneously schedule processes on parts of our application that are not thread-safe.

To ensure the building of robust and scalable systems, we use proper patterns. There are JDK packages just for concurrency. They are in the `java.util.concurrent` package, a result of JSR-166.

One of these patterns is the read-write lock pattern, which consists of is the interface `java.util.concurrent.locks.ReadWriteLock` and some implementations, one of which is `ReentrantReadWriteLock`.

The goal of `ReadWriteLock` is to allow the reading of an object from a virtually endless number of threads, while only one thread at a time can modify it. In this way, the state of the object can never be corrupted because threads reading the object's state will always read up-to-date data, and the thread modifying the state of the object in question will be able to act without the possibility of the object's state being corrupted. Another necessary feature is that the result of a thread's action can be visible to the other threads. The behavior is the same as we could have achieved using `synchronized`, but when using a read-write lock we are explicitly synchronizing the actions, whereas with `synchronized` synchronization is implicit.

Now let's see an example of `ReadWriteLock` on the `BankAccountThreadSafe` object.

Before the read operation that needs to be safe, we set the `read lock`. After the read operation, we release the `read lock`.

Before the write operation that needs to be safe, we set the `write lock`. After a state modification, we release the `write lock`.

```
package org.springaop.chapter.five.concurrent;

import java.util.Date;
import java.util.concurrent.locks.Lock;
import java.util.concurrent.locks.ReadWriteLock;
import java.util.concurrent.locks.ReentrantReadWriteLock;

public final class BankAccountThreadSafe {

    public BankAccountThreadSafe(Integer id) {
        this.id = id;
        balance = new Float(0);
        startDate = new Date();
    }

    public BankAccountThreadSafe(Integer id, Float balance) {
        this.id = id;
        this.balance = balance;
        startDate = new Date();
    }

    public BankAccountThreadSafe(Integer id, Float balance, Date start)
{
        this.id = id;
        this.balance = balance;
        this.startDate = start;
    }

    public boolean debitOperation(Float debit) {
        wLock.lock();
        try {

            float balance = getBalance();

            if (balance < debit) {

                return false;

            } else {

                setBalance(balance - debit);

                return true;
            }
        } finally {
```

```
            wLock.unlock();
        }
    }

    public void creditOperation(Float credit) {

        wLock.lock();
        try {
            setBalance(getBalance() + credit);

        } finally {

            wLock.unlock();
        }
    }

    private void setBalance(Float balance) {

        wLock.lock();
        try {
            balance = balance;

        } finally {

            wLock.unlock();
        }
    }

    public Float getBalance() {

        rLock.lock();

        try {
            return balance;

        } finally {

            rLock.unlock();
        }
    }

    public Integer getId() {
        return id;
    }

    public Date getStartDate() {

        return (Date) startDate.clone();
    }

    ...
```

```
    private Float balance;
    private final Integer id;
    private final Date startDate;
    private final ReadWriteLock lock = new ReentrantReadWriteLock();
    private final Lock rLock = lock.readLock();
    private final Lock wLock = lock.writeLock();
}
```

`BankAccountThreadSafe` is a class that doesn't allow a bank account to be overdrawn (that is, have a negative balance), and it's an example of a **thread-safe** class. The `final` fields are set in the constructors, hence implicitly thread-safe. The `balance` field, on the other hand, is managed in a thread-safe way by the `setBalance`, `getBalance`, `creditOperation`, and `debitOperation` methods.

In other words, this class is correctly programmed, concurrency-wise. The problem is that wherever we would like to have those characteristics, we have to write the same code (especially the `finally` block containing the lock's release).

We can solve that by writing an aspect that carries out that task for us.

- A state modification is `execution(void com.mycompany.BankAccount.set*(*))`

- A safe read is `execution(* com.mycompany.BankAccount.getBalance())`

```
package org.springaop.chapter.five.concurrent;

import java.util.concurrent.locks.Lock;
import java.util.concurrent.locks.ReadWriteLock;
import java.util.concurrent.locks.ReentrantReadWriteLock;

import org.aspectj.lang.annotation.After;
import org.aspectj.lang.annotation.Aspect;
import org.aspectj.lang.annotation.Before;
import org.aspectj.lang.annotation.Pointcut;

@Aspect
public class BankAccountAspect {

    /*pointcuts*/

    @Pointcut(
    "execution(* org.springaop.chapter.five.concurrent.BankAccount.
    getBalance())")
```

```
    public void safeRead(){}

    @Pointcut(
"execution(* org.springaop.chapter.five.concurrent.BankAccount.
set*(*))")
    public void stateModification(){}

    @Pointcut(
"execution(* org.springaop.chapter.five.concurrent.BankAccount.
getId())")
    public void getId(){}

@Pointcut("execution(* org.springaop.chapter.five.concurrent.
BankAccount.getStartDate()))
    public void getStartDate(){}

    /*advices*/

    @Before("safeRead()")
    public void beforeSafeRead() {

        rLock.lock();
    }

    @After("safeRead()")
    public void afterSafeRead() {

        rLock.unlock();
    }

    @Before("stateModification()")
    public void beforeSafeWrite() {

        wLock.lock();
    }

    @After("stateModification()")
    public void afterSafeWrite() {

        wLock.unlock();
    }

    private final ReadWriteLock lock = new
ReentrantReadWriteLock();
    private final Lock rLock = lock.readLock();
    private final Lock wLock = lock.writeLock();
}
```

The `BankAccountAspect` class applies the crosscutting functionality. In this case, the functionality is calling the `lock` and `unlock` methods on the `ReadLock` and the `WriteLock`. The `before` methods apply the locks with the `@Before` annotation, while the `after` methods release the locks as if they were in the final block, with the `@After` annotation that is always executed (an after-finally advice).

In this way the `BankAccount` class can become much easier, clearer, and briefer. It doesn't need any indication that it can be executed in a thread-safe manner.

```java
package org.springaop.chapter.five.concurrent;

import java.util.Date;

public class BankAccount {
    public BankAccount(Integer id) {
        this.id = id;
        this.balance = new Float(0);
        this.startDate = new Date();
    }

    public BankAccount(Integer id, Float balance) {
        this.id = id;
        this.balance = balance;
        this.startDate = new Date();
    }

    public BankAccount(Integer id, Float balance, Date start) {
        this.id = id;
        this.balance = balance;
        this.startDate = start;
    }

    public boolean debitOperation(Float debit) {

        float balance = getBalance();

        if (balance < debit) {

            return false;

        } else {

            setBalance(balance - debit);

            return true;

        }
    }

    public void creditOperation(Float credit) {

        setBalance(getBalance() + credit);
```

```
    }

    private void setBalance(Float balance) {

        this.balance = balance;
    }

    public Float getBalance() {

        return balance;
    }

    public Integer getId() {

        return id;
    }

    public Date getStartDate() {

        return (Date) startDate.clone();
    }

    private Float balance;
    private final Integer id;
    private final Date startDate;
}
```

Another good design choice, together with the use of `ReadWriteLock` when necessary, is using objects that once built are immutable, and therefore, not corruptible and can be easily shared between threads.

Transparent caching with AOP

Often, the objects that compose applications perform the same operations with the same arguments and obtain the same results. Sometimes, these operations are costly in terms of CPU usage, or may be there is a lot of I/O going on while executing those operations.

To get better results in terms of speed and resources used, it's suggested to use a **cache**. We can store in it the results corresponding to the methods' invocations as key-value pairs: `method` and `arguments` as key and `return object` as value.

Once you decide to use a cache you're just halfway. In fact, you must decide which part of the application is going to use the cache. Let's think about a web application backed by a database. Such a web application usually involves **Data Access Objects (DAOs)**, which access the relational database. Such objects are usually a bottleneck in the application as there is a lot of I/O going on. In other words, a cache can be used there.

The cache can also be used by the business layer that has already aggregated and elaborated data retrieved from repositories, or it can be used by the presentation layer putting formatted presentation templates in the cache, or even by the authentication system that keeps roles according to an authenticated username.

There are almost no limits as to how you can optimize an application and make it faster. The only price you pay is having RAM to dedicate the objects that are to be kept in memory, besides paying attention to the rules on how to manage the life of the objects in cache.

After these preliminary remarks, using a cache could seem common and obvious. A cache essentially acts as a hash into which key-value pairs are put. The keys are used to retrieve objects from the cache. Caching usually has configuration parameters that allow you to change its behavior.

Now let's have a look at an example with **ehcache** (`http://ehcache.sourceforge.net`). First of all let's configure it with the name `methodCache` so that we have at the most 1000 objects. The objects are inactive for a maximum of five minutes, with a maximum life of 10 minutes. If the objects count is over 1000, ehcache saves them on the filesystem, in `java.io.tmpdir`.

```
<ehcache>
    ...
    <diskStore path="java.io.tmpdir"/>
    ....
    <defaultCache

        maxElementsInMemory="10000"
        eternal="false"
        timeToIdleSeconds="120"
        timeToLiveSeconds="120"
        overflowToDisk="true"
        diskPersistent="false"
        diskExpiryThreadIntervalSeconds="120"

    />
    ...
    <cache      name="methodCache"
            maxElementsInMemory="1000"
            eternal="false"
            overflowToDisk="false"
            timeToIdleSeconds="300"
            timeToLiveSeconds="600"
    />
</ehcache>
```

Now let's create a `CacheAspect`. Let's define the `cacheObject` to which the `ProceedingJoinPoint` is passed. Let's recover an unambiguous key from the `ProceedingJoinPoint` with the method `getCacheKey`. We will use this key to put the objects into the cache and to recover them.

Once we have obtained the key, we ask to cache the `Element` with the instruction `cache.get(cacheKey)`. The `Element` has to be evaluated because it may be `null` if the cache didn't find an `Element` with the passed `cacheKey`.

If the `Element` is `null`, advice invokes the method `proceed()`, and puts in the cache the `Element` with the key corresponding to the invocation. Otherwise, if the `Element` recovered from the cache is not `null`, the method isn't invoked on the target class, and the value taken from the cache is returned to the caller.

```
package org.springaop.chapter.five.cache;

import it.springaop.utils.Constants;
import net.sf.ehcache.Cache;
import net.sf.ehcache.Element;

import org.apache.log4j.Logger;
import org.aspectj.lang.ProceedingJoinPoint;

public class CacheAspect {

    public Object cacheObject(ProceedingJoinPoint pjp) throws Throwable
{

        Object result;
        String cacheKey = getCacheKey(pjp);

        Element element = (Element) cache.get(cacheKey);
        logger.info(new StringBuilder("CacheAspect invoke:").append("\n
get:")
                .append(cacheKey).append(" value:").append(element).
toString());

        if (element == null) {

            result = pjp.proceed();

            element = new Element(cacheKey, result);

            cache.put(element);

            logger.info(new StringBuilder("\n put:").append(cacheKey).
append(
                " value:").append(result).toString());
        }
```

```java
            return element.getValue();
        }

    public void flush() {
        cache.flush();
        }

        private String getCacheKey(ProceedingJoinPoint pjp) {
            String targetName = pjp.getTarget().getClass().getSimpleName();
            String methodName = pjp.getSignature().getName();
            Object[] arguments = pjp.getArgs();

            StringBuilder sb = new StringBuilder();
            sb.append(targetName).append(".").append(methodName);
            if ((arguments != null) && (arguments.length != 0)) {
                for (int i = 0; i < arguments.length; i++) {
                    sb.append(".").append(arguments[i]);
                }
            }
            return sb.toString();
        }

        public void setCache(Cache cache) {
            this.cache = cache;
        }

        private Cache cache;
        private Logger logger = Logger.getLogger(Constants.LOG_NAME);
    }
```

Here is `applicationContext.xml`:

```xml
<beans xmlns=»http://www.springframework.org/schema/beans»
xmlns:xsi=»http://www.w3.org/2001/XMLSchema-instance»
xmlns:aop=»http://www.springframework.org/schema/aop»
xsi:schemaLocation=»http://www.springframework.org/schema/beans
http://www.springframework.org/schema/beans/spring-beans-2.5.xsd
http://www.springframework.org/schema/aop
http://www.springframework.org/schema/aop/spring-aop-2.5.xsd»>      …

    <bean id="rockerCacheAspect"  class="org.springaop.chapter.five.
cache.CacheAspect" >
    <property name="cache">
        <bean id="bandCache" parent="cache">
            <property name="cacheName" value="methodCache" />
        </bean>
    </property>
```

```
</bean>

<!-- CACHE config  -->

<bean id="cache" abstract="true"
   class="org.springframework.cache.ehcache.EhCacheFactoryBean">
   <property name="cacheManager" ref="cacheManager" />
</bean>

<bean id="cacheManager"
class="org.springframework.cache.ehcache.
EhCacheManagerFactoryBean">
      <property name="configLocation" value="classpath:org/springaop/
chapter/five/cache/ehcache.xml" />
   </bean>

   ...
</beans>
```

The idea about the caching aspect is to avoid repetition in our code base and have a consistent strategy for identifying objects (for example using the hash code of an object) so as to prevent objects from ending up in the cache twice.

Employing an around advice, we can use the cache to make the method invocations return the cached result of a previous invocation of the same method in a totally transparent way. In fact, to the methods of the classes defined in the interception rules in pointcuts will be given back the return values drawn from the cache or, if these are not present, they will be invoked and inserted in the cache. In this way, the classes and methods don't have any knowledge of obtaining values retrieved from the cache.

Let's define the pointcut that intercepts the methods of the class DummyClass.

```
<beans xmlns="http://www.springframework.org/schema/beans"
xmlns:xsi="http://www.w3.org/2001/XMLSchema-instance"
xmlns:aop="http://www.springframework.org/schema/aop"
xsi:schemaLocation="http://www.springframework.org/schema/beans
http://www.springframework.org/schema/beans/spring-beans-2.5.xsd
http://www.springframework.org/schema/aop
http://www.springframework.org/schema/aop/spring-aop-2.5.xsd">
    ...

<aop:config>

<!--  Pointcuts -->
<aop:pointcut id="readOperation" expression=
"execution(* org.springaop.chapter.five.cache.DummyClass.get*(..))"
/>
```

```
<aop:pointcut id="exitOperation" expression=
"execution(void org.springaop.chapter.five.cache.DummyClass.exit())"
/>

<!-- Aspects -->
<aop:aspect id="dummyCacheAspect" ref="rockerCacheAspect">
<aop:around pointcut-ref="readOperation" method="cacheObject" />
    <aop:after pointcut-ref="exitOperation" method="flush" />
</aop:aspect>

</aop:config>
    …
</beans>
```

Class DummyClass used to check the cache's working:

```
package org.springaop.chapter.five.cache;

public class DummyClass {

    public String getFooFighters(){
        return "My hero";
    }

    public String getHives(String year){
        if(year.equals("2004")){
        return "Walk idiot walk !";}else{
            return "Abra Cadaver";
        }
    }

    public String getDandyWarhols(){
        return "Ride";
    }

public void exit(){
        System.out.println("The end.");
    }
}
```

Here is `ApplicationContext.xml` complete:

```
<beans xmlns=»http://www.springframework.org/schema/beans»
xmlns:xsi=»http://www.w3.org/2001/XMLSchema-instance»
xmlns:aop=»http://www.springframework.org/schema/aop»
xsi:schemaLocation=»http://www.springframework.org/schema/beans
http://www.springframework.org/schema/beans/spring-beans-2.5.xsd
```

```
http://www.springframework.org/schema/aop
http://www.springframework.org/schema/aop/spring-aop-2.5.xsd»>

<bean id="dummy" class="org.springaop.chapter.five.cache.DummyClass"/>

   <aop:config>
      <!--  Pointcuts -->

      <aop:pointcut id="readOperation"
            expression="execution(* org.springaop.chapter.five.cache.
DummyClass.get*(..))" />

      <aop:pointcut id="exitOperation"
            expression="execution(void org.springaop.chapter.five.
cache.DummyClass.exit())" />

      <!-- Aspects -->

      <aop:aspect id="dummyCacheAspect" ref="rockerCacheAspect">
         <aop:around pointcut-ref="readOperation" method="cacheObject"
/>
         <aop:after pointcut-ref="exitOperation" method="flush" />
      </aop:aspect>

   </aop:config>

   <bean id="rockerCacheAspect" class="org.springaop.chapter.five.
cache.CacheAspect" >
      <property name="cache">
         <bean id="bandCache" parent="cache">
            <property name="cacheName" value="methodCache" />
         </bean>
      </property>
   </bean>

   <!-- CACHE config  -->

   <bean id="cache" abstract="true"
      class="org.springframework.cache.ehcache.EhCacheFactoryBean">
      <property name="cacheManager" ref="cacheManager" />
   </bean>

   <bean id="cacheManager"
      class="org.springframework.cache.ehcache.
EhCacheManagerFactoryBean">
      <property name="configLocation" value="classpath:org/springaop/
chapter/five/cache/ehcache.xml" />
   </bean>

</beans>
```

`ApplicationContext` contains the following beans:

1. The `dummy` bean, used to test the cache's working.

2. The `readOperation` and `exitOperation` pointcuts.

3. The `dummyCacheAspect` aspect, with around and after advices.

4. The `rockerCacheAspect`, which is the implementation of the aspect class that contains the logic of recovery from and insertion into the cache.

5. The `cache` bean, which is an `EhCacheFactoryBean`.

6. The `cacheManager` bean, which is an `EhCacheManagerFactoryBean`.

Here is the test class:

```
package org.springaop.chapter.five.cache;

import org.springframework.context.ApplicationContext;
import org.springframework.context.support.
ClassPathXmlApplicationContext;

public class CacheTest {

    public static void main(String[] args){

        String[] paths = { "org/springaop/chapter/five/cache/
applicationContext.xml" };

        ApplicationContext ctx = new ClassPathXmlApplicationContext
(paths);

        DummyClass dummy = (DummyClass) ctx.getBean("dummy");
        dummy.getFooFighters();
        dummy.getHives("2004");
        dummy.getDandyWarhols();

        dummy.getFooFighters();
        dummy.getHives("2004");
        dummy.getDandyWarhols();

dummy.exit();
    }
}
```

The result will be:

```
  Problems  Ju JUnit   Console ✕      Spring Explorer   Spring AOP Event Trace
<terminated> CacheTest [Java Application] /usr/local/jdk1.6.0_07/bin/java (Sep 14, 2008 8:37:20 PM)
 INFO [main] - Refreshing org.springframework.context.support.ClassPathXmlApplicationContext@2bb514: display
 INFO [main] - Loading XML bean definitions from class path resource [org/springaop/chapter/five/cache/appli
 INFO [main] - Bean factory for application context [org.springframework.context.support.ClassPathXmlApplica
 INFO [main] - Pre-instantiating singletons in org.springframework.beans.factory.support.DefaultListableBean
 INFO [main] - Initializing EHCache CacheManager
 INFO [main] - CacheAspect invoke:
get:DummyClass.getFooFighters value:null
 INFO [main] -
put:DummyClass.getFooFighters value:My hero!
 INFO [main] - CacheAspect invoke:
get:DummyClass.getHives.2004 value:null
 INFO [main] -
put:DummyClass.getHives.2004 value:Walk idiot walk !
 INFO [main] - CacheAspect invoke:
get:DummyClass.getDandyWarhols value:null
 INFO [main] -
put:DummyClass.getDandyWarhols value:Ride
 INFO [main] - CacheAspect invoke:
get:DummyClass.getFooFighters value:[ key = DummyClass.getFooFighters, value=My hero!, version=1, hitCount=
 INFO [main] - CacheAspect invoke:
get:DummyClass.getHives.2004 value:[ key = DummyClass.getHives.2004, value=Walk idiot walk !, version=1, hi
 INFO [main] - CacheAspect invoke:
get:DummyClass.getDandyWarhols value:[ key = DummyClass.getDandyWarhols, value=Ride, version=1, hitCount=1,
The end.
```

As we can see from the log, the first invocations of methods are always followed by put because the cache didn't contain the results of invocations.

On the second calls, the values are instead recovered by the cache with key className.method.arguments. The number of hits, the date of creation, and the last access are shown as well.

Security with AOP

Security is one of the most important elements of an application. The word "security" covers two concepts:

- Authentication is the verification's process of a principal's identity; a principal is typically a user. A principal in order to be authenticated provides a credential that is the password.

- Authorization, on the other hand, is the process of granting authorities, which are usually roles, to an authenticated user.

Once a user is authenticated and has roles, he or she can work on the application and perform the actions permitted by an access control list, which according to the user's roles allows certain operations.

Before **Spring Security**, the rules of who can do what were usually implemented using custom code and an in-house framework, or using JAAS. Usually, the first type of implementation was a consequence of the second type's difficulty. Unfortunately, though custom-type security fits its purposes, it lacks in its main aim. This is because it's safer to employ a much-used framework that is constantly updated and corrects security problems, rather than having an in-house framework that might be barely tested. Beside these considerations, which should be carefully take into account, defining and applying security rules without AOP means causing code tangling and code scattering.

In fact, AOP applied to security solves most of the common practical problems concerning security. In order to solve them we use Spring Security 2.0.x (formerly Acegi Security System for Spring), configuring it properly to carry out most of the work according to the application's needs. We will see its configuration in Chapter 7. Now let's look just at some parts where AOP intervenes in its configuration.

For now, we will not deal with the authentications and roles attribution. Instead, we will start from the point at which the decision is taken to authorize a user and to provide him or her with roles to access a certain resource. Taking an actual decision whether or not to allow the user (based on its roles) gain access to the secure resource is the responsibility of the access decision manager.

An access decision manager implements the `AccessDecisionManager` interface, and in order to carry out his or her job, the manager needs a group of voters which implement the `AccessDecisionVoter` interface.

The `AccessDecisionManagers` provided by Spring are:

- `AffirmativeBased`: At least one voter votes to grant access
- `ConsensusBased`: A consensus of voters votes to grant access
- `UnanimousBased`: All voters vote to abstain or grant access

If none of them is specified, we employ `AffirmativeBased` with two voters, `RoleVoter` and `AuthenticatedVoter`. A voter can vote to grant, deny, or abstain.

- `RoleVoter`: This bases its vote on role. If the user has the required role by the required resource, it votes `ACCESS_GRANTED`. But if the resource doesn't have a specified role, it votes `ACCESS_ABSTAIN`. If the resource has a role the user doesn't have, then it votes `ACCESS_DENIED`.
- `AuthenticatedVoter`: This votes on the strength of the user's authentication. A user can be authenticated with:
  - `IS_AUTHENTICATED_FULLY`
  - `IS_AUTHENTICATED_REMEMBERED`

- ○ IS_AUTHENTICATED_ANONYMOUSLY

- ○ AuthenticatedVoter votes ACCESS_GRANTED if the authentication level is higher than the level requested by the resource. The highest one is IS_AUTHENTICATED_FULLY.

In the following XML, we see the declaration of the access decision manager:

```
<beans xmlns="http://www.springframework.org/schema/beans"
xmlns:xsi="http://www.w3.org/2001/XMLSchema-instance"
xmlns="http://www.springframework.org/schema/security"
xsi:schemaLocation="http://www.springframework.org/schema/beans
http://www.springframework.org/schema/security
http://www.springframework.org/schema/security/spring-security-
2.0.4.xsd
http://www.springframework.org/schema/beans/spring-beans-2.5.xsd">
...
    <bean id="accessDecisionManager" class="org.springframework.
security.vote.AffirmativeBased">
        <property name="decisionVoters">
            <list>
    <bean class="org.springframework.security.vote.RoleVoter" />
    <bean class="org.springframework.security.vote.AuthenticatedVoter"
/>
            </list>
        </property>
    </bean>

</beans>
```

Once we have defined the AccessDecisionManager, we can use AOP to decide the roles that are necessary to call the several beans' methods.

We can employ three strategies:

1. Securing methods with security interceptors.

2. Securing methods with pointcuts.

3. Securing methods with annotations.

 In order to employ interceptors, the aspectjrt.jar and aspectjweaver.jar JARs must be in the classpath. For the annotations, there must be the JAR spring-security-core-tiger-2.0.x.jar.

Securing methods with security interceptors

With security interceptors we can define the roles necessary to execute methods on the bean.

Let's have the interface:

```
public interface FooService {

    public Integer getBalance(Integer idAccount);
    public void setBalanceAccount(Integer id, Integer balance);
    public boolean suspendAccount(Integer id);

}
```

`FooService` is implemented by `FooServiceImpl`, that is configured as follows :

```
<beans xmlns="http://www.springframework.org/schema/beans"
xmlns:xsi="http://www.w3.org/2001/XMLSchema-instance"
xmlns:security="http://www.springframework.org/schema/security"
xsi:schemaLocation="http://www.springframework.org/schema/beans
http://www.springframework.org/schema/beans/spring-beans-2.5.xsd
http://www.springframework.org/schema/security
http://www.springframework.org/schema/security/spring-security-
2.0.4.xsd">
...

    <bean id="accessDecisionManager" class="org.springframework.
security.vote.AffirmativeBased">
        <property name="decisionVoters">
            <list>
             <bean class="org.springframework.security.vote.RoleVoter"
/>
     <bean class="org.springframework.security.vote.AuthenticatedVoter"
/>
            </list>
        </property>
    </bean>
...

<bean class="org.springaop.chapter.five.security.FooServiceImpl">
      <security:intercept-methods
        access-decision-manager-ref="accessDecisionManager">
        <security:protect method="org.springaop.chapter.five.
security.FooService.getBalance"
            access="ROLE_USER" />
        <security:protect
```

```
                    method="org.springaop.chapter.five.security.FooService.
        setBalanceAccount"
                access="ROLE_ACCOUNTING,ROLE_ADMIN" />
            <security:protect method="org.springaop.chapter.five.
        security.FooService.suspendAccount"
                access="ROLE_ADMIN" />
        </security:intercept-methods>
    </bean>
...
</beans>
```

We have defined some roles (separated by a comma) that can execute those method
we want to be executed by a user that has a particular role. This choice permits us to
define roles on methods directly on beans, but makes the configuration files too long.

Securing methods with pointcuts

With this strategy, it's possible to define the roles required for the different pointcuts
with AspectJ syntax that we define with the tag `global-method-security`.

We use the same rules on the same methods of the interface `FooService`.

```
    <global-method-security
            access-decision-manager-ref="accessDecisionManager">
        <protect-pointcut
            expression="execution(* org.springaop.chapter.five.security.
        FooService.getBalance(..))"
            access="ROLE_USER" />
        <protect-pointcut
            expression="execution(* org.springaop.chapter.five.security.
        FooService.set*(..))"
            access="ROLE_ACCOUNTING,ROLE_ADMIN" />
        <protect-pointcut
            expression="execution(* org.springaop.chapter.five.security.
        FooService.suspendAccount(..))"
            access="ROLE_ADMIN" />
    </global-method-security>
```

When using pointcuts, we don't have to use interceptors if they can be in conflict
with the execution of methods that we have defined in the configuration. This
modality of configuration is consistent with AspectJ syntax for the definition of
pointcuts, making the modality of configuration of aspects homogeneous.

Compared to interceptors, the configuration is less prolix and dispersive as it
concentrates the methods that can be invoked with the different roles at one point.

Securing methods with annotations

We can use annotations to define which roles can be executed by the methods of our classes. We will use the same rules on the same methods of the interface `FooService`.

```
package org.springaop.chapter.five.security;

import org.springframework.security.annotation.Secured;

public class FooServiceImplWithAnnotations implements FooService{

    @Secured("ROLE_USER")
    public Integer getBalance(Integer idAccount) {
        Integer result = 0;
        // do something
        return result;
    }

    @Secured( { "ROLE_ACCOUNTING", "ROLE_ADMIN" })
    public void setBalanceAccount(Integer id, Integer balance) {
        // do something
    }

    @Secured("ROLE_ADMIN")
    public boolean suspendAccount(Integer id) {
        boolean result = false;
        // do something
        return result;
    }
}
```

With this strategy, we define the roles within the class, needed for the execution of methods. With this choice we don't have to configure any XML, but we lose the possibility of seeing the roles for the methods present defined in a single place.

Summary

In this chapter we've seen how to implement crosscutting functionalities, such as concurrency control, the employment of a cache, and security management. Without AOP those functionalities would be scattered across the application, with the same code duplicated in different modules. With AOP we can have cleaner code, much more concise and easier to maintain and debug. We've seen how it is possible to implement these functionalities without having tangled or scattered code, implementing functionalities with aspects and advices.

Other important functionalities are transactions management, application logging, exception management, layout, and others. They will be illustrated in the next two chapters in a complete and working application.

6
Three-tier Spring Application, Domain-Driven Design

This chapter presents an overview of the **Domain-Driven Design** (DDD) concept and explains its capabilities and features. Here is a brief outline of the topics covered in this chapter:

- Domain-Driven Design
- The Domain layer of the sample application
- The Infrastructure layer of the sample application

Domain-Driven Design

DDD is not a technology or methodology. It is a way of thinking and a set of priorities aimed at accelerating software projects that have to deal with complicated domains (http://www.domaindrivendesign.org).

For many years, designing and realizing JEE application has meant moving **Data Transfer Objects** (DTO) and **Value Objects** (VO) between layers and writing procedural code to allow **Enterprise JavaBeans** (EJB) to do their work.

This led to the use of classes that were defined as *anemic* by Martin Fowler (http://martinfowler.com/bliki/AnemicDomainModel.html), that's to say, classes where the business logic is completely separate from the domain objects; usually it is in a service layer, which uses the domain classes as classes of data.

The business logic is contained in services using anemic domain models. But as we have seen, the application works in a procedural way, and is not object-oriented. The objects are mere carriers of data realized as DTO or VO, with only the methods `get` and `set`. They have no behavior.

As well as being an anti-pattern, this is a misuse of the **Object-Oriented Programming (OOP)** paradigm. OOP provides concepts and constructs that simplify and rationalize the design of application model and business logic.

DDD proposes a lot of little domain classes, instead of the big service classes, that generate anemic domain models. We have indeed gone back to the origins of OOP, when the objects had states and behaviors as models of the entities of a particular domain.

DDD uses all of the OOP concepts to define the business logic in the domain classes, making it easier to modify the application as requirements change and where needed.

The application is extendable, modular, and easy to change. Also, the testability is improved, and the customer and the development team use a common language (ubiquitous language).

Using anemic classes, a fat service layer is created where we have **façade** classes to move anemic objects that are used only as data containers. (For details about façade pattern `http://en.wikipedia.org/wiki/Facade_pattern`.)

This leads to the same problems for which we apply AOP with the OOP: duplicated code that is scattered in several classes, façade classes in this case.

In the rest of the chapter, we will see how AOP and Dependency Injection support the design obtained with DDD and make class testing easier.

Roles and responsibilities

In this section we are going to see a generic organization to define the roles and responsibilities of objects with DDD. This organization should be considered open. If we need to act in a different way, we are free to do so.

Entities

These are objects that have their own identity and almost always correspond to real concepts. They are the core of the domain model, and are realized as **Plain Old Java Objects (POJO)**.

Aggregates

The domain model can be composed of several associated entities. If aggregated, they can be considered as a unique entity that must be accessible from a unique point to preserve the integrity of the objects contained. An aggregation is accessible only through the root, that is, an entity.

The root internally keeps the references to all the objects that compose the aggregation, which in some cases have an identity only as parts of the aggregation.

If we have to act on the aggregation, it's the root that makes the modifications in a controlled way. As the entities inside the aggregation can't be accessed from outside, their state can't be corrupted.

If we need to pass data to the external code, a copy (and not the reference) is passed just to make the aggregation impenetrable to external modifications. Everything has to pass through the root. If the root is removed, all the objects of the aggregation are removed. The root guarantees the maintenance of invariance.

Modules

When the application gets bigger, the model grows consequently. To manage the organization and complexity, the domain model is divided into modules that are interrelated.

Value objects

These are objects defined only by the value of their attributes and have no behavior and identity.

They are often unchangeable, and since they are defined only by the value of their attributes, they are interchangeable.

Factories

These define methods to create entities that may need many operations to be built. Above all, in this case, it would be necessary to build a complex graph of objects.

The factory becomes responsible for the encapsulation of the logic behind the creation of object graphs that are linked and work together to perform necessary business logic.

This encapsulation enables the caller class to have the entities needed to perform its work.

Repositories

The repository classes manage the entity collections and `read/write/update/delete` methods.

The exposed methods are declared in the interface, which masks the implementation, which uses the framework for persistence.

Defining the operations through the interface in terms of domain objects eliminates the need to focus on the details of persistence.

Services

Services are objects that have responsibilities that can't be contained in a class of a single domain model, and so act on several objects, nearly always in a transactional way.

A service has three characteristics:

- The operation is related to a domain concept that is not a natural part of an `entity` or `VO`
- The interface is defined in terms of other elements of the domain model
- The operation is stateless

Architecture

After seeing the division of responsibilities, we will see the conceptual architecture.

User interface

This is the presentation layer. Its task is presenting information from the application to the user, and acquiring commands from the user to the application.

Application layer

The application layer's task is to coordinate the application's activities. It doesn't contain any business logic or object status, but rather maintains the progress status of the application tasks such as navigation in the **User Interface** (**UI**) and validation of the fields received by the application.

Domain layer

This layer contains the business domain and the status of the business objects, which contain the status and behavior of business entities, and the business rules.

If it is necessary to execute several steps to perform a business use case, it maintains information about status among the steps.

In addition to domain objects, it also contains services that implement logic that can't be contained in a single domain object.

The objects contained in this layer do not depend on any framework employed in other layers because it must be completely isolated from the other layers.

In this layer we find entities, VO, services, and factories.

All the concepts of OOP have been used in the implementation of this layer: interfaces, inheritance, encapsulation, and polymorphism. Entities have status (attributes) and behavior (methods that act on the state) because they have to model concepts of the real world.

However, by using all the features of OOP we fall again into the problems explained in the first chapter, such as code scattering and tangling.

In order to support the domain layer, AOP and Dependency Injection are employed.

Infrastructure layer

This layer provides support to the other layers, such as persistence, support for the UI, and allowing communication between layers. This layer contains the repositories.

Sample application

The application we are going to prototype creates an online wholesale fresh-fruit shop, a market where in the evening goods that will be delivered to customers the next morning are traded. In this way, goods are not collected and handled until there is actually a buyer. The buyer buys goods that are actually available and will collect them the next morning to sell at a retail market.

Farmers inform about the availability of a certain quantity of fruit they offer, pointing out the main features that qualify the product.

Certified customers buy a certain quantity of different kinds of fruits.

At the time of ordering, the system ensures the full availability of goods (orders take place in real time). The order will be put in ACCEPTED status and the customer will be immediately notified. The customer can pay by credit card and get the goods early the next morning.

The following image contains an overview of the application:

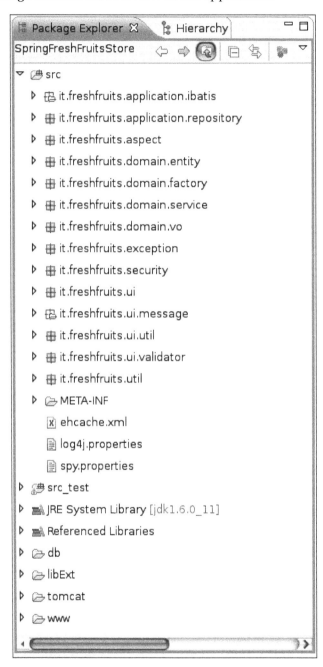

Design

The first step in the use of DDD is the location of entities.

Let's define a method that is shared between all the entities to identify them univocally.

```
package it.freshfruits.domain.entity;

public interface BaseEntity {

    public Integer getId();
}
```

Let's identify the customer in the domain, since the sale of the produce is the first reason for the application's existence.

```
package it.freshfruits.domain.entity;

public interface NamedEntity extends BaseEntity{

    public String getName();
}
```

`NamedEntity` adds a `getName` to `BaseEntity`:

```
package it.freshfruits.domain.entity;

import it.freshfruits.domain.vo.Address;
import it.freshfruits.domain.vo.ContactInformation;

import java.util.List;

public interface Customer extends NamedEntity{

    public Address getAddress();

    public ContactInformation getContact();

    public void modifyContactInformation(ContactInformation contact);

    public void modifyAddress(Address address);

    public Boolean saveCustomer();

    public Boolean createOrder();

    public Boolean saveOrder();

    public Order getOrder();

    public List<Order> getOrders();
}
```

Customer interface define the customer's behaviors.

The entity Customer uses internally VO Address and VO ContactInformation.

Let's identify the fruit type in the domain. It may seem a VO, but it represents the type of object bought by the customer; vice versa, the real VO is the item in the order.

```
package it.freshfruits.domain.entity;

import java.math.BigDecimal;

public interface FruitType extends NamedEntity{

    public String getLocation();

    public String getColor();

    public String getFlavour();

    public BigDecimal getPrice();
}
```

The entity FruitType represents a type of fruit with its characteristics.

The following Order class represents an order from a customer.

```
package it.freshfruits.domain.entity;

import it.freshfruits.domain.vo.OrderItem;

import java.math.BigDecimal;
import java.util.Date;
import java.util.Set;

public interface Order extends BaseEntity{

    public String getStatus();

    public String getIdCustomer();

    public Set<OrderItem> getOrderItems();

    public Integer getNumberItems();

    public void addOrderItem(OrderItem item);

    public void saveOrder();

    public BigDecimal getOrderAmount();

    public Date getDateOrder();

    public Boolean removeOrderItem(String idItem);
}
```

The entity `Order` contains a Set of VO `OrderItem`. Any `OrderItem` contains the information about the quantity and amount of a certain `FruitType`.

Each `OrderItem` contains a `FruitType` different from others. An `Order` can't contain two instances of `OrderItem` with the same `FruitType`.

The `OrderItem` represents one of the elements that compose the `Order` of a `Customer`.

```java
package it.freshfruits.domain.vo;

import java.math.BigDecimal;

import it.freshfruits.domain.entity.FruitType;

public interface OrderItem {

    public FruitType getFruitType();

    public Integer getQuantity();

    public Integer getIdOrder();

    public BigDecimal getAmountItem();
}
```

An `Address` object acts as a VO object that contains address information.

The `Address` represents the address of a `Customer`.

```java
package it.freshfruits.domain.vo;

public interface Address {

    public String getStreet();

    public String getCity();

     public String getState();
}
```

`ContactInformation` represents contact information about the `Customer`.

```java
package it.freshfruits.domain.vo;

public interface ContactInformation {

    public String getPhoneNumber();

    public String getMobilePhoneNumber();

    public String getFaxNumber();

    public String getEmail();
}
```

It is important to underline that, apart from being an entity, Customer is also an aggregate that performs the work of root towards Address and ContactInformation. In fact, the interfaces of Address and ContactInformation provide only accessors method to avoid compromising their internal state.

Let's see the implementations of Customer and the VO that it contains (Address and ContactInformation).

```
package it.freshfruits.domain.entity;

import it.freshfruits.application.repository.CustomerRepository;
import it.freshfruits.application.repository.OrderRepository;
import it.freshfruits.domain.vo.Address;
import it.freshfruits.domain.vo.AddressImpl;
import it.freshfruits.domain.vo.ContactInformation;
import it.freshfruits.domain.vo.ContactInformationImpl;
import it.freshfruits.util.Constants;

import java.io.Serializable;
import java.util.Date;
import java.util.List;

import org.springframework.beans.factory.annotation.Autowire;
import org.springframework.beans.factory.annotation.Autowired;
import org.springframework.beans.factory.annotation.Configurable;
import org.springframework.beans.factory.annotation.Qualifier;

@Configurable(dependencyCheck = true, autowire = Autowire.BY_TYPE)
public class CustomerImpl implements Customer, Serializable {

    public Boolean createOrder() {
        Boolean result = false;
        if (order == null) {
            order = new OrderImpl.Builder(Constants.ID_NEW, new
Date(), id.toString()).build();
            result = true;
        }
        return result;
    }

    public Boolean saveCustomer() {
        return customerRepository.saveCustomer(this);
    }

    public Address getAddress() {
        return address;
    }

    public ContactInformation getContact() {
```

```
            return contactInformation;
    }

    public Integer getId() {
        return id;
    }

    public String getName() {
        return name;
    }

    public void modifyContactInformation(ContactInformation contact) {
        contactInformation = contact;
    }

    public void modifyAddress(Address address) {
        this.address = address;
    }

    public List<Order> getOrders() {
        return orderRepository.getOrders(id.toString());
    }

    public Order getOrder() {
        return order;
    }

    public Boolean saveOrder() {
        return orderRepository.saveOrder(order);
    }

    public String toString() {
        return new StringBuilder().append("\nid:").append(id).
append("\nname:").append(name).append("\n<-address->").
append(address).append("\n<-contactInformation->").append(
contactInformation)
                .toString();
    }

    public static class Builder {
        // Required parameters
        private String name = "";
        private Integer id = 0;

        // Optional parameters
        private Address address;
        private ContactInformation contactInformation;
        private OrderRepository orderRepository;
        private CustomerRepository customerRepository;
```

```
        public Builder(String name, String id) {
            this.name = name;
            this.id = Integer.valueOf(id);
        }

        public Builder(String name, String id, Address address,
ContactInformation contact) {
            this.name = name;
            this.id = Integer.valueOf(id);
            this.address = address;
            this.contactInformation = contact;
        }

        public Builder address(String street, String city, String
state) {
            address = new AddressImpl.Builder(street, city, state).
build();
            return this;
        }

        public Builder contactInfo(String phoneNumber, String
mobilePhoneNumber, String faxNumber, String email) {
            contactInformation = new ContactInformationImpl.
Builder(phoneNumber, mobilePhoneNumber, faxNumber, email).build();
            return this;
        }

        public Builder orderRepository(OrderRepository
orderRepository) {
            this.orderRepository = orderRepository;
            return this;
        }

        public Builder customerRepository(CustomerRepository
customerRepository) {
            this.customerRepository = customerRepository;
            return this;
        }

        public CustomerImpl build() {
            return new CustomerImpl(this);
        }
    }

    private CustomerImpl(Builder builder) {
        id = builder.id;
        name = builder.name;
        address = builder.address;
        contactInformation = builder.contactInformation;
        orderRepository = builder.orderRepository;
```

```
            customerRepository = builder.customerRepository;
        }

        @Autowired
        public void setCustomerRepository(@Qualifier("customerRepository")
    CustomerRepository customerRepository) {
            this.customerRepository = customerRepository;
        }

        @Autowired
        public void setOrderRepository(@Qualifier("orderRepository")
    OrderRepository orderRepository) {
            this.orderRepository = orderRepository;
        }

        private CustomerRepository customerRepository;
        private OrderRepository orderRepository;
        private Address address;
        private Order order;
        private ContactInformation contactInformation;
        private String name;
        private Integer id;
        private static final long serialVersionUID = 6512264975502119631L;
    }
```

`Customer` is one of the main objects questioned by the application layer. To let it perform its work, the dependencies are injected at the moment of the creation of the `Customer` through the annotation `@Configurable`(dependencyCheck = true, autowire=Autowire.BY_TYPE)

It does not have public constructors and new instances are built using a `Builder`. It interacts with two repositories to perform operations: the `OrderRepository` and the `CustomerRepository`. It allows placing a new order and saving the customer's address. Using the order provided by customer, it is possible to perform all the operations defined by the `Order` interface.

The `AddressImpl` class implements the VO interface Address.

```
    package it.freshfruits.domain.vo;

    import it.freshfruits.util.ValidationUtils;

    public final class AddressImpl implements Address {

        public static class Builder {
            private String street = "";
            private String city = "";
            private String state = "";
```

```java
        public Builder(String street, String city, String state) {
            ValidationUtils.validateStreet(street);
             ValidationUtils.validateCity(city);
            ValidationUtils.validateState(state);
            this.street = street;
            this.city = city;
            this.state = state;
        }

        public AddressImpl build() {
            return new AddressImpl(this);
        }
    }

    public String getStreet() {
        return street;
    }

    public String getCity() {
        return city;
    }

    public String getState() {
        return state;
    }

    public String toString() {
        return new StringBuilder().append("\nstreet:").append(street).
append(
            "\ncity:").append(city).append("\nstate:").append(state)
            .toString();
    }

    private AddressImpl(Builder builder) {
        city = builder.city;
        state = builder.state;
        street = builder.street;
    }

    private String street = "";
    private String city = "";
    private String state = "";
}
```

`ContactInformationImpl` implements the VO interface `ContactInformation`.

```
package it.freshfruits.domain.vo;

import it.freshfruits.util.ValidationUtils;

public final class ContactInformationImpl implements
ContactInformation {

    public static class Builder {
        private String phoneNumber = "";
        private String mobilePhoneNumber = "";
        private String faxNumber = "";
        private String email = "";

        public Builder(String phoneNumber, String mobilePhoneNumber,
                String faxNumber, String email) {
    ValidationUtils.validatePhoneNumber(phoneNumber);
        ValidationUtils.validateMobilePhoneNumber(mobilePhoneNumber);
            ValidationUtils.validateFaxNumber(faxNumber);
            ValidationUtils.validateEmail(email);
            this.phoneNumber = phoneNumber;
            this.mobilePhoneNumber = mobilePhoneNumber;
            this.faxNumber = faxNumber;
            this.email = email;
        }

        public ContactInformationImpl build() {
            return new ContactInformationImpl(this);
        }
    }

    public String getPhoneNumber() {
        return phoneNumber;
    }

    public String getMobilePhoneNumber() {
        return mobilePhoneNumber;
    }

    public String getFaxNumber() {
        return faxNumber;
    }

    public String getEmail() {
        return email;
    }
```

```
    public String toString() {
        return new StringBuilder().append("\nphoneNumber:").
append(phoneNumber)

    .append("\nmobilePhoneNumber:").append(mobilePhoneNumber)

    .append("\nfaxNumber:").append(faxNumber).append("\nemail:")
            .append(email).toString();
    }

    private ContactInformationImpl(Builder builder) {
        this.email = builder.email;
        this.faxNumber = builder.faxNumber;
        this.mobilePhoneNumber = builder.mobilePhoneNumber;
        this.phoneNumber = builder.phoneNumber;
    }

    private String phoneNumber = "";
    private String mobilePhoneNumber = "";
    private String faxNumber = "";
    private String email = "";
}
```

These implementations (CustomerImpl, AddressImpl, ContactInformationImpl) don't have public constructors, but internal builders and validators.

Even though AddressImpl and ContactInformationImpl are simple VO, they contain minimal validation rules to ensure building with values that make sense for the application. In fact, the fields are either empty or have a minimal pre-established length. The validation on the UI will then decide if they must have values or not and if the type is correct (numeric or text). In any case, the validation on the UI is made both on the builder and mutator methods. The class is final to prevent the possibility of the creation of subclasses. In the class, the override of toString is done to allow a communicative visualization when it's needed.

AddressImpl and ContactInformationImpl are the implementations of the VO that are used in the interface Customer.

Now let's see the other entities, such as FruitType, Order, and OrderItem.

```
package it.freshfruits.domain.entity;

import it.freshfruits.application.repository.FruitTypeRepository;
import it.freshfruits.util.ValidationUtils;

import java.io.Serializable;
import java.math.BigDecimal;
```

```java
import org.springframework.beans.factory.annotation.Autowired;
import org.springframework.beans.factory.annotation.Configurable;

@Configurable(dependencyCheck = true)
public class FruitTypeImpl implements FruitType, Serializable {

    @Autowired
    public void setFruitTypeRepository(FruitTypeRepository
    fruitTypeRepository) {
        this.fruitTypeRepository = fruitTypeRepository;
    }

    public void save() {
        if (id == 0) {
            fruitTypeRepository.insert(this);
        } else {
            fruitTypeRepository.update(this);
        }
    }

    public String getColor() {
        return color;
    }

    public String getFlavour() {
        return flavour;
    }

    public String getLocation() {
        return location;
    }

    public String getName() {
        return name;
    }

    public BigDecimal getPrice() {
        return price;
    }

    public Integer getId() {
        return id;
    }

    public String toString() {
        return new StringBuilder().append("\nid:").append(id).append(
"\nname:")
                .append(name).append("\ncolor:").append(color).append(
```

```
      "\nflavour:").append(flavour).append("\nlocation:")
            .append(location).toString();
   }

   public static class Builder {
      // Required parameters
      private String name = "";
      private Integer id = 0;
      private BigDecimal price;

      // optional parameters
      private String color = "";
      private String flavour = "";
      private String location = "";
      private FruitTypeRepository fruitTypeRepository;

      private void validatePrice(BigDecimal price) {

         if (price == null || (price.compareTo(BigDecimal.ZERO) <= 0))

            throw new IllegalArgumentException("price argument < 0 :"+
price);
      }

      private void validateName(String name) {
         if (name == null || name.length() != 0 && name.length() < 3)
            throw new IllegalArgumentException("name argument < 3 :" +
name);
      }

      private void validateColor(String color) {
         if (color == null || color.length() != 0 && color.length() <
3)
            throw new IllegalArgumentException("color argument < 3 :"+
color);
      }

      private void validateFlavour(String flavour) {
         if (flavour == null || flavour.length() != 0
               && flavour.length() < 4)
            throw new IllegalArgumentException("flavour argument < 4 :"+
flavour);
      }

      private void validateLocation(String location) {
         if (location == null || location.length() != 0
               && location.length() < 3)
```

```
                    throw new IllegalArgumentException("location argument < 3
    :"+ location);
        }

    public Builder(String name, Integer id, BigDecimal price) {
        ValidationUtils.validateId(id.toString());
        validateName(name);
        validatePrice(price);
        this.name = name;
        this.id = id;
        this.price = price;
    }

    public Builder color(String val) {
        validateColor(val);
        color = val;
        return this;
    }

    public Builder flavour(String val) {
        validateFlavour(val);
        flavour = val;
        return this;
    }

    public Builder location(String val) {
        validateLocation(val);
        location = val;
        return this;
    }

    public Builder fruitTypeRepository(
            FruitTypeRepository fruitTypeRepository) {
        this.fruitTypeRepository = fruitTypeRepository;
        return this;
    }

    public FruitTypeImpl build() {
        return new FruitTypeImpl(this);
    }
    }

    private FruitTypeImpl(Builder builder) {
        id = builder.id;
        name = builder.name;
        price = builder.price;
        color = builder.color;
```

```
        flavour = builder.flavour;
    location = builder.location;
        fruitTypeRepository = builder.fruitTypeRepository;
    }

    private Integer id;
    private BigDecimal price;
    private String color, flavour, location, name;
    private FruitTypeRepository fruitTypeRepository;
}
```

FruitTypeImpl represents a type of product with unambiguous features and contains information about the price for the sale item.

```
package it.freshfruits.domain.entity;

import it.freshfruits.application.repository.OrderRepository;
import it.freshfruits.domain.service.SupplyService;
import it.freshfruits.domain.vo.OrderItem;
import it.freshfruits.util.Constants;
import it.freshfruits.util.ValidationUtils;

import java.io.Serializable;
import java.math.BigDecimal;
import java.util.Date;
import java.util.HashSet;
import java.util.Set;

import org.springframework.beans.factory.annotation.Autowired;
import org.springframework.beans.factory.annotation.Configurable;

@Configurable(dependencyCheck = true)
public class OrderImpl implements Order, Serializable {

    public String getIdCustomer() {
        return idCustomer.toString();
    }

    public void saveOrder() {
        orderRepository.saveOrder(this);
    }

    public Integer getNumberItems() {
        return orderItems.size();
    }

    public String getStatus() {
        return status;
    }

    public boolean addOrderItem(OrderItem item) {
        return supplyService.isAvailable(item) ? orderItems.add(item)
: false;
```

```
    }

    public Date getDateOrder() {
        return new Date(dateOrder.getTime());
    }

    public Set<OrderItem> getOrderItems() {
        return orderItems;
    }

    public BigDecimal getOrderAmount() {
        if ((amount.compareTo(BigDecimal.ZERO) == 0) && orderItems.
size() != 0) {
            for (OrderItem item : orderItems) {
                amount = amount.add(item.getAmountItem());
            }
        }
        return amount;
    }

    public Boolean removeOrderItem(String idOrder, String idItem) {
        Boolean result = false;
        for (OrderItem item : orderItems) {
            if (item.getFruitType().getId().toString().equals(idItem))
{
                result = orderItems.remove(item);
                if (result)
                    supplyService.release(idOrder, idItem);
                continue;
            }
        }
        return result;
    }

    public Integer getId() {
        return id;
    }

    public String toString() {

        StringBuilder sb = new StringBuilder().append("\nid:").
append(id).append("\nidCustomer:").append(idCustomer).append("\
ndateOrder:").append(dateOrder).append("\namount:").append(amount);

        if (orderItems != null && orderItems.size() > 0) {
            sb.append("\n");
            for (OrderItem item : orderItems) {
                sb.append(item);
            }
        }
        return sb.toString();
    }
```

```
@Autowired
public void setOrderRepository(OrderRepository orderRepository) {
    this.orderRepository = orderRepository;
}

@Autowired
public void setSupplyService(SupplyService supplyService) {
    this.supplyService = supplyService;
}

public static class Builder {
    // Required parameters
    private Integer id, idCustomer;
    private Date dateOrder;

    // Optional parameters
    private BigDecimal amount = new BigDecimal("0");
    private Set<OrderItem> orderItems = new HashSet<OrderItem>();

    public Builder(String id, Date dateOrder, String idCustomer) {
        ValidationUtils.validateId(id);
        ValidationUtils.validateId(idCustomer);
        ValidationUtils.validateDate(dateOrder);
        this.dateOrder = dateOrder;
        this.id = Integer.valueOf(id);
        this.idCustomer = Integer.valueOf(idCustomer);
    }

    public Builder amount(BigDecimal val) {
        ValidationUtils.validateAmount(val);
        amount = val;
        return this;
    }

    public Builder orderItems(Set<OrderItem> values) {
        orderItems = values;
        return this;
    }

    public OrderImpl build() {
        return new OrderImpl(this);
    }
}

private OrderImpl(Builder builder) {
    id = builder.id;
    idCustomer = builder.idCustomer;
    dateOrder = builder.dateOrder;
    amount = builder.amount;
    orderItems = builder.orderItems;
}

private Integer id, idCustomer;
private String status = Constants.ORDER_NEW;
```

```
      private BigDecimal amount;
      private Set<OrderItem> orderItems;
      private Date dateOrder;
      private OrderRepository orderRepository;
      private SupplyService supplyService;
      private static final long serialVersionUID = 2525105011114628958L;
}
```

Order represents the order of a Customer, who can make only one new order at a time. It returns a visualization of items, implements the addition and removal of an OrderItem, and maintains the state of the order.

An Order contains some OrderItem that contains information about the type of product and the amount bought.

Services

There are important domain operations that can't find a natural home in an ENTITY or VO. Some of these are intrinsically activities or actions.

The name service explains the relationship with other objects.

Our SupplyService provides an availability check and reservation service.

```
package it.freshfruits.domain.service;

import it.freshfruits.domain.vo.OrderItem;
import it.freshfruits.domain.vo.QuantityAndItemVO;

import java.util.List;
import java.util.Map;

public interface SupplyService {

    public Boolean isAvailable(OrderItem item);

    public Boolean retainItem(OrderItem item);

    public Boolean release(String idOrder, String idItem);

    public Map<String, QuantityAndItemVO> getItemsAvailable();

    public void init();

    public Map<String, List<OrderItem>> getReservedItems();
}
```

This is the `SupplyService` implementation:

```
package it.freshfruits.domain.service;

import it.freshfruits.domain.entity.FruitType;
import it.freshfruits.domain.entity.FruitTypeImpl;
import it.freshfruits.domain.vo.OrderItem;
import it.freshfruits.domain.vo.OrderItemImpl;
import it.freshfruits.domain.vo.QuantityAndItemVO;

import java.math.BigDecimal;
import java.util.ArrayList;
import java.util.HashMap;
import java.util.List;
import java.util.Map;

public class SupplyServiceImpl implements SupplyService {

    public SupplyServiceImpl(){
        this.availableItems = new HashMap<String, QuantityAndItemVO>();
        this.reservedItems = new HashMap<String, List<OrderItem>>();
    }

    public void init() { //test purpose only
        FruitType fruit = new FruitTypeImpl.Builder("orange", new
Integer(2), new BigDecimal("0.20")).build();
        OrderItem item = new OrderItemImpl.Builder(fruit, 400, "1").
build();
        availableItems.put(item.getFruitType().getId().toString(), new
QuantityAndItemVO(item));
        FruitType fruitTwo = new FruitTypeImpl.Builder("lemon", new
Integer(3), new BigDecimal("0.15")).build();
        OrderItem itemTwo = new OrderItemImpl.Builder(fruitTwo, 350,
"1").build();
        availableItems.put(itemTwo.getFruitType().getId().toString(),
new QuantityAndItemVO(itemTwo));
    }

    public Map<String, QuantityAndItemVO> getItemsAvailable() {
        return availableItems;
    }

    public Map<String, List<OrderItem>> getReservedItems() {
        return reservedItems;
    }

    public Boolean isAvailable(OrderItem item) {
```

```
            return availableItems.containsKey(item.getFruitType().getId().
toString());
    }

    public Boolean release(String idOrder, String idItem) {
        Boolean result = false;

        List<OrderItem> listItems = reservedItems.get(idOrder);

        if (listItems != null && listItems.size() > 0) {

            for (int index = 0; index < listItems.size(); index++) {

                OrderItem item = listItems.get(index);
                if (item.getFruitType().getId().toString().
equals(idItem)) {

                    listItems.remove(item);
                    QuantityAndItemVO qat = availableItems.
get(idItem);

                    qat.add(item.getQuantity());
                    availableItems.put(idItem, qat);
                    reservedItems.put(idOrder, listItems);
                    result = true;

                }

            }

        }

        return result;
    }

    public Boolean retainItem(OrderItem item) {

        Boolean result = false;

        QuantityAndItemVO qat = availableItems.get(item.
getFruitType().getId().toString());

        if (qat != null) {

            if (qat.getQuantity() >= item.getQuantity()) {

                List<OrderItem> items = reservedItems.get(item.
getIdOrder().toString());
                if (items == null) {
                    items = new ArrayList<OrderItem>();
                }
                items.add(item);
                reservedItems.put(item.getIdOrder().toString(),
items);
```

```
                qat.setQuantity(qat.getQuantity() - item.
    getQuantity());
                availableItems.put(qat.getItem().getFruitType().
    getId().toString(), qat);
                result = true;
            }
        }
        return result;
    }

    private Map<String, QuantityAndItemVO> availableItems;
    private Map<String, List<OrderItem>> reservedItems;
}
```

Factories

In the interaction of the user with the application layer, the domain object must be available because its creation/instantiation may involve several objects. Therefore, factory objects are used.

```
package it.freshfruits.domain.factories;

public interface CustomerFactory {

    public Customer getCustomer(String idCustomer);

    public Customer getCurrentCustomer();
}

package it.freshfruits.domain.factory;

import org.springframework.beans.factory.annotation.Autowired;
import org.springframework.stereotype.Component;

import it.freshfruits.application.repository.CustomerRepository;
import it.freshfruits.domain.entity.Customer;
import it.freshfruits.security.SecurityUtils;

// good candidate for customerCache
@Component("customerFactory")
public class CustomerFactoryImpl implements CustomerFactory {

    public Customer getCurrentCustomer() {
        return customerRepository.selectCustomer(SecurityUtils.
    getIdCustomer());
    }

    public Customer getCustomer(String idCustomer) {
```

```
            return customerRepository.selectCustomer(idCustomer);
      }

      @Autowired
      private CustomerRepository customerRepository;

}
```

As we can see from the implementation of `CustomerFactory`, we could recover it during the interactions with the UI. But after the creation, it is better to keep it in cache instead of recovering it every time from the database. In fact, this is an excellent class for a cache that is transparent with AOP.

In this way, the result we obtain is that the `Customer` object remains alive and available in the cache. When the `Customer` object is persisted, it will be eliminated from the cache.

A good strategy is to retrieve the `Customer` after the login and to put it in the cache.

A Spring handler interceptor makes this `Customer` available as a request attribute to the UI to provide its functionality to the application's users.

At the end of the session, a session listener removes the customer from the cache.

In the next chapter, we will see these operations of insertion and elimination from the AOP cache.

Repositories

Repositories are the classes that deal with persistence and are used by the domain classes. In the implementation of `Customer`, we have seen that two repositories are used: `OrderRepository`, which persists the order of a `Customer` and its `OrderItems`, or populates an order with the different items from the database; and `CustomerRepository`:

```
package it.freshfruits.application.repository;

import it.freshfruits.domain.entity.Customer;

import java.util.List;

public interface CustomerRepository {

    public String getIdCustomer(String username);

    public Boolean saveCustomer(Customer customer);

    public String insertCustomer(Customer customer);

    public Boolean updateCustomer(Customer customer);
```

```
    public Boolean disableCustomer(String id);

    public Boolean deleteCustomer(String id);

    public Customer selectCustomer(String id);

    public List<CustomerView> selectCustomers();

    public List<CustomerView> selectDisabledCustomers();

    public Boolean isPresent(String name);
}
```

The following `CustomerRepositoryImpl` is the implementation of the `CustomerRepository`. This implementation uses Apache iBATIS (`http://ibatis. apache.org`), a data mapper, to perform the storage on database.

```
package it.freshfruits.application.repository;

import it.freshfruits.domain.entity.Customer;
import it.freshfruits.domain.entity.CustomerImpl;
import it.freshfruits.util.Constants;

import java.util.List;

import org.springframework.beans.factory.annotation.Autowired;
import org.springframework.beans.factory.annotation.Qualifier;
import org.springframework.orm.ibatis.SqlMapClientTemplate;
import org.springframework.stereotype.Repository;

import com.ibatis.sqlmap.client.SqlMapClient;

@Repository("customerRepository")
public class CustomerRepositoryImpl extends SqlMapClientTemplate
implements CustomerRepository {

    public Boolean saveCustomer(Customer customer) {

        if (customer.getId().toString().equals(Constants.ID_NEW)) {

            return !insertCustomer(customer).equals(null) ? true : false;

        } else {

            return updateCustomer(customer);
        }
    }

    public Boolean deleteCustomer(String id) {
```

```
        return delete("deleteCustomerVO", Integer.valueOf(id)) == 1 ?
true
            : false;
    }

    public String insertCustomer(Customer customer) {
        return insert("insertCustomerVO", new CustomerMap(customer)).
toString();
    }

    public Boolean isPresent(String name) {
        return queryForObject("selectIdCustomerByName", name) != null ?
true : false;
    }

    public Customer selectCustomer(String id) {
        CustomerMap vo = (CustomerMap) queryForObject("selectCustomerVO
",
            Integer.valueOf(id));
        return new CustomerImpl.Builder(vo.getName(), vo.getId().
toString(), vo.getAddress(), vo.getContactInformation()).
build();
    }

    public Boolean updateCustomer(Customer customer) {
        return update("updateCustomerVO", new CustomerMap(customer)) ==
1 ? true : false;
    }

    public Boolean disableCustomer(String id) {
        return update("disableCustomer", Integer.valueOf(id)) == 1 ?
true : false;
    }

    @SuppressWarnings("unchecked")
    public List<CustomerView> selectCustomers() {
        return queryForList("selectCustomers");
    }

    @SuppressWarnings("unchecked")
    public List<CustomerView> selectDisabledCustomers() {
        return queryForList("selectDisabledCustomers");
    }

    public String getIdCustomer(String username) {
        return queryForObject("selectIdByUsername", username).
toString();
    }
```

```
    @Autowired @Override
    public void setSqlMapClient(
          @Qualifier("sqlMapClient") SqlMapClient sqlMapClient) {
        super.setSqlMapClient(sqlMapClient);
    }
}
```

The `OrderRepository` persists the orders of the customers.

```
package it.freshfruits.application.repository;

import it.freshfruits.domain.entity.Order;
import it.freshfruits.exception.OrderItemsException;

import java.util.List;

public interface OrderRepository {

    public String insertOrder(Order order) throws OrderItemsException;

    public Boolean saveOrder(Order order);

    public Boolean updateOrder(Order order);

    public Order getOrder(String id, String idCustomer);

    public List<Order> getOrders(String idCustomer);
}
```

The following `OrderRepositoryImpl` is the implementation of `OrderRepository`.

```
package it.freshfruits.application.repository;

import it.freshfruits.domain.entity.Order;
import it.freshfruits.domain.entity.OrderImpl;
import it.freshfruits.domain.vo.OrderItem;
import it.freshfruits.domain.vo.OrderItemImpl;
import it.freshfruits.exception.OrderItemsException;
import it.freshfruits.util.Constants;

import java.sql.SQLException;
import java.util.HashMap;
import java.util.Iterator;
import java.util.List;
import java.util.Map;
import java.util.Set;

import org.apache.log4j.Logger;
import org.springframework.beans.factory.annotation.Autowired;
import org.springframework.beans.factory.annotation.Qualifier;
```

```
import org.springframework.orm.ibatis.SqlMapClientCallback;
import org.springframework.orm.ibatis.SqlMapClientTemplate;
import org.springframework.stereotype.Repository;

import com.ibatis.sqlmap.client.SqlMapClient;
import com.ibatis.sqlmap.client.SqlMapExecutor;

@Repository("orderRepository")
public class OrderRepositoryImpl extends SqlMapClientTemplate
implements OrderRepository {

    public Boolean saveOrder(Order order) {
        if (order.getId().toString().equals(Constants.ID_NEW)) {
            return !insertOrder(order).equals(null) ? true : false;
        } else {
            return updateOrder(order);
        }
    }

    public Order getOrder(String id, String idCustomer) {
        Map<String, Integer> params = new HashMap<String, Integer>();
        params.put("id", Integer.valueOf(id));
        params.put("idCustomer", Integer.valueOf(idCustomer));
        OrderMap dto = (OrderMap) queryForObject("selectOrderVO",
params);
        return new OrderImpl.Builder(dto.getId().toString(),
                dto.getDateOrder(), dto.getIdCustomer().toString()).
orderItems(
                dto.getOrderItems()).build();
    }

    @SuppressWarnings("unchecked")
    public List<Order> getOrders(String idCustomer) {
        return queryForList("selectOrdersVO", Integer.
valueOf(idCustomer));
    }

    public Boolean updateOrder(Order order) {
        return update("updateOrderVO", new OrderMap(order)) == 1
? true : false;
    }

    @Autowired
    @Override
    public void setSqlMapClient(
            @Qualifier("sqlMapClient") SqlMapClient sqlMapClient) {
```

```
            super.setSqlMapClient(sqlMapClient);
        }

    public String insertOrder(Order order) throws OrderItemsException {
        Integer idOrder = (Integer) insert("insertOrderVO", new
OrderMap(order));
        if (order.getNumberItems() > 0) {
            int result = insertOrderItems(order.getOrderItems(),
idOrder);
            if (result != order.getNumberItems()) {
                throw new OrderItemsException();
            }
        }
        return idOrder.toString();
    }

    private Integer insertOrderItems(final Set<OrderItem> items,
            final Integer idOrder) {
        return (Integer) execute(new SqlMapClientCallback() {
            public Object doInSqlMapClient(SqlMapExecutor executor) {
                int ris = 0;
                try {
                    executor.startBatch();
                    Iterator<OrderItem> iter = items.iterator();

                    while (iter.hasNext()) {
                        OrderItem item = iter.next();
                        executor.insert("insertOrderItemVO",
                                new OrderItemImpl.Builder(item.getFruitType(),
                                        item.getQuantity(), idOrder.toString())
                                        .build());
                    }
                    ris = executor.executeBatch();
                } catch (SQLException e) {
                    Logger log = Logger.getLogger(this.getClass());
                    StringBuffer sb = new StringBuffer(
                            "insertOrderItem failed \n").append(
                            "num items batch:").append(items.size()).append(
                            "\n").append(e.getNextException());
                    log.error(sb.toString());
                    ;
                }
                return ris;
            }
        });
    }

}
```

The `RepositoryImpl` classes are implemented with iBATIS to realize persistence.

Its configuration files (`customer.xml`, `order.xml`) follow. In them we can see the order fields that correspond to `orderItems` populated with `selectOrderItems`, and fruit populated with `selectFruitType` (present in another file).

iBatis maps the row of the `resultset` with an object.

In the following file, we see an alias (`typeAlias` tag) of the `Customer` class with the name `customer`.

In the tag `resultMap` we see the effective mapping between the column of the table in the database and the properties available through set* and get* methods of the object (`Customer` in this case). This mapping has the name `resultCustomer`.

After this mapping, we see the query in the database and the `resultMap` to map the row during the select and the insert/update/delete operations.

The following XML configuration map `customer.xml` acts on the table "customers".

```xml
<?xml version="1.0" encoding="UTF-8"?>
<!DOCTYPE sqlMap PUBLIC "-//ibatis.apache.org//DTD SQL Map 2.0//EN"
"http://ibatis.apache.org/dtd/sql-map-2.dtd">
<sqlMap>

    <typeAlias type="it.freshfruits.application.repository.CustomerMap"
alias="customerVO" />

    <resultMap class="customerVO" id="resultCustomerVO">
        <result column="id" property="id" jdbcType="BIGINT" />
        <result column="name" property="name" jdbcType="VARCHAR" />
        <result column="city" property="city" jdbcType="VARCHAR" />
        <result column="email" property="email" jdbcType="VARCHAR" />
        <result column="fax" property="faxNumber" jdbcType="VARCHAR" />
        <result column="state" property="state" jdbcType="VARCHAR" />
        <result column="street" property="street" jdbcType="VARCHAR" />
        <result column="mobile" property="mobilePhoneNumber"
            jdbcType="VARCHAR" />
        <result column="phone" property="phoneNumber"
            jdbcType="VARCHAR" />
    </resultMap>


    <!--  S E L E C T -->

    <select id="selectKeyCustomer" resultClass="int">
```

```
        select nextval('customers_id_seq') ;
    </select>

    <select id="selectCustomerVO" resultMap="resultCustomerVO">
        SELECT id, name, city, email, fax, mobile,
        phone, state, street FROM customers WHERE id = #value# ;
    </select>

    <select id="selectCustomers" resultMap="resultCustomerVO">
        SELECT id, name, city, email, fax, mobile,
        phone, state, street FROM customers WHERE enabled = true;
    </select>

    <select id="selectIdCustomerByName" resultClass="int">
        SELECT id FROM customers WHERE name = #value# ;
    </select>

    <!--  I N S E R T -->

    <insert id="insertCustomerVO" parameterClass="customerVO">
        <selectKey keyProperty="id" resultClass="int">
            select nextval('customers_id_seq')
         </selectKey>
        INSERT INTO customers (id, name, city, email, fax,
        mobile, phone, state, street) VALUES
        (#id:BIGINT#, #name:VARCHAR#, #city:VARCHAR#, #email:VARCHAR#,
        #faxNumber:VARCHAR#, #mobilePhoneNumber:VARCHAR#,
        #phoneNumber:VARCHAR#, #address.state:VARCHAR#, #address.street:
VARCHAR#) ;
    </insert>


    <!--  U P D A T E -->

    <update id="updateCustomerVO" parameterClass="customerVO">
        UPDATE customers SET
        name = #name:VARCHAR#,
        city = #city:VARCHAR#,
        email = #email:VARCHAR#,
        fax = #faxNumber:VARCHAR#,
        mobile = #mobilePhoneNumber:VARCHAR#,
        phone = #phoneNumber:VARCHAR#,
        state = #state:VARCHAR#,
        street = #street:VARCHAR#
        WHERE id = #id:BIGINT# AND enabled = true;
    </update>

    <update id="disableCustomer" parameterClass="int">
```

```
      UPDATE customers SET
      enabled = false
      WHERE id = #id:BIGINT# ;
   </update>

   <update id="enableCustomer" parameterClass="int">
      UPDATE customers SET
      enabled = true
      WHERE id = #id:BIGINT# ;
   </update>


   <!--  D E L E T E -->

   <delete id="deleteCustomerVO" parameterClass="int">
      DELETE FROM customers WHERE id = #value# ;
   </delete>

</sqlMap>
```

The following XML configuration map `order.xml` acts on the table `orders`.

```
<?xml version="1.0" encoding="UTF-8"?>
<!DOCTYPE sqlMap PUBLIC "-//ibatis.apache.org//DTD SQL Map 2.0//EN"
"http://ibatis.apache.org/dtd/sql-map-2.dtd">
<sqlMap>
   <typeAlias type="it.freshfruits.application.repository.OrderMap"
alias="orderVO" />
   <typeAlias type="it.freshfruits.application.repository.
OrderItemMap" alias="orderItemVO" />

   <resultMap class="orderVO" id="resultOrder">
      <result column="id" property="id" jdbcType="BIGINT" />
      <result column="id_customer" property="idCustomer"
jdbcType="BIGINT" />
      <result column="date" property="dateOrder" jdbcType="DATE" />
      <result  property="orderItems" select="selectOrderItems"
column="id"/>
   </resultMap>

   <resultMap class="orderItemVO" id="resultOrderItem">
      <result column="id_order" property="idOrder" jdbcType="BIGINT"
/>
      <result column="quantity" property="quantity" jdbcType="INT" />
      <result property="fruit" select="selectFruitTypeVO" column="id_
fruit"/>
   </resultMap>
```

```xml
<!--  S E L E C T -->

<select id="selectKeyOrder" resultClass="int">
    select nextval('orders_id_seq') ;
</select>


<select id="selectOrderVO" resultMap="resultOrder">
    SELECT id, id_customer, date FROM orders WHERE id = #id# AND
id_customer = #idCustomer# ;
</select>


<select id="selectOrdersVO" resultMap="resultOrder">
    SELECT id, id_customer, date FROM orders WHERE id_customer =
#value# ;
</select>


<select id="selectOrderItems" resultMap="resultOrderItem">
    SELECT id_fruit, id_order, quantity FROM orderitems WHERE id_
order = #value# ;
</select>


<!--  I N S E R T -->

<insert id="insertOrderVO" parameterClass="orderVO">
    <selectKey keyProperty="id" resultClass="int">
       select nextval('orders_id_seq')
     </selectKey>
    INSERT INTO orders (id, id_customer, date) VALUES
    (#id:BIGINT#, #idCustomer:BIGINT#, #dateOrder:DATE#) ;
</insert>


<insert id="insertOrderItemVO" parameterClass="orderItemVO">
    INSERT INTO orderitems (id_order, id_fruit, quantity) VALUES
    (#idOrder:BIGINT#, #fruit.id:BIGINT#, #quantity:INT#) ;
</insert>


<!--  U P D A T E -->

<update id="updateOrderVO" parameterClass="orderVO">
    UPDATE orders SET
    date = #dateOrder:DATE#
    WHERE id = #id:BIGINT# AND id_customer = #idCustomer:BIGINT# ;
</update>

</sqlMap>
```

Summary

In this chapter, we have seen how use Domain-Driven Design to have an effective object-oriented design for the sample application and the components and definitions of the DDD.

We have seen how to use the annotation `@Configurable` to use IoC in domain objects that aren't Spring bean, and how provide persistence to the entities with Apache iBATIS.

In the next chapter, we will see the other parts of the sample application.

7
Three-tier Spring Application, Tests and AOP

This chapter continues the sample application described in Chapter 6.

Here is a brief outline of the topics that will be covered in this chapter:

- Application layer and user interface
- Tests
- AOP

Application layer and user interface

To be used by the users, the **Domain Classes** have to be used by the controllers that form the application layer. This layer coordinates and interprets the commands given on the **User Interface (UI)**, which is the HTML pages seen by the final user.

Now we will see some controllers that are part of the UI.

`CustomerController` lets the customer interact with the store. The names of the methods of the Controller are:

- `Create`: To perform creation of a new order
- `save`: To save the order
- `show`: To show the customer details
- `order`: To show the content of the order
- `items`: To show the items contained in the order
- `remove`: To remove an item from the order

The controller is built through Spring MVC annotation. The class is marked as controller with the @Controller annotation with the name customerController. Each method is marked with @RequestMapping to assign the HTTP URL used to call the method on the controller.

Every method returns a ModelAndView object that contains the logical template name and the name and value of the objects to show in the template.

To perform actions on the Customer object, every method uses UiUtils to obtain the customer object corresponding to user logged in.

```
package it.freshfruits.ui;

import it.freshfruits.domain.entity.Order;
import it.freshfruits.ui.util.UiUtils;

import javax.servlet.http.HttpServletRequest;

import org.springframework.stereotype.Controller;
import org.springframework.web.bind.annotation.RequestMapping;
import org.springframework.web.bind.annotation.RequestParam;
import org.springframework.web.servlet.ModelAndView;

@Controller("customerController")
public class CustomerController{

    @RequestMapping("/customer.create.page")
    public ModelAndView create(HttpServletRequest req) {
        return new ModelAndView("customer/create", "result", UiUtils.
getCustomer(req).createOrder());
    }

    @RequestMapping("/customer.save.page")
    public ModelAndView save(HttpServletRequest req) {
        return new ModelAndView("customer/save", "result", UiUtils.
getCustomer(req).saveOrder());
    }

    @RequestMapping("/customer.show.page")
    public ModelAndView show(HttpServletRequest req) {
        return new ModelAndView("customer/show", "customer", UiUtils.
getCustomer(req));
    }

    @RequestMapping("/customer.order.page")
    public ModelAndView order(HttpServletRequest req) {
        return new ModelAndView("customer/order", "order", UiUtils.
getOrder(req));
```

```
    }

    @RequestMapping("/customer.items.page")
    public ModelAndView items(HttpServletRequest req) {
        return new ModelAndView("customer/items", "items", UiUtils.
getOrder(req).getOrderItems());
    }

    @RequestMapping("/customer.remove.page")
    public ModelAndView remove(@RequestParam("id") String id,
HttpServletRequest req)
            throws Exception {

        Order order = UiUtils.getOrder(req);
        return order.removeOrderItem(order.getId().toString(), id) ?
            new ModelAndView("customer/items", "items", order.
getOrderItems()):
            new ModelAndView("customer/remove", "result", false);

    }
}
```

To support the controller in its task, the CustomerInterceptor adds the Customer object to the request before the work of the controller (CustomerInterceptor acts as a servlet filter).

In this way, the controller code is cleaner and has only one responsibility.

The intercepor contains the method preHandle, which is executed before the controller. The interceptor sets the Customer object as an attribute of the HttpServletRequest.

The CustomerFactory that provides the Customer object is injected with the @Autowired Spring annotation.

```
package it.freshfruits.ui.interceptor;

import it.freshfruits.domain.factory.CustomerFactory;

import javax.servlet.http.HttpServletRequest;
import javax.servlet.http.HttpServletResponse;

import org.springframework.beans.factory.annotation.Autowired;
import org.springframework.web.servlet.handler.
HandlerInterceptorAdapter;

import it.freshfruits.util.Constants;

public class CustomerInterceptor extends HandlerInterceptorAdapter{
```

```
    @Override
    public boolean preHandle(HttpServletRequest req,
            HttpServletResponse res, Object handler) throws Exception {
        req.setAttribute(Constants.CUSTOMER,customerFactory.
getCurrentCustomer());
        return true;
    }

    @Autowired
    private CustomerFactory customerFactory;
}
```

Another controller is the `AddOrderItemController`, which is used to add an `orderItem` to the order object.

The method `handle`, which responds to the `/customer.add.page` URL, receives the order object (bound to the `HttpRequest` parameters), and adds the items to the order.

```
package it.freshfruits.ui;

import it.freshfruits.domain.vo.OrderItemImpl;
import it.freshfruits.ui.util.UiUtils;

import javax.servlet.http.HttpServletRequest;

import org.springframework.stereotype.Controller;
import org.springframework.web.bind.annotation.ModelAttribute;
import org.springframework.web.bind.annotation.RequestMapping;
import org.springframework.web.servlet.ModelAndView;

@Controller("addOrderItemController")
public class AddOrderItemController {

    @RequestMapping("/customer.add.page")
    public ModelAndView handle(@ModelAttribute("order") OrderItemImpl
order,
            HttpServletRequest req) throws Exception {

        UiUtils.getOrder(req).addOrderItem(order);
        return new ModelAndView("redirect:items.htm");
    }
}
```

Now let's create a form controller to handle the `FruitType` form (creation and update):

```
FruitController.

package it.freshfruits.ui;

import it.freshfruits.application.repository.FruitTypeRepository;
import it.freshfruits.domain.vo.FruitMap;
import it.freshfruits.ui.validator.FruitValidator;
import it.freshfruits.util.Constants;

import org.springframework.beans.factory.annotation.Autowired;
import org.springframework.beans.factory.annotation.Qualifier;
import org.springframework.beans.propertyeditors.StringTrimmerEditor;
import org.springframework.stereotype.Controller;
import org.springframework.ui.ModelMap;
import org.springframework.validation.BindingResult;
import org.springframework.web.bind.WebDataBinder;
import org.springframework.web.bind.annotation.InitBinder;
import org.springframework.web.bind.annotation.ModelAttribute;
import org.springframework.web.bind.annotation.RequestMapping;
import org.springframework.web.bind.annotation.RequestMethod;
import org.springframework.web.bind.annotation.RequestParam;
import org.springframework.web.bind.annotation.SessionAttributes;
import org.springframework.web.bind.support.SessionStatus;

@Controller("fruitController")
@RequestMapping("/fruit.edit.admin")
@SessionAttributes("fruit")
public class FruitController {

    @RequestMapping(method = RequestMethod.POST)
    public String processSubmit(@ModelAttribute("fruit") FruitMap
fruit, BindingResult result, SessionStatus status) {

        validator.validate(fruit, result);
        if (result.hasErrors()) {
           return "userForm";
        } else {
           fruit.save();
           status.setComplete();
           return "redirect:role.list.admin";
        }
    }

    @InitBinder()
```

```
public void initBinder(WebDataBinder binder) throws Exception {
    binder.registerCustomEditor(String.class,
        new StringTrimmerEditor(false));
}

@RequestMapping(method = RequestMethod.GET)
public String setupForm(
        @RequestParam(required = false, value = "id") Integer id,
        ModelMap model) {
    model.addAttribute(Constants.FRUIT, id == null ? new FruitMap()
            : fruitRepository.getFruitType(id));
    return "role/form";
}

@Autowired @Qualifier("fruitRepository")
private FruitTypeRepository fruitRepository;

@Autowired @Qualifier("fruitValidator")
FruitValidator validator;
}
```

Test

Now that we've seen the implementation, let's look at the tests.

As a testing framework we use JUnit 4.5 with the use of annotations and for the preparation of repositories before and after tests we employ DbUnit. (For details about JUnit see: `http://www.junit.org`, for details about DbUnit see: `http://dbunit.sourceforge.net`.)

The main class is `AllTests`, marked with `@RunWith(Suite.class)` to act as `TestSuite`.

In the `@SuiteClasses` annotation, we put the classes that contain the tests.

The annotated setup method with `@BeforeClass` contains the initialization of Spring `applicationContext`; the annotated `tearDown` method with `@AfterClass` destroys the `ApplicationContext` and closes the `DbUnit` connection.

The folders that contain the tests have packages identical to the classes. This is to have access to the classes that have visibility only for the package, so that the test classes can test their targets.

We have three main classes to perform the tests: first, the unit tests; second, the integration tests where Spring and the application context are used; and a third suite that performs all the tests together.

```
package it.freshfruits;

import it.freshfruits.conf.dbunit.DbUnit;
import it.freshfruits.domain.entity.CustomerUnitTest;
import it.freshfruits.domain.entity.FruitTypeUnitTest;
import it.freshfruits.domain.entity.OrderUnitTest;
import it.freshfruits.domain.factory.CustomerFactoryTest;
import it.freshfruits.domain.repository.CustomerRepositoryTest;
import it.freshfruits.domain.repository.OrderRepositoryTest;
import it.freshfruits.domain.service.SupplyServiceTest;
import it.freshfruits.domain.vo.AddressUnitTest;
import it.freshfruits.domain.vo.ContactInformationUnitTest;
import it.freshfruits.domain.vo.OrderItemUnitTest;
import it.freshfruits.ui.CustomerControllerTest;
import it.freshfruits.ui.FruitControllerTest;
import it.freshfruits.utils.ValidationUtilsTest;

import org.junit.AfterClass;
import org.junit.BeforeClass;
import org.junit.runner.RunWith;
import org.junit.runners.Suite;
import org.junit.runners.Suite.SuiteClasses;

@RunWith(Suite.class)
@SuiteClasses( { AddressUnitTest.class, ContactInformationUnitTest.
class,
      CustomerUnitTest.class, FruitTypeUnitTest.class,
      ValidationUtilsTest.class, OrderUnitTest.class,
      OrderItemUnitTest.class, CustomerRepositoryTest.class,
      OrderRepositoryTest.class, CustomerFactoryTest.class,
      CustomerControllerTest.class, FruitControllerTest.class,
      SupplyServiceTest.class })
public class AllTests {

   @BeforeClass
   public static void setUp() throws Exception {
      SpringFactory.setUpXmlWebApplicationContext();
   }

   @AfterClass
   public static void tearDown() throws Exception {
      DbUnit.closeConnection();
      SpringFactory.destroyXmlWebApplicationContext();
   }
}
```

Now we have some domain tests on domain classes.

The following `AddressUnitTest` tests the correctness of the VO `Address`.

JUnit 4.5 executes any method annotated with `@Test` as a test method.

```
package it.freshfruits.domain.vo;

import static org.junit.Assert.assertEquals;
import it.freshfruits.domain.vo.Address;
import it.freshfruits.domain.vo.AddressImpl;

import org.junit.Test;

public class AddressUnitTest {

    @Test
    public void testConstructorCorrect() {
        Address address = new AddressImpl.Builder("Viale Europa",
"Cagliari",
                "Italy").build();
        assertEquals(address.getCity(), "Cagliari");
        assertEquals(address.getState(), "Italy");
        assertEquals(address.getStreet(), "Viale Europa");
    }

    @Test(expected = IllegalArgumentException.class)
    public void testNullStreet() {
        new AddressImpl.Builder(null, "Cagliari", "Italy").build();
    }

    @Test(expected = IllegalArgumentException.class)
    public void testNullCity() {
        new AddressImpl.Builder("Viale Europa", null, "Italy").build();
    }

    @Test(expected = IllegalArgumentException.class)
    public void testNullState() {
        new AddressImpl.Builder("Viale Europa", "Cagliari", null).
build();
    }

}
```

The `ContactInformationUnitTest` tests the correctness of the
VO `ContactInformation`.

```
package it.freshfruits.domain.vo;

import static org.junit.Assert.assertEquals;
import it.freshfruits.domain.vo.ContactInformation;
```

```
import it.freshfruits.domain.vo.ContactInformationImpl;

import org.junit.Test;

public class ContactInformationUnitTest {

    @Test
    public void testConstructorCorrect() {

        ContactInformation contact = new ContactInformationImpl.Builder(
                "+39070123456", "3391234567", "", "foo[at]yahoo[dot]it")
                .build();
        assertEquals(contact.getEmail(), "foo[at]yahoo[dot]it");
        assertEquals(contact.getFaxNumber(), "");
        assertEquals(contact.getMobilePhoneNumber(), "3391234567");
        assertEquals(contact.getPhoneNumber(), "+39070123456");
    }

    @Test(expected = IllegalArgumentException.class)
    public void testNullEmail() {

        new ContactInformationImpl.Builder("+39070123456", "3391234567",
"",
                null).build();

    }

    @Test(expected = IllegalArgumentException.class)
    public void testNullPhoneNumber() {

        new ContactInformationImpl.Builder(null, "3391234567", "",
                "foo[at]yahoo[dot]it").build();

    }

    @Test(expected = IllegalArgumentException.class)
    public void testNullMobilePhoneNumber() {

        new ContactInformationImpl.Builder("+39070123456", null, "",
                "foo[at]yahoo[dot]it").build();

    }

    @Test(expected = IllegalArgumentException.class)
    public void testNullFaxNumber() {

        new ContactInformationImpl.Builder("+39070123456", "3391234567",
null,
                "foo[at]yahoo[dot]it").build();

    }
}
```

The `OrderItemUnitTest` tests the correctness of the VO `OrderItemUnit`.

```
package it.freshfruits.domain.vo;

import static org.junit.Assert.assertEquals;
import it.freshfruits.domain.entity.FruitType;
import it.freshfruits.domain.entity.FruitTypeImpl;
import it.freshfruits.domain.vo.OrderItem;
import it.freshfruits.domain.vo.OrderItemImpl;

import java.math.BigDecimal;

import org.junit.Test;

public class OrderItemUnitTest {

    @Test
    public void testConstructorCorrect() {
        FruitType fruit = new FruitTypeImpl.Builder("orange", new
Integer(2),
                new BigDecimal("0.20")).build();
        OrderItem item = new OrderItemImpl.Builder(fruit, 20, "1").
build();

        assertEquals(item.getFruitType(), fruit);
        assertEquals(item.getAmountItem().toString(), "4.00");
        assertEquals(item.getQuantity(), new Integer(20));
    }

    @Test(expected = IllegalArgumentException.class)
    public void testNullFruitType() {
        new OrderItemImpl.Builder(null, 20, "1").build();
    }

    @Test(expected = IllegalArgumentException.class)
    public void testNullQuantity() {

        FruitType fruit = new FruitTypeImpl.Builder("orange", new
Integer(2),
                new BigDecimal("0.20")).build();
        new OrderItemImpl.Builder(fruit, null, "1").build();
    }
}
```

The `FruitTypeUnitTest` tests the correctness of the VO `FruitType`.

```
package it.freshfruits.domain.entity;

import static org.junit.Assert.assertEquals;
import static org.junit.Assert.assertTrue;
import it.freshfruits.domain.entity.FruitType;
import it.freshfruits.domain.entity.FruitTypeImpl;

import java.math.BigDecimal;

import org.junit.Test;

public class FruitTypeUnitTest {

    @Test
    public void testBasicBuilder() {
        FruitType fruit = new FruitTypeImpl.Builder("orange", new
Integer(10),
                new BigDecimal("0.30")).build();

        assertEquals(fruit.getId().toString(), "10");
        assertEquals(fruit.getName(), "orange");
        assertEquals(fruit.getColor(), "");
        assertEquals(fruit.getFlavour(), "");
        assertEquals(fruit.getLocation(), "");
        assertTrue(fruit.getPrice().toString().equals("0.30"));
    }

    @Test
    public void testFullBuilder() {

        FruitType fruit = new FruitTypeImpl.Builder("orange", new
Integer(10),
                new BigDecimal("0.30")).color("red").flavour("sweet").
location(
                "Italy").build();

        assertEquals(fruit.getId().toString(), "10");
        assertEquals(fruit.getName(), "orange");
        assertEquals(fruit.getColor(), "red");
        assertEquals(fruit.getFlavour(), "sweet");
        assertEquals(fruit.getLocation(), "Italy");
        assertTrue(fruit.getPrice().toString().equals("0.30"));

    }

    @Test(expected = IllegalArgumentException.class)
    public void testNullName() {
```

```
        new FruitTypeImpl.Builder(null, new Integer(10), new
BigDecimal("0.30"))
            .color("red").flavour("sweet").location("Italy").build();

    }

    @Test(expected = IllegalArgumentException.class)
    public void testNullPrice() {

        new FruitTypeImpl.Builder("orange", new Integer(10), null).
color("red")
            .flavour("sweet").location("Italy").build();

    }

    @Test(expected = IllegalArgumentException.class)
    public void testNullColor() {

        new FruitTypeImpl.Builder("orange", new Integer(10), new
BigDecimal(
            "0.30")).color(null).flavour("sweet").location("Italy").
build();

    }

    @Test(expected = IllegalArgumentException.class)
    public void testNullFlavour() {

        new FruitTypeImpl.Builder("orange", new Integer(10), new
BigDecimal(
            "0.30")).color("red").flavour(null).location("Italy").
build();

    }

    @Test(expected = IllegalArgumentException.class)
    public void testNullLocation() {

        new FruitTypeImpl.Builder("orange", new Integer(10), new
BigDecimal(
            "0.30")).color("red").flavour("sweet").location(null).
build();

    }

    @Test(expected = IllegalArgumentException.class)
    public void testWrongPrice() {
```

```
        new FruitTypeImpl.Builder("orange", new Integer(10), new
BigDecimal(
            "-0.01")).color("red").flavour("sweet").location("Italy")
            .build();

    }

    @Test(expected = IllegalArgumentException.class)
    public void testWrongName() {

        new FruitTypeImpl.Builder("or", new Integer(10), new
BigDecimal("0.30"))
            .color("red").flavour("sweet").location("Italy").build();

    }

    @Test(expected = IllegalArgumentException.class)
    public void testWrongColor() {

        new FruitTypeImpl.Builder("orange", new Integer(10), new
BigDecimal(
            "0.30")).color("re").flavour("sweet").location("Italy").
build();

    }

    @Test(expected = IllegalArgumentException.class)
    public void testWrongFlavour() {

        new FruitTypeImpl.Builder("orange", new Integer(10), new
BigDecimal(
            "0.30")).color("red").flavour("sw").location("Italy").
build();
    }

    @Test(expected = IllegalArgumentException.class)
    public void testWrongLocation() {

        new FruitTypeImpl.Builder("orange", new Integer(10), new
BigDecimal(
            "0.30")).color("red").flavour("sweet").location("It").
build();

    }
}
```

The GUI of JUnit will report the results of the unit tests.

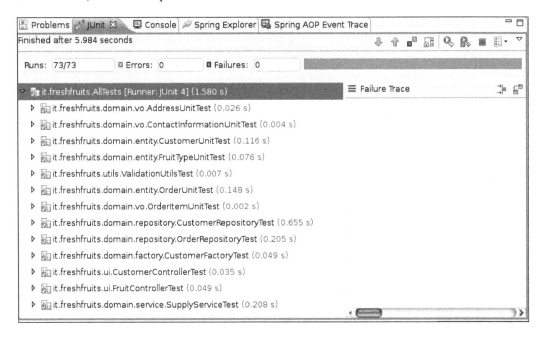

The internal changes to an aggregate all pass through the root, which exposes its content where needed and some methods to modify its content in a controlled way. But in no way does it expose the internal state of the objects contained in the aggregate to external modification.

Now let's see the test of `Customer`.

```
package it.freshfruits.domain.entity;

import static org.junit.Assert.assertEquals;
import it.freshfruits.domain.entity.Customer;
import it.freshfruits.domain.entity.CustomerImpl;
import it.freshfruits.domain.vo.Address;
import it.freshfruits.domain.vo.AddressImpl;
import it.freshfruits.domain.vo.ContactInformation;
import it.freshfruits.domain.vo.ContactInformationImpl;

import org.junit.Test;

public class CustomerUnitTest {

    @Test
    public void testBuilder() {
```

```
        Customer customer = new CustomerImpl.Builder("max", "1").
address(
            "Viale Europa", "Cagliari", "Italy").contactInfo(
            "+39070123456", "3391234567", "", "foo[at]yahoo[dot]it")
            .build();

        assertEquals(customer.getId().toString(), "1");
        assertEquals(customer.getName(), "max");

        Address address = customer.getAddress();
        assertEquals(address.getCity(), "Cagliari");
        assertEquals(address.getState(), "Italy");
        assertEquals(address.getStreet(), "Viale Europa");

        ContactInformation contact = customer.getContact();
        assertEquals(contact.getEmail(), "foo[at]yahoo[dot]it");
        assertEquals(contact.getFaxNumber(), "");
        assertEquals(contact.getMobilePhoneNumber(), "3391234567");
        assertEquals(contact.getPhoneNumber(), "+39070123456");

    }

    @Test(expected = IllegalArgumentException.class)
    public void testWrongLenghtAddress() {

        new CustomerImpl.Builder("max", "1").address("Vi", "Cagliari",
"Italy")
            .contactInfo("+39070123456", "3391234567", "",
                "foo[at]yahoo[dot]it").build();

    }

    @Test(expected = IllegalArgumentException.class)
    public void testWrongLenghtCity() {

        new CustomerImpl.Builder("max", "1").address("Via", "Ca",
"Italy")
            .contactInfo("+39070123456", "3391234567", "",
                "foo[at]yahoo[dot]it").build();

    }

    @Test(expected = IllegalArgumentException.class)
    public void testWrongLenghtState() {

        new CustomerImpl.Builder("max", "1").address("Via", "Cagliari",
"It")
            .contactInfo("+39070123456", "3391234567", "",
                "foo[at]yahoo[dot]it").build();
```

```
    }

    @Test(expected = IllegalArgumentException.class)
    public void testWrongLenghtPhone() {

        new CustomerImpl.Builder("max", "1").address("Via", "Cagliari",
                "Italia").contactInfo("+39", "3391234567", "",
                "foo[at]yahoo[dot]it").build();

    }

    @Test(expected = IllegalArgumentException.class)
    public void testWrongLenghtMobilePhone() {

        new CustomerImpl.Builder("max", "1").address("Via", "Cagliari",
                "Italia").contactInfo("+39070123456", "339", "",
                "foo[at]yahoo[dot]it").build();

    }

    @Test
    public void testModifyAddressCorrect() {

        Customer customer = new CustomerImpl.Builder("max", "1").
address(
                "Viale Europa", "Cagliari", "Italy").contactInfo(
                "+39070123456", "3391234567", "", "foo[at]yahoo[dot]it")
                .build();

        Address newAddress = new AddressImpl.Builder("Viale Europa",
                "Cagliari", "Italy").build();
        customer.modifyAddress(newAddress);
    }

    @Test
    public void testModifyAddressWrong() {

        Customer customer = new CustomerImpl.Builder("max", "1").
address(
                "Viale Europa", "Cagliari", "Italy").contactInfo(
                "+39070123456", "3391234567", "", "foo[at]yahoo[dot]it")
                .build();

        Address newAddress = new AddressImpl.Builder("Viale Europa",
                "Cagliari", "Italy").build();
        customer.modifyAddress(newAddress);
    }

    @Test
```

```
    public void testModifyContactInformationCorrect() {

        Customer customer = new CustomerImpl.Builder("max", "1").
address(
                "Viale Europa", "Cagliari", "Italy").contactInfo(
                "+39070123456", "3391234567", "", "foo[at]yahoo[dot]it")
                .build();

        ContactInformation newContactInformation = new
ContactInformationImpl.Builder(
                "+39070123456", "3391234567", "", "foo[at]yahoo[dot]it")
                .build();
        customer.modifyContactInformation(newContactInformation);
    }

    @Test
    public void testModifyContactInformationWrong() {

        Customer customer = new CustomerImpl.Builder("max", "1").
address(
                "Viale Europa", "Cagliari", "Italy").contactInfo(
                "+39070123456", "3391234567", "", "foo[at]yahoo[dot]it")
                .build();

        ContactInformation newContactInformation = new
ContactInformationImpl.Builder(
                "+39070123456", "3391234567", "", "foo[at]yahoo[dot]it")
                .build();
        customer.modifyContactInformation(newContactInformation);
    }

}
```

Now let's see the test of Order.

```
package it.freshfruits.domain.entity;

import static org.junit.Assert.*;
import it.freshfruits.domain.entity.FruitType;
import it.freshfruits.domain.entity.FruitTypeImpl;
import it.freshfruits.domain.entity.OrderImpl;
import it.freshfruits.domain.vo.OrderItem;
import it.freshfruits.domain.vo.OrderItemImpl;
import it.freshfruits.util.DateTimeUtils;

import java.math.BigDecimal;
import java.util.Date;
import java.util.Iterator;
import java.util.Set;
```

```
import org.junit.Test;

public class OrderUnitTest {

    @Test
    public void testBasicBuilder() {

        Date date = DateTimeUtils.getDateNowToNextDays(2).toDate();
        OrderImpl order = new OrderImpl.Builder(new Integer(11).
toString(),
                date, "2").build();
        assertEquals(order.getId().toString(), "11");
        assertEquals(order.getDateOrder(), date);

    }

    @Test
    public void testFullBuilder() {

        Date now = new Date();
        OrderImpl order = new OrderImpl.Builder(new Integer(11).
toString(),
                now, "2").amount(new BigDecimal("5000")).build();
        assertEquals(order.getId().toString(), "11");
        assertEquals(order.getDateOrder(), now);
        assertEquals(order.getOrderAmount().toString(), "5000");
    }

    @Test
    public void testFruitItems() {

        Date date = DateTimeUtils.getDateNowToNextDays(2).toDate();
        OrderImpl order = new OrderImpl.Builder(new Integer(11).
toString(),
                date, "2").build();

        FruitType fruit = new FruitTypeImpl.Builder("orange", new
Integer(2),
                new BigDecimal("0.20")).build();
        OrderItem item = new OrderItemImpl.Builder(fruit, 20, order.
getId()
                .toString()).build();
        assertTrue(order.addOrderItem(item));

        assertTrue(order.getNumberItems() == 1);
        assertEquals(order.getOrderAmount().toString(), ("4.00"));

        Set<OrderItem> items = order.getOrderItems();
        assertTrue(items.size() == 1);
        Iterator<OrderItem> iterator = items.iterator();
```

```
            while (iterator.hasNext()) {
                OrderItem current = iterator.next();
                assertEquals(item.getFruitType().getName(), current.
getFruitType()
                        .getName());
                assertEquals(item.getFruitType().getId(), current.
getFruitType()
                        .getId());
                assertEquals(item.getIdOrder(), current.getIdOrder());
                assertEquals(item.getQuantity(), current.getQuantity());
            }

            assertTrue(order
                    .removeOrderItem(order.getId().toString(), item.
getFruitType().getId().toString()));
        }

    @Test
    public void testNullAmount() {

        boolean result = false;
        try {
            new OrderImpl.Builder(new Integer(11).toString(), new Date(),
"2")
                    .amount(null).build();
        } catch (IllegalArgumentException e) {
            if (e.getMessage().equals("amount < 0:null")) {
                result = true;
            }
        }
        assertTrue(result);
    }

    @Test
    public void testNullDate() {

        boolean result = false;
        try {
            new OrderImpl.Builder(new Integer(11).toString(), null, "2")
                    .amount(new BigDecimal("5000")).build();
        } catch (IllegalArgumentException e) {
            if (e.getMessage().equals("dateOrder not correct")) {
                result = true;
            }
        }
        assertTrue(result);
    }
```

```
    @Test
    public void testNullIdCustomer() {

        boolean result = false;
        try {
            new OrderImpl.Builder(new Integer(11).toString(), new Date(),
null)
                    .amount(new BigDecimal("5000")).build();
        } catch (IllegalArgumentException e) {
            if (e.getMessage().equals("id argument null")) {
                result = true;
            }
        }
        assertTrue(result);
    }

    @Test
    public void testWrongAmount() {

        boolean result = false;
        try {
            new OrderImpl.Builder(new Integer(11).toString(), new Date(),
"2")
                    .amount(new BigDecimal("-1.0")).build();
        } catch (IllegalArgumentException e) {
            if (e.getMessage().equals("amount < 0:-1.0")) {
                result = true;
            }
        }
        assertTrue(result);
    }

    @Test
    public void testWrongDate() {

        boolean result = false;
        try {
            new OrderImpl.Builder(new Integer(11).toString(), null, "2").
amount(
                    new BigDecimal("4000")).build();
        } catch (IllegalArgumentException e) {
            if (e.getMessage().equals("dateOrder not correct")) {
                result = true;
            }
        }
        assertTrue(result);
    }
}
```

The `CustomerControllerUnitTest` tests the controller with mock objects such as `MockHttprequest` that simulate the user's browser interaction with the application.

```
package it.freshfruits.ui;

import static org.junit.Assert.assertEquals;
import static org.junit.Assert.assertTrue;
import it.freshfruits.conf.dbunit.DBCustomer;
import it.freshfruits.conf.dbunit.DBOrder;
import it.freshfruits.conf.dbunit.DBOrderItems;
import it.freshfruits.domain.entity.Customer;
import it.freshfruits.domain.entity.CustomerImpl;
import it.freshfruits.domain.entity.FruitType;
import it.freshfruits.domain.entity.FruitTypeImpl;
import it.freshfruits.domain.vo.OrderItemImpl;
import it.freshfruits.util.Constants;

import java.math.BigDecimal;

import org.junit.After;
import org.junit.Before;
import org.junit.Test;
import org.springframework.mock.web.MockHttpServletRequest;
import org.springframework.web.servlet.ModelAndView;

public class CustomerControllerTest {

    private CustomerController customerController;
    private Customer customer;
    private FruitType fruit;

    @Before
    public void setup() {
        customerController = new CustomerController();
    }

    @After
    public void tearDown() {
        customerController = null;
        customer = null;
        fruit = null;
    }

    @Test
    public void create() throws Exception {
        customer = new CustomerImpl.Builder("max", "26").address(
                "Viale Europa", "Cagliari", "Italy").contactInfo(
```

```
                    "+39070123456", "3391234567", "", "foo[at]yahoo[dot]it")
                    .build();
        MockHttpServletRequest req = new MockHttpServletRequest();
        req.setMethod("GET");
        req.setAttribute(Constants.CUSTOMER, customer);
        ModelAndView modelAndView = customerController.create(req);
        assertEquals(modelAndView.getViewName(), "customer/create");
        assertTrue(modelAndView.getModel().containsKey("result"));
    }

    @Test
    public void items() throws Exception {
        customer = new CustomerImpl.Builder("max", "26").address(
                "Viale Europa", "Cagliari", "Italy").contactInfo(
                "+39070123456", "3391234567", "", "foo[at]yahoo[dot]it")
                .build();
        assertTrue(customer.createOrder());
        MockHttpServletRequest req = new MockHttpServletRequest();
        req.setMethod("GET");
        req.setAttribute(Constants.CUSTOMER, customer);
        ModelAndView modelAndView = customerController.items(req);
        assertEquals(modelAndView.getViewName(), "customer/items");
        assertTrue(modelAndView.getModel().containsKey("items"));
    }

    @Test
    public void order() throws Exception {
        customer = new CustomerImpl.Builder("max", "26").address(
                "Viale Europa", "Cagliari", "Italy").contactInfo(
                "+39070123456", "3391234567", "", "foo[at]yahoo[dot]it")
                .build();
        assertTrue(customer.createOrder());
        MockHttpServletRequest req = new MockHttpServletRequest();
        req.setMethod("GET");
        req.setAttribute(Constants.CUSTOMER, customer);
        ModelAndView modelAndView = customerController.order(req);
        assertEquals(modelAndView.getViewName(), "customer/order");
        assertTrue(modelAndView.getModel().containsKey("order"));
    }

    @Test
    public void remove() throws Exception {
        customer = new CustomerImpl.Builder("max", "26").address(
                "Viale Europa", "Cagliari", "Italy").contactInfo(
                "+39070123456", "3391234567", "", "foo[at]yahoo[dot]it")
```

```
                    .build();
        assertTrue(customer.createOrder());
        fruit = new FruitTypeImpl.Builder("orange", new Integer(10),
                new BigDecimal("0.30")).build();
        customer.getOrder().addOrderItem(
                new OrderItemImpl.Builder(fruit, 13, customer.getOrder()
                    .getId().toString()).build());
        MockHttpServletRequest req = new MockHttpServletRequest();
        req.setMethod("GET");
        req.setAttribute(Constants.CUSTOMER, customer);
        ModelAndView modelAndView = customerController.remove(fruit.
getId()
            .toString(), req);
        assertEquals(modelAndView.getViewName(), "customer/items");
        assertTrue(modelAndView.getModel().containsKey("items"));
    }

    @Test
    public void save() throws Exception {
        DBCustomer dbCustomer = new DBCustomer();
        DBOrder dbOrder = new DBOrder();
        DBOrderItems dbItems = new DBOrderItems();
        dbCustomer.prepareDb();

        customer = new CustomerImpl.Builder("max", "26").address(
                "Viale Europa", "Cagliari", "Italy").contactInfo(
                "+39070123456", "3391234567", "", "foo[at]yahoo[dot]it")
                .build();
        assertTrue(customer.createOrder());
        fruit = new FruitTypeImpl.Builder("orange", new Integer(10),
                new BigDecimal("0.30")).build();
        customer.getOrder().addOrderItem(
                new OrderItemImpl.Builder(fruit, 13, customer.getOrder()
                    .getId().toString()).build());
        MockHttpServletRequest req = new MockHttpServletRequest();
        req.setMethod("GET");
        req.setAttribute(Constants.CUSTOMER, customer);
        ModelAndView modelAndView = customerController.save(req);
        assertEquals(modelAndView.getViewName(), "customer/save");
        assertTrue(modelAndView.getModel().containsKey("result"));

        dbItems.cleanDb();
        dbOrder.cleanDb();
        dbCustomer.cleanDb();
        dbCustomer = null;
    }
}
```

Now we see the integration test for `CustomerRepository`. An integration test is a test of the object with runtime conditions, such as db connection, or interaction with other objects. The following `CustomerRepositoryTest` tests the repository operations in the database.

Before each operation, DbUnit prepares the table on which the test operates by populating it with data. The data used for the read operations is prepared in the `db.prepareDb()` method of the `CustomerRepositoryTest` class, and is as follows:

```
<!DOCTYPE dataset SYSTEM "src_test/it/freshfruits/conf/dbunit/
database-schema.dtd">
<dataset>
    <customers id="26" name="max" street="Viale Europa" city="Cagliari"
        state="Italy" email="foo[at]yahoo[dot]it" fax=""
mobile="3391234567"
        phone="+39070123456" enabled="true" />
    <customers id="27" name="matt" street="Viale Europa 2"
city="Cagliari"
        state="Italy" email="foo[at]yahoo[dot]com" fax=""
mobile="3391234568"
        phone="+39070123458" enabled="true" />
</dataset>
```

Each integration test that involves repository operations has its own dedicated DbUnit classes and XML with data (in the package `it.freshfruits.conf.dbunit`).

```
package it.freshfruits.domain.repository;

import static org.junit.Assert.assertTrue;
import static org.junit.Assert.fail;
import it.freshfruits.SpringFactory;
import it.freshfruits.application.repository.CustomerRepository;
import it.freshfruits.conf.dbunit.DBCustomer;
import it.freshfruits.domain.entity.Customer;
import it.freshfruits.domain.entity.CustomerImpl;
import it.freshfruits.domain.entity.CustomerView;
import it.freshfruits.domain.vo.Address;
import it.freshfruits.domain.vo.ContactInformation;
import it.freshfruits.util.Constants;

import java.util.List;

import org.junit.After;
import org.junit.Before;
import org.junit.Test;
import org.springframework.context.ApplicationContext;
import org.springframework.dao.DataAccessException;
```

```
public class CustomerRepositoryTest {

    @Before
    public void setUp() throws Exception {
        ctx = SpringFactory.getXmlWebApplicationContext();
        repo = (CustomerRepository) ctx.getBean("customerRepository");
    }

    @After
    public void tearDown() throws Exception {
        db.cleanDb();
        ctx = null;
        repo = null;
    }

    @Test
    public void testInsertCustomer() {

    Customer customer = new CustomerImpl.Builder("max", Constants.
ID_NEW)
            .address("Viale Europa", "Cagliari", "Italy")
            .contactInfo("+39070123456", "3391234567", "",
                "foo[at]yahoo[dot]it").build();

        try {
            repo.insertCustomer(customer);
        } catch (DataAccessException e) {
            fail("unexpected exception");
        }
        return;
    }

    @Test
    public void testSaveCustomer() {

    Customer customer = new CustomerImpl.Builder("max", Constants.
ID_NEW)
            .address("Viale Europa", "Cagliari", "Italy")
            .contactInfo("+39070123456", "3391234567", "",
                "foo[at]yahoo[dot]it").build();

        assertTrue(repo.saveCustomer(customer));

    }

    @Test
    public void testSelectCustomer() {
        db.prepareDb();
```

```java
        Customer customer = repo.selectCustomer("26");
        Address address = customer.getAddress();
        ContactInformation contact = customer.getContact();

        assertTrue(customer.getName().equals("max"));
        assertTrue(customer.getId().toString().equals("26"));

        assertTrue(address.getCity().equals("Cagliari"));
        assertTrue(address.getState().equals("Italy"));
        assertTrue(address.getStreet().equals("Viale Europa"));

        assertTrue(contact.getEmail().equals("foo[at]yahoo[dot]it"));
        assertTrue(contact.getFaxNumber().equals(""));
        assertTrue(contact.getMobilePhoneNumber().equals("3391234567"));
        assertTrue(contact.getPhoneNumber().equals("+39070123456"));

        db.cleanDb();
    }

    @Test
    public void testSelectCustomers() {
        db.prepareDb();
        List<CustomerView> customers = repo.selectCustomers();
        assertTrue(customers.size() == 2);
    }

    @Test
    public void testSelectDisabledCustomers() {
        db.prepareDb();
        assertTrue(repo.disableCustomer("26"));
        List<CustomerView> customers = repo.selectCustomers();
        assertTrue(customers.size() == 1);
    }

    @Test
    public void testIsPresent() {
        db.prepareDb();
        assertTrue(!repo.isPresent("mike"));
        assertTrue(repo.isPresent("max"));
    }

    @Test
    public void testDeleteCustomer() {
        db.prepareDb();
        assertTrue(repo.deleteCustomer("26"));
    }

    @Test
```

```
    public void testdisableCustomer() {
       db.prepareDb();
       assertTrue(repo.disableCustomer("26"));
    }

    @Test
    public void testUpdateCustomer() {
       db.prepareDb();
       Customer customer = new CustomerImpl.Builder("max", "26").
address(
              "Via Scano", "Monserrato", "Italy").
contactInfo("+39070654321",
              "3397654321", "07012345678", "foo[at]yahoo[dot]com").
build();
       assertTrue(repo.updateCustomer(customer));
    }

    private DBCustomer db = new DBCustomer();
    private CustomerRepository repo;
    private ApplicationContext ctx;

}
```

The following `OrderRepositoryTest` tests the `OrderRepository` in the database.

```
package it.freshfruits.domain.repository;

import static org.junit.Assert.*;
import it.freshfruits.SpringFactory;
import it.freshfruits.application.repository.OrderRepository;
import it.freshfruits.conf.dbunit.DBCustomer;
import it.freshfruits.conf.dbunit.DBFruitType;
import it.freshfruits.conf.dbunit.DBOrder;
import it.freshfruits.conf.dbunit.DBOrderItems;
import it.freshfruits.domain.entity.Order;
import it.freshfruits.domain.entity.OrderImpl;
import it.freshfruits.domain.vo.OrderItem;
import it.freshfruits.util.Constants;
import it.freshfruits.util.DateTimeUtils;

import java.math.BigDecimal;

import org.junit.After;
import org.junit.Before;
import org.junit.Test;
import org.springframework.context.ApplicationContext;

public class OrderRepositoryTest {
```

```java
@Before
public void setUp() throws Exception {
    ctx = SpringFactory.getXmlWebApplicationContext();
    repo = (OrderRepository) ctx.getBean("orderRepository");
}

@After
public void tearDown() throws Exception {
    ctx = null;
    repo = null;
}

@Test
public void testInsertOrder() {
    DBCustomer dbCustomer = new DBCustomer();
    DBOrder dbOrders = new DBOrder();
    dbCustomer.prepareDb();

    Order order = new OrderImpl.Builder(Constants.ID_NEW,
DateTimeUtils
            .getDateNowToNextDays(2).toDate(), "26").amount(
            new BigDecimal("5000")).build();
    try {
        String id = repo.insertOrder(order);
        Order retrieve = repo.getOrder(id, "26");
        assertNotNull(retrieve);
    } catch (Exception e) {
        fail("exception unexpected");
    }
    dbOrders.cleanDb();
    dbCustomer.cleanDb();
}

@Test
public void testUpdateOrder() {
    DBCustomer dbCustomer = new DBCustomer();
    DBOrder dbOrders = new DBOrder();

    dbCustomer.prepareDb();
    dbOrders.prepareDb();

    Order order = new OrderImpl.Builder("34", DateTimeUtils
            .getDateNowToNextDays(2).toDate(), "26").amount(
            new BigDecimal("5000")).build();

    assertTrue(repo.updateOrder(order));
    Order retrieve = repo.getOrder("34", "26");
    assertNotNull(retrieve);
```

```
            dbOrders.cleanDb();
            dbCustomer.cleanDb();
        }

        @Test
        public void testSelectOrders() {
            DBCustomer dbCustomer = new DBCustomer();
            DBOrder dbOrders = new DBOrder();

            dbCustomer.prepareDb();
            dbOrders.prepareDb();

            assertTrue(repo.getOrders("26").size() == 1);
            assertTrue(repo.getOrders("27").size() == 0);

            dbOrders.cleanDb();
            dbCustomer.cleanDb();
        }

        @Test
        public void testSelectOrder() {
            DBCustomer dbCustomer = new DBCustomer();
            dbCustomer.prepareDb();
            DBFruitType dbFruit = new DBFruitType();
            dbFruit.prepareDb();
            DBOrder dbOrder = new DBOrder();
            dbOrder.prepareDb();
            DBOrderItems dbOrderItems = new DBOrderItems();
            dbOrderItems.prepareDb();

            Order order = repo.getOrder("34", "26");
            assertEquals(order.getNumberItems().toString(), "1");
            assertTrue(order.getNumberItems() == 1);

            for (OrderItem item : order.getOrderItems()) {
                assertEquals(item.getQuantity(), new Integer(8));
                assertEquals(item.getAmountItem(), new BigDecimal("9.6"));
            }

            dbOrderItems.cleanDb();
            dbOrder.cleanDb();
            dbFruit.cleanDb();
            dbCustomer.cleanDb();
        }

        private OrderRepository repo;
        private ApplicationContext ctx;

    }
```

To perform integration tests, so that the injection in the domain class works, we have to use the JARs that Spring gives for the **Load Time Weaver**.

In the `dist/weaving` folder of the distribution of Spring we have three JARs:

- `spring-agent.jar`
- `spring-aspects.jar`
- `spring-tomcat-weaver.jar`

In this case, to run the test we have to use `spring-agent.jar` and pass the following parameter to the virtual machine :

```
-javaagent:<path to jar>/spring-agent.jar
```

We pass this command through the configuration window of Eclipse to run JUnit.

On Linux:

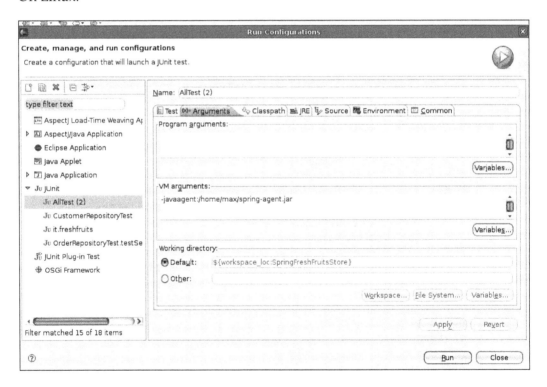

On Windows:

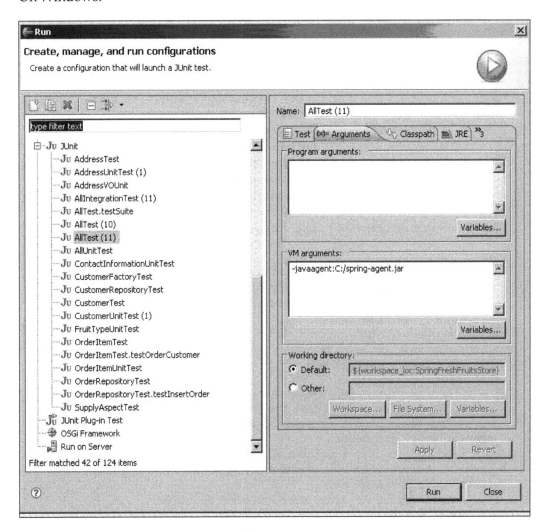

AOP

Now let's go on to explain how AOP plays an important role in the application, in domain classes with `@Configurable` annotation, and with the other features seen in the previous chapters.

The following configuration enables the aspect classes:

```
sffs-aop-domain.xml:

<?xml version="1.0" encoding="UTF-8"?>
<beans xmlns="http://www.springframework.org/schema/beans"
xmlns:xsi="http://www.w3.org/2001/XMLSchema-instance"
xmlns:context="http://www.springframework.org/schema/context"
xmlns:aop="http://www.springframework.org/schema/aop"
xmlns:p="http://www.springframework.org/schema/p"
xsi:schemaLocation="http://www.springframework.org/schema/beans
http://www.springframework.org/schema/beans/spring-beans-2.5.xsd
http://www.springframework.org/schema/context
http://www.springframework.org/schema/context/spring-context-2.5.xsd
http://www.springframework.org/schema/aop
http://www.springframework.org/schema/aop/spring-aop-2.5.xsd">

    <!--
        Enable @Configurable Annotation in conjunction with LTW jvm:
        (test) -javaagent:<path>/spring-agent.jar
        (tomcat) <tomcat6>/lib/spring-tomcat-weaver.jar-->
    <context:load-time-weaver /> <!-- enable the use of META-INF/aop.
xml -->
    <context:annotation-config />
    <context:spring-configured />

    <aop:config proxy-target-class="true">
        <aop:pointcut id="customerFactoryReadOperation"
 expression="execution(* it.freshfruits.domain.factory.
CustomerFactoryImpl.get*(..))" />
        <aop:pointcut id="customerRepoReadOperation"
expression="execution(* it.freshfruits.application.repository.
CustomerRepositoryImpl.select*(..))" />
        <aop:pointcut id="customerRepoInsertOperation"
expression="execution(* it.freshfruits.application.repository.
CustomerRepositoryImpl.insert*(..))" />
        <aop:pointcut id="customerRepoUpdateOperation"
expression="execution(* it.freshfruits.application.repository.
CustomerRepositoryImpl.update*(..))" />
        <aop:pointcut id="customerRepoDisableOperation"
expression="execution(* it.freshfruits.application.repository.
CustomerRepositoryImpl.disable*(..))" />
        <aop:pointcut id="fruitReadOperation" expression="execution(*
it.freshfruits.application.repository.FruitTypeRepositoryImpl.
get*(..))" />
```

```xml
        <aop:pointcut id="fruitInsertOperation" expression="execution(*
it.freshfruits.application.repository.FruitTypeRepositoryImpl.
insert*(..))" />
        <aop:pointcut id="fruitUpdateOperation" expression="execution(*
it.freshfruits.application.repository.FruitTypeRepositoryImpl.
update*(..))" />

        <aop:aspect id="customerAspect" ref="customerCacheAspect">
            <aop:around pointcut-ref="customerFactoryReadOperation"
method="invoke" />
            <aop:around pointcut-ref="customerRepoReadOperation"
method="invoke" />
            <aop:before pointcut-ref="customerRepoInsertOperation"
method="flush" />
            <aop:before pointcut-ref="customerRepoUpdateOperation"
method="flush" />
            <aop:before pointcut-ref="customerRepoDisableOperation"
method="flush" />
        </aop:aspect>

        <aop:aspect id="fruitAspect" ref="fruitCacheAspect">
            <aop:around pointcut-ref="fruitReadOperation" method="invoke"
/>
            <aop:before pointcut-ref="fruitInsertOperation"
method="flush" />
            <aop:before pointcut-ref="fruitUpdateOperation"
method="flush" />
        </aop:aspect>
    </aop:config>

    <bean id="customerCacheAspect" class="it.freshfruits.aspect.
CacheAspect" >
        <property name="cache">
            <bean id="customerCache" parent="cache">
                <property name="cacheName" value="customerCache" />
            </bean>
        </property>
    </bean>

    <bean id="fruitCacheAspect" class="it.freshfruits.aspect.
CacheAspect" >
        <property name="cache">
            <bean id="fruitCache" parent="cache">
                <property name="cacheName" value="fruitCache" />
            </bean>
        </property>
    </bean>
```

```
    <bean id="customer" scope="prototype" class="it.freshfruits.domain.
entity.CustomerImpl"/>

    <bean id="fruitType"  scope="prototype" class="it.freshfruits.domain.
entity.FruitTypeImpl" />

    <bean id="order"  scope="prototype" class="it.freshfruits.domain.
entity.OrderImpl"/>

        <bean id="supplyService" class="it.freshfruits.domain.service.
SupplyServiceImpl"/>

</beans>
```

Besides the normal configurations, since the injection of domain classes (outside Spring control) implies the action of AspectJ's weaver, we have to put file aop.xml inside META-INF in order to configure AspectJ. Here is aop.xml:

```
<!DOCTYPE aspectj PUBLIC "-//AspectJ//DTD//EN"
"http://www.eclipse.org/aspectj/dtd/aspectj.dtd">
<aspectj>
<weaver options="-showWeaveInfo
-XmessageHandlerClass:org.springframework.aop.aspectj.
AspectJWeaverMessageHandler">
    <!-- only weave classes in our application-specific packages -->
    <include within="it.freshfruits.domain.entity.*"/>
    <include within="it.freshfruits.domain.factory.*"/>
    <include within="it.freshfruits.domain.service.*"/>
    <include within="it.freshfruits.domain.vo.*"/>
    <include within="it.freshfruits.application.repository.*"/>
    <include within="it.freshfruits.ui.*"/>
    <exclude within="it.freshfruits.aspect.*"/>
</weaver>
<!-- Be careful, those Aspects lose injected
    properties (AspectJ ignore Spring at LWT),
    otherwise consider aspect xml definition -->
<aspects>
        <aspect name="it.freshfruits.aspect.ConcurrentAspect" />
        <aspect name="it.freshfruits.aspect.LogManagedAspect" />
        <aspect name="it.freshfruits.aspect.
TimeExecutionManagedAspect" />
</aspects>
</aspectj>
```

(For detail about ltw configuration see: http://www.eclipse.org/aspectj/doc/ released/devguide/ltw-configuration.html.)

The behavior of the agent and of the weaver are exposed by the tests and by the message on the console:

```
DbUnit setUpConnection
12 classes under test
67 test case
 INFO [main] - Refreshing
… org.springframework.beans.factory.support.DefaultListableBeanFactor
y@811c88
 INFO [main] - Found Spring's JVM agent for instrumentation
 INFO [main] - [AspectJ] AspectJ Weaver Version 1.6.2 built on
Saturday  Oct 4, 2008 at 05:47:07 GMT
….
```

Besides the application IoC on domain classes, now we employ aspects containing transversal.

Now let's add some aspects, such as the cache and concurrent aspects, introduced in Chapter 5.

Cache

Let's see the aspect that manages the cache.

This class has been extensively described in Chapter 5.

```
package it.freshfruits.aspect;

import it.freshfruits.util.Constants;
import net.sf.ehcache.Cache;
import net.sf.ehcache.Element;

import org.apache.log4j.Logger;
import org.aspectj.lang.ProceedingJoinPoint;

public class CacheAspect {

    public void flush() {
        cache.flush();
    }

    public Object invoke(ProceedingJoinPoint pjp) throws Throwable {

        Object result;
        String cacheKey = getCacheKey(pjp);

        Element element = (Element) cache.get(cacheKey);
```

```
        logger.info(new StringBuilder("CacheAspect invoke:").append("\n
get:")
            .append(cacheKey).append(" value:").append(element).
toString());

        if (element == null) {

            result = pjp.proceed();

            element = new Element(cacheKey, result);
            cache.put(element);
            logger.info(new StringBuilder("\n put:").append(cacheKey).
append(
                " value:").append(result).toString());

        }
        return element.getValue();
    }

    private String getCacheKey(ProceedingJoinPoint pjp) {

        String targetName = pjp.getTarget().getClass().getSimpleName();
        String methodName = pjp.getSignature().getName();
        Object[] arguments = pjp.getArgs();

        StringBuilder sb = new StringBuilder();
        sb.append(targetName).append(".").append(methodName);
        if ((arguments != null) && (arguments.length != 0)) {
            for (int i = 0; i < arguments.length; i++) {
                sb.append(".").append(arguments[i]);
            }
        }
        return sb.toString();
    }

    public void setCache(Cache cache) {
        this.cache = cache;
    }

    private Cache cache;
    private Logger logger = Logger.getLogger(Constants.LOG_NAME);

}
```

Concurrent

Let's see the aspect that manages the concurrency.

This class has been extensively described in Chapter 5.

```
package it.freshfruits.aspect;

import it.freshfruits.util.Constants;

import java.util.concurrent.locks.Lock;
import java.util.concurrent.locks.ReadWriteLock;
import java.util.concurrent.locks.ReentrantReadWriteLock;

import org.apache.log4j.Logger;
import org.aspectj.lang.annotation.After;

import org.aspectj.lang.annotation.Aspect;
import org.aspectj.lang.annotation.Before;
import org.aspectj.lang.annotation.Pointcut;
import org.springframework.core.annotation.Order;

@SuppressWarnings("unused")
@Aspect()
@Order(0)
public class ConcurrentAspect {

    @Pointcut("execution (* isAvailable(..))")
    private void isAvailable() {}

    @Pointcut("execution (* retainItem(..))")
    private void retainItem() {}

    @Pointcut("execution (* release(..))")
    private void release() {}

    @Pointcut("release() || retainItem()")
    private void releaseOrRetain() {}

    @Before("isAvailable()")
    public void setReadLock() {
        log.info("setReadLock");
        rLock.lock();
    }

    @After("isAvailable()")
    public void releaseReadLock() {
        rLock.unlock();
        log.info("releaseReadLock");
```

```
    }

    @Before("releaseOrRetain()")
    public void setWriteLock() {
        log.info("setWriteLock");
        wLock.lock();
    }

    @After("releaseOrRetain()")
    public void releaseWriteLock() {
        wLock.unlock();
        log.info("releaseWriteLock");
    }

    private final ReadWriteLock lock = new ReentrantReadWriteLock();
    private final Lock rLock = lock.readLock();
    private final Lock wLock = lock.writeLock();
    private Logger log = Logger.getLogger(Constants.LOG_NAME);;
}
```

TimeExecutionManagedAspect

To perform its work of measuring a method's average execution time, TimeExecutionmanagedAspect uses the class StopWatch, provided by Spring. The methods of the aspects are JMX exposed as attributes or operations.

```
package it.freshfruits.aspect;

import it.freshfruits.util.Constants;

import org.apache.log4j.Logger;
import org.aspectj.lang.ProceedingJoinPoint;
import org.aspectj.lang.annotation.Around;
import org.aspectj.lang.annotation.Aspect;
import org.springframework.core.annotation.Order;
import org.springframework.jmx.export.annotation.ManagedAttribute;
import org.springframework.jmx.export.annotation.ManagedOperation;
import org.springframework.jmx.export.annotation.ManagedResource;
import org.springframework.util.StopWatch;

@ManagedResource("freshfruitstore:type=TimeExecutionManagedAspect")
@Aspect() @Order(2)
public class TimeExecutionManagedAspect {

    @ManagedAttribute
    public boolean isLogEnabled() {
        return isLogEnabled;
```

```
    }

    @ManagedAttribute
    public void setLogEnabled(boolean isLogEnabled) {
       this.isLogEnabled = isLogEnabled;
    }

    @ManagedAttribute
    public boolean isTimeExecutionEnabled() {
       return isTimeExecutionEnabled;
    }

    @ManagedAttribute
    public void setTimeExecutionEnabled(boolean isTimeExecutionEnabled)
{
       this.isTimeExecutionEnabled = isTimeExecutionEnabled;
    }

    @ManagedAttribute
    public long getAverageCallTime() {
       return (this.callCount > 0 ? this.accumulatedCallTime / this.
callCount
              : 0);
    }

    @ManagedOperation
    public void resetCounters() {
       this.callCount = 0;
       this.accumulatedCallTime = 0;
    }

    @Around("within(it.freshfruits.domain.entity.CustomerImpl )")
    public Object invoke(ProceedingJoinPoint joinPoint) throws
Throwable {

       if (this.isTimeExecutionEnabled) {
          StopWatch sw = new StopWatch(joinPoint.toString());

          sw.start("invoke");
          try {
             return joinPoint.proceed();
          } finally {
             sw.stop();
             synchronized (this) {
                this.accumulatedCallTime += sw.getTotalTimeMillis();
             }
             if (isLogEnabled) {
```

```
                    logger.info(sw.prettyPrint());
                }
            }
        } else {
            return joinPoint.proceed();
        }
    }

    private boolean isTimeExecutionEnabled = true;
    private boolean isLogEnabled = true;
    private long accumulatedCallTime = 0;
    private int callCount = 0;
    private Logger logger = Logger.getLogger(Constants.LOG_NAME);
}
```

Here is the configuration to enable the `TimeExecutionManagedAspect` aspect to the JMX `MBeanServer`:

```
<!-- JMX -->
<bean id="mbeanServer" class="org.springframework.jmx.support.
MBeanServerFactoryBean"
    p:locateExistingServerIfPossible="true"/>

<bean id="exporter" class="org.springframework.jmx.export.
MBeanExporter"
    p:assembler-ref="assembler" p:namingStrategy-
ref="namingStrategy" p:autodetect="true"/>

<bean id="jmxAttributeSource" class="org.springframework.jmx.
export.annotation.AnnotationJmxAttributeSource"/>

<bean id="assembler" class="org.springframework.jmx.export.
assembler.MetadataMBeanInfoAssembler"
    p:attributeSource-ref="jmxAttributeSource"/>

<bean id="namingStrategy" class="org.springframework.jmx.export.
naming.MetadataNamingStrategy"
    p:attributeSource-ref="jmxAttributeSource"/>
```

Transactions

All the operations executed on the database must take place in a transactional way. Let's see how we configure Spring to perform this task.

```
<?xml version="1.0" encoding="UTF-8"?>
<beans xmlns="http://www.springframework.org/schema/beans"
xmlns:xsi="http://www.w3.org/2001/XMLSchema-instance"
```

```
xmlns:p="http://www.springframework.org/schema/p"
xmlns:aop="http://www.springframework.org/schema/aop"
xmlns:tx="http://www.springframework.org/schema/tx"
xsi:schemaLocation="http://www.springframework.org/schema/beans
http://www.springframework.org/schema/beans/spring-beans-2.5.xsd
http://www.springframework.org/schema/tx
http://www.springframework.org/schema/tx/spring-tx-2.5.xsd
http://www.springframework.org/schema/aop
http://www.springframework.org/schema/aop/spring-aop-2.5.xsd">
    ...


    <!-- D A T A S O U R C E -->

   <bean id="dataSource" class="org.apache.commons.dbcp.
BasicDataSource" destroy-method="close"
       p:url="${jdbc.url}" p:username="${jdbc.username}" p:
password="${jdbc.password}"
       p:driverClassName="${jdbc.production.driver}" p:maxIdle="3" p:
maxWait="50" p:removeAbandoned="true"
       p:removeAbandonedTimeout="550" p:logAbandoned="true" p:
maxActive="20"/>

    <!-- iBATIS -->

   <bean id="sqlMapClient" class="org.springframework.orm.ibatis.
SqlMapClientFactoryBean"
      p:dataSource-ref="dataSource"
        p:configLocation="/sffs-sqlMapConfig.xml"/>

   <bean id="transactionManager" class="org.springframework.jdbc.
datasource.DataSourceTransactionManager"
       p:dataSource-ref="dataSource"/>


    <!-- T R A N S A C T I O N S  Spring Classic -->
<!--
   <bean id="matchAllTxInterceptor" class="org.springframework.
transaction.interceptor.TransactionInterceptor"
      p:transactionManager-ref="transactionManager"
      p:transactionAttributeSource-ref="txAttributes"/>

   <bean id="txAttributes" class="org.springframework.transaction.
interceptor.NameMatchTransactionAttributeSource">
      <property name="properties">
        <props>
           <prop key="*">PROPAGATION_SUPPORTS,readOnly</prop>
```

```
                <prop key="save*">PROPAGATION_REQUIRED,-Exception</prop>
                <prop key="insertOrder">PROPAGATION_REQUIRED,-
OrderItemsException</prop>
                <prop key="insert*">PROPAGATION_REQUIRED,-Exception</prop>
                <prop key="update*">PROPAGATION_REQUIRED,-Exception</prop>
                <prop key="delete*">PROPAGATION_REQUIRED,-Exception</prop>
                <prop key="disable*">PROPAGATION_REQUIRED,-Exception
</prop>
            </props>
        </property>
    </bean>


    <bean id="autoProxyCreator"
        class="org.springframework.aop.framework.autoproxy.
BeanNameAutoProxyCreator">
        <property name="interceptorNames">
            <list>
              <idref local="matchAllTxInterceptor"/>
            </list>
        </property>
        <property name="beanNames">
            <list>
                <value>customerRepository</value>
                <value>orderRepository</value>
                <value>fruitRepository</value>
            </list>
        </property>
    </bean>-->


    <tx:advice id="txAdvice" transaction-manager="transactionManager">
      <tx:attributes>
        <tx:method name="save*" propagation="REQUIRED" rollback-
for="Exception"/>
        <tx:method name="insertOrder" propagation="REQUIRED"
rollback-for="OrderItemsException"/>
        <tx:method name="insert*" propagation="REQUIRED" rollback-
for="Exception"/>
        <tx:method name="update*" propagation="REQUIRED" rollback-
for="Exception"/>
        <tx:method name="delete*" propagation="REQUIRED" rollback-
for="Exception"/>
         <tx:method name="disable*" propagation="REQUIRED" rollback-
for="Exception"/>
        <tx:method name="*" read-only="true"/>
      </tx:attributes>
```

```
    </tx:advice>

    <aop:config>
        <aop:pointcut id="repoOperations" expression="execution(*
it.freshfruits.application.repository.*.*(..))" />
        <aop:advisor advice-ref="txAdvice" pointcut-ref="repoOperations
"/>
    </aop:config>

    ...
</beans>
```

Security

Now let's see the configuration that allows us, once authenticated, to be able to use the user's information without him or her knowing it and in a totally transparent way.

Our user will extend the User of Spring Security (formerly known as Acegi).

```
package it.freshfruits.security;

import org.springframework.security.GrantedAuthority;
import org.springframework.security.userdetails.User;

public class FreshFruitUser extends User {

    public FreshFruitUser(String username, String password, boolean
isEnabled,
            GrantedAuthority[] authorities, Object user) {
        super(username, password, isEnabled, true, true, true,
authorities);
        this.setUserInfo(user);
    }

    public FreshFruitUser(String username, String password, boolean
isEnabled,
            GrantedAuthority[] arrayAuths) {
        super(username, password, isEnabled, true, true, true,
arrayAuths);
    }

    public Object getUserInfo() {
        return userInfo;
    }

    public void setUserInfo(Object userInfo) {
        this.userInfo = userInfo;
```

```
    }

    private Object userInfo;
    private static final long serialVersionUID = -343812156239227785L;
}
```

Here is the class that loads the user's data and ID during authentication:

```
package it.freshfruits.security;

import it.freshfruits.application.repository.CustomerRepository;
import it.freshfruits.util.Constants;

import java.util.HashMap;
import java.util.Map;

import org.springframework.dao.DataAccessException;
import org.springframework.security.userdetails.UserDetails;
import org.springframework.security.userdetails.
UsernameNotFoundException;
import org.springframework.security.userdetails.jdbc.JdbcDaoImpl;

public class AuthenticationJdbcDaoImpl extends JdbcDaoImpl {

    public UserDetails loadUserByUsername(String username) {
        try {
            UserDetails user = super.loadUserByUsername(username);
            Map userInfo = new HashMap();
            userInfo.put(Constants.ID_CUSTOMER, repo.getIdCustomer(
username));
            return new FreshFruitUser(user.getUsername(), user.
getPassword(),
                    user.isEnabled(), user.getAuthorities(), userInfo);
        } catch (UsernameNotFoundException ex1) {
            ex1.printStackTrace();
            throw ex1;
        } catch (DataAccessException ex2) {
            ex2.printStackTrace();
            throw ex2;
        }
    }

    public void setRepo(CustomerRepository repo) {
        this.repo = repo;
    }

    private CustomerRepository repo;
}
```

Now the class allows us to get information about the user's ID from whichever class the call comes from, thanks to the pieces of information made available on the current execution thread and displayed by the SecurityContextHolder.

```
package it.freshfruits.security;

import it.freshfruits.util.Constants;

import java.util.Map;

import org.springframework.security.context.SecurityContextHolder;

public class SecurityUtils {

    public static String getIdCustomer() {
        FreshFruitUser user = (FreshFruitUser) SecurityContextHolder.
getContext().getAuthentication().getPrincipal();
        Map userInfo = (Map) user.getUserInfo();
        return userInfo.get(Constants.ID_CUSTOMER).toString();

    }

    public static String getCustomerName() {
        return SecurityContextHolder.getContext().getAuthentication().
getName();
    }
}
```

sffs-security.xml:

```
<?xml version="1.0" encoding="UTF-8"?>
<beans xmlns="http://www.springframework.org/schema/beans"
xmlns:xsi="http://www.w3.org/2001/XMLSchema-instance"
xmlns:p="http://www.springframework.org/schema/p"
xmlns:sec="http://www.springframework.org/schema/security"
xsi:schemaLocation="http://www.springframework.org/schema/beans
http://www.springframework.org/schema/beans/spring-beans-2.5.xsd
http://www.springframework.org/schema/security
http://www.springframework.org/schema/security/spring-security-
2.0.4.xsd">

    <sec:http>
        <sec:intercept-url pattern="/log*.jsp" filters="none" />
        <sec:intercept-url pattern="/*.page" access="ROLE_ADMIN" />
        <sec:form-login login-page="/login.jsp"
            default-target-url="/" login-processing-url="/j_security_
check"
            authentication-failure-url="/loginError.jsp" />
        <sec:logout logout-url="/logout.jsp" invalidate-session="true"
```

```
                logout-success-url="/login.jsp" />
        <sec:remember-me />
        <sec:intercept-url pattern="*.htm"
            access="ROLE_USER,ROLE_ANONYMOUS" />
        <sec:intercept-url pattern="*.page" access="ROLE_USER,ROLE_
ADMIN" />
        <sec:intercept-url pattern="*.edit" access="ROLE_USER,ROLE_
ADMIN" />
        <sec:intercept-url pattern="*.admin" access="ROLE_ADMIN" />
    </sec:http>

    <sec:authentication-provider
        user-service-ref="sffsUserDetailservice">
        <sec:password-encoder hash="sha" />
    </sec:authentication-provider>

    <bean id="accessManager" class="org.springframework.security.vote.
AffirmativeBased">
        <property name="decisionVoters">
            <list>
                <bean class="org.springframework.security.vote.RoleVoter"
/>
                <bean class="org.springframework.security.vote.
AuthenticatedVoter" />
            </list>
        </property>
    </bean>

    <bean id="sffsUserDetailservice" class="it.freshfruits.security.
AuthenticationJdbcDaoImpl">
        <property name="rolePrefix" value="ROLE_" />
        <property name="dataSource" ref="dataSource" />
        <property name="usersByUsernameQuery"
            value="SELECT id AS username, password, enabled FROM riot_
users WHERE id = ? " />
        <property name="authoritiesByUsernameQuery"
            value="SELECT id AS username, role FROM riot_users WHERE id =
? " />
    </bean>

    <bean id="accessDecisionManager" class="org.springframework.
security.vote.AffirmativeBased">
        <property name="decisionVoters">
            <list>
                <bean class="org.springframework.security.vote.RoleVoter"
/>
```

```
            <bean class="org.springframework.security.vote.
AuthenticatedVoter" />
            </list>
        </property>
    </bean>

    <sec:global-method-security
        access-decision-manager-ref="accessDecisionManager">
        <sec:protect-pointcut
            expression="execution(* it.freshfruits.domain.
entity.*.*(..))"
            access="ROLE_USER,ROLE_ADMIN" />
    </sec:global-method-security>

</beans>
```

The following files show the configurations explained in this chapter.

The file sffs-servlet.xml:

```
<beans xmlns="http://www.springframework.org/schema/beans"
xmlns:xsi="http://www.w3.org/2001/XMLSchema-instance"
xmlns:p="http://www.springframework.org/schema/p"
xmlns:context="http://www.springframework.org/schema/context"
xsi:schemaLocation="http://www.springframework.org/schema/beans
http://www.springframework.org/schema/beans/spring-beans-2.5.xsd
http://www.springframework.org/schema/context
http://www.springframework.org/schema/context/spring-context-2.5.xsd">

    <context:component-scan base-package="it.freshfruits.ui"/>

    <bean name="urlMapping" class="org.springframework.web.servlet.
mvc.annotation.DefaultAnnotationHandlerMapping">
        <property name="interceptors">
            <list>
                <ref bean="customerInterceptor"/>
            </list>
        </property>
    </bean>

    <bean name="customerInterceptor" class=" it.freshfruits.ui
CustomerInterceptor"/>

    <!-- M E S S A G E S  -->
    <bean id="messageSource" class="org.springframework.context.
support.ResourceBundleMessageSource"
        p:basename=" it.freshfruits.ui.message"/>
```

```
    <!-- V I E W   R E S O L V E R -->
    <bean name="viewResolver" class="org.springframework.web.servlet.
view.InternalResourceViewResolver"
        p:viewClass="org.springframework.web.servlet.view.JstlView" p:
prefix="WEB-INF/jsp/" p:suffix=".jsp"/>

</beans>
```

The file `sffs-application.xml`:

```
<?xml version="1.0" encoding="UTF-8"?>
<beans xmlns="http://www.springframework.org/schema/beans"
xmlns:xsi="http://www.w3.org/2001/XMLSchema-instance"
xmlns:p="http://www.springframework.org/schema/p"
xmlns:aop="http://www.springframework.org/schema/aop"
xmlns:tx="http://www.springframework.org/schema/tx"
xmlns:context="http://www.springframework.org/schema/context"
xsi:schemaLocation="http://www.springframework.org/schema/beans
http://www.springframework.org/schema/beans/spring-beans-2.5.xsd
http://www.springframework.org/schema/tx
http://www.springframework.org/schema/tx/spring-tx-2.5.xsd
http://www.springframework.org/schema/aop
http://www.springframework.org/schema/aop/spring-aop-2.5.xsd
http://www.springframework.org/schema/context
http://www.springframework.org/schema/context/spring-context-2.5.xsd">

    <context:component-scan base-package="it.freshfruits"/>
    <context:property-placeholder location="/config.properties" />

    <bean id="cache" abstract="true" class="org.springframework.cache.
ehcache.EhCacheFactoryBean"
        p:cacheManager-ref="cacheManager" />

    <bean id="cacheManager" class="org.springframework.cache.ehcache.
EhCacheManagerFactoryBean"
        p:configLocation="classpath:ehcache.xml" />

    <bean id="messageSource" class="org.springframework.context.
support.ResourceBundleMessageSource"
        p:basename="it.freshfruits.messages.msg"/>

    <bean id="viewResolver" class="org.springframework.web.servlet.
view.InternalResourceViewResolver"
        p:viewClass="org.springframework.web.servlet.view.JstlView" p:
prefix="WEB-INF/jsp/" p:suffix=".jsp"/>
```

```
    <bean id="exceptionResolver" class="org.springframework.web.
servlet.handler.SimpleMappingExceptionResolver">
        <property name="exceptionMappings">
            <props>
                <prop key="java.lang.Exception">errors/exception</prop>
            </props>
        </property>
    </bean>

    <bean id="dataSource" class="org.apache.commons.dbcp.
BasicDataSource" destroy-method="close"
        p:url="${jdbc.url}" p:username="${jdbc.username}" p:
password="${jdbc.password}"
        p:driverClassName="${jdbc.production.driver}" p:maxIdle="3" p:
maxWait="50" p:removeAbandoned="true"
        p:removeAbandonedTimeout="550" p:logAbandoned="true" p:
maxActive="20"/>

    <bean id="sqlMapClient" class="org.springframework.orm.ibatis.
SqlMapClientFactoryBean"
        p:dataSource-ref="dataSource" p:configLocation="/sffs-
sqlMapConfig.xml"/>

    <bean id="transactionManager" class="org.springframework.jdbc.
datasource.DataSourceTransactionManager"
        p:dataSource-ref="dataSource"/>

  <tx:advice id="txAdvice" transaction-manager="transactionManager">
     <tx:attributes>
        <tx:method name="save*" propagation="REQUIRED" rollback-
for="Exception"/>
        <tx:method name="insertOrder" propagation="REQUIRED"
rollback-for="OrderItemsException"/>
        <tx:method name="insert*" propagation="REQUIRED" rollback-
for="Exception"/>
        <tx:method name="update*" propagation="REQUIRED" rollback-
for="Exception"/>
        <tx:method name="delete*" propagation="REQUIRED" rollback-
for="Exception"/>
         <tx:method name="disable*" propagation="REQUIRED" rollback-
for="Exception"/>
        <tx:method name="*" read-only="true"/>
     </tx:attributes>
  </tx:advice>

  <aop:config>
     <aop:pointcut id="repoOperations" expression="execution(*
it.freshfruits.application.repository.*.*(..))" />
```

```
        <aop:advisor advice-ref="txAdvice" pointcut-ref="repoOperations
"/>
    </aop:config>

    <!-- JMX -->
    <bean id="mbeanServer" class="org.springframework.jmx.support.
MBeanServerFactoryBean"
        p:locateExistingServerIfPossible="true"/>

    <bean id="exporter" class="org.springframework.jmx.export.
MBeanExporter"
        p:assembler-ref="assembler" p:namingStrategy-
ref="namingStrategy" p:autodetect="true"/>

    <bean id="jmxAttributeSource" class="org.springframework.jmx.
export.annotation.AnnotationJmxAttributeSource"/>

    <bean id="assembler" class="org.springframework.jmx.export.
assembler.MetadataMBeanInfoAssembler"
        p:attributeSource-ref="jmxAttributeSource"/>

    <bean id="namingStrategy" class="org.springframework.jmx.export.
naming.MetadataNamingStrategy"
        p:attributeSource-ref="jmxAttributeSource"/>
</beans>
```

The file `config.properties`:

```
jndi.datasource=java:comp/env/jdbc/sffs
jdbc.url=jdbc:postgresql://localhost:5432/sffs
jdbc.username=sffs
jdbc.password=sffs
jdbc.production.driver=org.postgresql.Driver
jdbc.debug.driver=com.p6spy.engine.spy.P6SpyDriver
jdbc.driver=org.postgresql.Driver
```

Summary

In this chapter we've used AOP and IoC with Spring to create in a minimal way an application with DDD Test Driver Development.

We've seen what DDD is and what its philosophy is, and how it can be applied using AOP and Spring to use IoC on domain objects instantiated outside Spring using AspectJ's weaver.

We've seen how to adopt Aspects to improve implementation by centralizing the logic of crosscutting functionalities among classes.

We've improved the application's speed, avoiding calls to the database in a transparent way, which without AOP would have been unavoidable for the application layer.

We've also employed AOP for the authorization part with Spring Security.

As an exercise, the reader will be able to apply the other aspects described in the previous chapters as well, which we left out for the sake of brevity in this partial application.

We've used JUnit, DbUnit, Spring, and SpringIDE AJDT in Eclipse.

In the next chapter will see in detail how to install the whole development environment on Ubuntu Linux, on apple MacOSX, and on Windows XP, and how to make the best use of these tools during development.

8
Develop with AOP Tools

To create a working environment for Spring AOP development on Canonical Ubuntu Linux 8.10, Apple MacOSX 10.5.6, or Windows XP, we need to:

- Download and install the Integrated Development Environment (IDE) Eclipse, Spring IDE, and AJDT plug-ins
- Download and install the Apache Tomcat servlet container
- Download and install the PostgreSQL database
- Download the Spring full distribution

In this chapter we will see how to install the whole development environment on Canonical Ubuntu Linux 8.10, Apple MacOSX 10.5.6, and Windows XP, including the Java Development Kit, the IDE Eclipse, the Eclipse plug-ins Spring IDE, and AJDT, which allow Checking the Spring and AOP configurations.

We're also going to see how to install the database PostgreSQL 8.3, create the application's database, and install the servlet engine Tomcat 6.0.x.

Our aim is to have a development environment, and not a production one. Therefore, we won't deal with the permissions that must be correctly set in a production.

At the end of the chapter, we'll have an environment ready to employ and modify the example application of Chapter 6.

Java Development Kit
A prerequisite is to have Java Development Kit 1.5 or upward on your PC/Mac.

Spring

Go to http://www.springsource.org/ and click on the entry "**Downloads**", and download the latest version of Spring (Spring 2.5.6 at the time of writing this book), choose the "**with dependencies**" package that contains the JARs of all the projects supported by Spring.

This distribution also contains the JARs of the third-party software that we will use in all the examples of the book.

Source code for the examples described in the book is available online.

For each chapter there is a folder where you can find the file which_jars.txt that lists the JAR files from the Spring distribution you have to include in each project to make it run. For 3rd-party libraries not included in the Spring with-dependencies distribution, you can find instructions to get them on the Web.

Eclipse

After downloading Eclipse (3.4.1 or upward) unpack and run it. You must install some plug-ins.

In this section we will see which plug-ins should be installed, and how to install and use them.

Eclipse plug-ins (Linux, MacOSX, and Windows)

The Eclipse plug-ins provide rich features such as code autocompletion of Spring beans, a visual explorer for bean dependencies, management of resources and automatic syntax checking for configuration files.

We're going to see two plug-ins: SpringIDE and AJDT (AspectJ Development Tool).

SpringIDE

SpringIDE provides an autocompletion of the beans in the XML files, and checks if the classes exist and if the XML is well-formed. A "red signal" on the wrong XML line appears if an error is found.

SpringIDE provides a visual graph to see the dependencies between your beans.

To install the SpringIDE in your eclipse installation, go to `http://springide.org/blog`, and copy the link to the latest version of the plug-in.

The current link is `http://springide.org/updatesite/`. Copy this link in your clipboard.

Now, to install the plug-in, let's go in Eclipse to **Help | Software Update | Add site** and copy the link `http://springide.org/updatesite/`.

After reading the remote site, Eclipse shows the available options provided by the plug-in.

We select the visible entries and we confirm the choice.

Once the installation is complete, we have a Spring tab in Eclipse, always reachable with **Window | Show view | Spring explorer**.

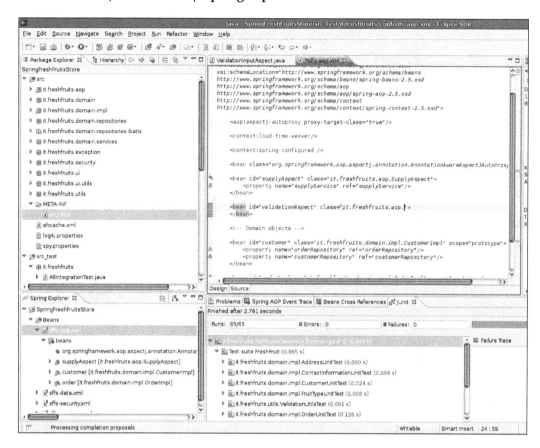

To enable the plug-in on the current project, add the **Spring nature** command.

Go to the project name and right-click the mouse. You can see a **Spring tool** label that has an arrow with some label. Click **Add Spring nature**, a small blue **S** appears near the project name.

Now a folder with project name and Spring symbols appears inside Spring explorer. If you click on the folder a menu appears. Now you can choose the type of work you want SpringIDE do for you after you add the configuration files to the project.

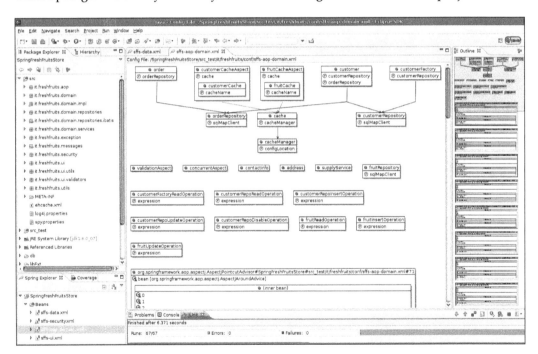

SpringIDE enables bean searching and is useful when you have a large number of beans, or if you find pointcuts in the XML configuration.

You can find all the SpringIDE features in **Window | Customize perspective**, and in the voice Shortcuts and Commands in the label that starts with Spring.

AJDT

AspectJ Development Tool (AJDT) allows us to check whether the pointcuts are correctly written, indicating on which methods they act. This is shown by arrows beside of the methods.

AJDT checks both annotations and XML, using different arrow icons to indicate the target of an advice.

This is indicated by small arrows with different orientation to indicate the type of advice (before, after, and around). This is very helpful to understand whether a pointcut is well-formed or not.

Another feature is an AOP trace view that shows how AspectJ performs.

Now to install the plug-in, let's go in Eclipse to **Help | Software Update | Available Software**.

In the following image, Eclipse shows the selectable items; choose the **AspectJ Development Tools** items.

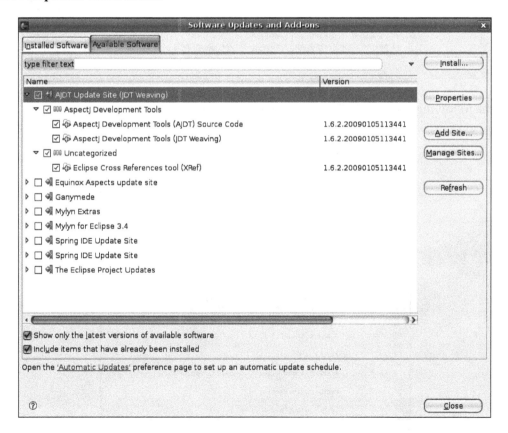

Check and install.

In the Spring explorer window, AJDT adds the arrows to indicate "advised" when the pointcut advises some classes, and on the Spring beans to tell "advised by" pointcut.

In the following image AJDT is in action in the Spring config files:

In the following image, AJDT acts on annotated classes:

The arrows enabled by AJDT indicate the type of advice.

AJDT doesn't work on aspects declared in `META-INF/aop.xml`.

Apache Tomcat

Apache Tomcat is a Servlet container and allows deployment of web applications, based on the servlet application model.

Spring MVC, used in Chapter 7, is based on Spring `DispatcherServlet`.

Now we'll see how to download, install, and configure Tomcat on Linux, MacOSX, and Microsoft Windows.

Ubuntu Linux

Go to the Tomcat site at `http://tomcat.apache.org/`.

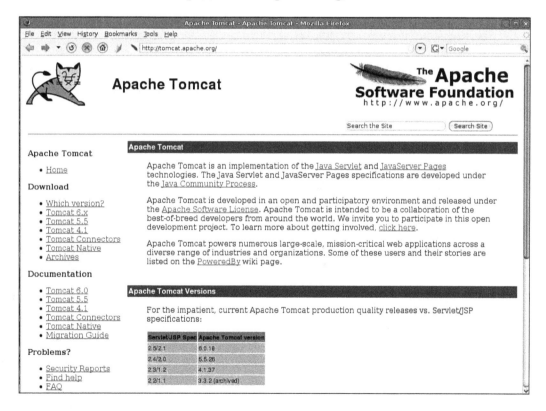

The Apache Tomcat home page shows the Tomcat version, according to the Servlet and JSP specification version.

We choose the latest version (6.0.18 at the time of writing the book) from `apache-tomcat-6.0.18.tar.gz` and download it, as shown in the following image:

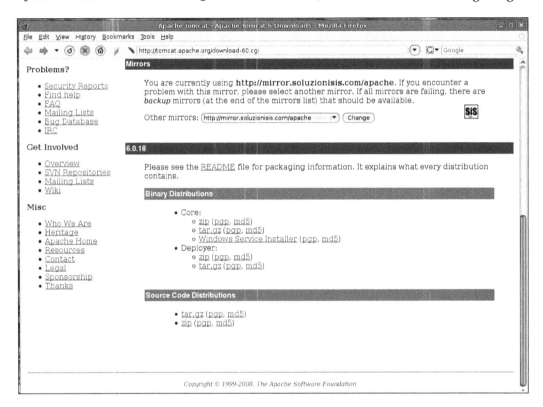

Before unpacking and running Tomcat, we must create a Tomcat user with limited privileges to execute it.

Create the Tomcat user with the following shell command:

```
sudo adduser tomcat
```

In the following image we see the result of the **adduser** command, like adding the new group **tomcat**, and setting the password for this new user.

```
max@mac-magicbox: ~
File  Edit  View  Terminal  Tabs  Help
max@mac-magicbox:~$ sudo adduser tomcat
Adding user `tomcat' ...
Adding new group `tomcat' (1001) ...
Adding new user `tomcat' (1001) with group `tomcat' ...
Creating home directory `/home/tomcat' ...
Copying files from `/etc/skel' ...
Enter new UNIX password:
Retype new UNIX password:
passwd: password updated successfully
Changing the user information for tomcat
Enter the new value, or press ENTER for the default
        Full Name []: tomcat
        Room Number []:
        Work Phone []:
        Home Phone []:
        Other []:
Is the information correct? [Y/n] y
max@mac-magicbox:~$
```

After creating the Tomcat user, we unpack the Tomcat distribution with this command (the **sudo** command requires administration privileges) :

```
sudo tar -xvzf apache-tomcat-6.0.18.tar.gz
```

In the following image we see the unpacked folders inside Tomcat:

Now we move the output directory `apache-tomcat-6.0.18` and rename it for convenience as `tomcat-6.0.18` (renaming it is an optional step).

```
sudo mv ./apache-tomcat-6.0.18 /usr/local/tomcat-6.0.18
```

Now we move to the new Tomcat location with this command:

```
cd /usr/local
```

Then we change the folder's owner with the command:

```
sudo chown -R tomcat ./tomcat-6.0.18/
```

Now we can log in as a Tomcat user with:

```
su tomcat
```

and start Tomcat with the command:

```
sh ./startup.sh
```

In the following image we see all these commands and their output:

To see if Tomcat is up and verify that everything is fine, let's open a web browser at `http://localhost:8080`:

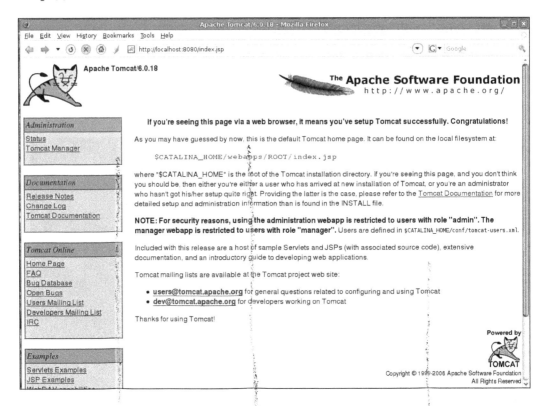

MacOSX

Now we see the installation of Apache Tomcat on MacOSX. The steps are less, but it is more insecure, and is suggested only for a development machine.

To get Apache Tomcat, go to `http://tomcat.apache.org/` and then under **download**, click on the **Tomcat 6.x** build (6.0.18 at the time of writing the book) `apache-tomcat-6.0.18.tar.gz` and download it.

Create a folder in the filesystem `tomcat_home` (`/Users/max/developer/tomcat_home` in the example) and unpack it inside.

In the shell, go to the folder `bin` and launch `startup.sh` with the command:

```
sh startup.sh &
```

```
Shell — java — 80×24
Last login: Sat Sep 13 00:17:45 on ttys000
magicbox:~ max$ cd developer/tomcat_home/tomcat-6.0.18/bin/
magicbox:bin max$ sh startup.sh &
[1] 1049
magicbox:bin max$ Using CATALINA_BASE:   /Users/max/developer/tomcat_home/tomcat
-6.0.18
Using CATALINA_HOME:    /Users/max/developer/tomcat_home/tomcat-6.0.18
Using CATALINA_TMPDIR: /Users/max/developer/tomcat_home/tomcat-6.0.18/temp
Using JRE_HOME:         /Library/Java/Home/
[]
```

To see if Tomcat is up, let's open a web browser at `http://localhost:8080` to verify that everything is fine.

Microsoft Windows

Now we shall see the installation of Apache Tomcat on Microsoft Windows XP, the steps are fewer, but it is more unsecure, and suggested only for a development machine.

To download Tomcat go to `http://tomcat.apache.org/`, click on the **Download Tomcat 6.x** item, choose `apache-tomcat-6.0.18.zip` and download it. Now, create a directory `tomcat_home` and extract the ZIP file in this folder.

The following image shows the Tomcat folder content.

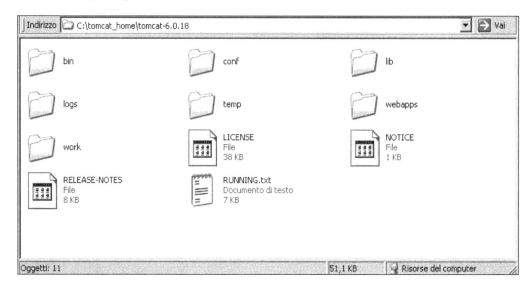

Execute the `startup.bat` script in the `bin\` folder.

To see if Tomcat is up, let's open a web browser at URL `http://localhost:8080` to verify that everything was fine.

Common steps for Linux, MacOSX, and Windows

Now we will see how to deploy the prototype application `freshfruitstore` shown in Chapters 6 and 7.

Create, in `<tomcat_dir>/conf`, the folder `Catalina` and `localhost` inside it, so that you will have `conf\Catalina\localhost` where you will copy the file `sffs.xml` contained in the `tomcat` folder of the `SpringFreshFruitStore` application.

In `SpringFreshFruitStore`, you can find the structure and the files as shown in the following image:

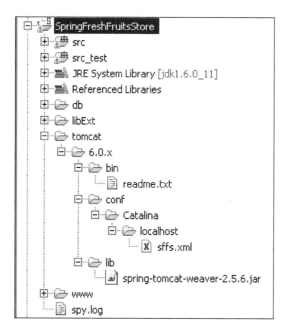

In the `tomcat/6.0.x/bin` folder you can find a **readme** with instructions to enable JMX support in Tomcat.

In the `conf/Catalina/localhost` folder you can find the `sffs.xml` deployment file.

You only need to put the path in the filesystem in the `<path_to>` and change username/password/url if needed, according to your installation after putting the `sffs.xml` inside `<tomcat_dir>Tomcat/conf/Catalina/localhost`.

The tag `<loader..>` is a class that has the same effect as `javaagent:<path_to>/spring-agent.jar` in the test classes. In other words, it is responsible for the Load-Time Weaver in Tomcat.

```
<Context docBase="<path_to>/SpringFreshFruitsStore/www/" debug="0">

<Loader loaderClass="org.springframework.instrument.classloading.
tomcat.TomcatInstrumentableClassLoader"
    useSystemClassLoaderAsParent="false"/>

<Resource name="jdbc/sffs" auth="Container" type="javax.sql.
DataSource"
            username="sffs"
            password="sffs"
```

```
            driverClassName="org.postgresql.Driver"
            url="jdbc:postgresql://localhost:5432/sffs"
            removeAbandoned="true"
            removeAbandonedTimeout="60"

            maxWait="500"
            maxActive="20"
            logAbandoned="true"

            maxIdle="5"
            minEvictableIdleTimeMillis="4000"
            timeBetweenEvictionRunsMillis="5000"/>

    <Manager className="org.apache.catalina.session.PersistentManager"
    saveOnRestart="false"/>

    </Context>
```

In `<tomcat_dir>` `/lib` you must put the `spring-tomcat-weaver-2.5.6.jar` (available in Spring distribution), which contains the class mapped in the `<Loader..>` tag.

PostgreSQL

PostgreSQL is an open-source object-relational database system.

We use PostgreSQL to store the information used by the `SpringFreshfruitStore` application and to run the tests.

We will see how to download and install PostgreSQL on Linux `MacOSX`, and Microsoft Windows.

Ubuntu Linux

Let's see how to install PostgreSQL as a service on Linux with Ubuntu Package Manager.

Open the Synaptic Package Manager and search for PostgreSQL.

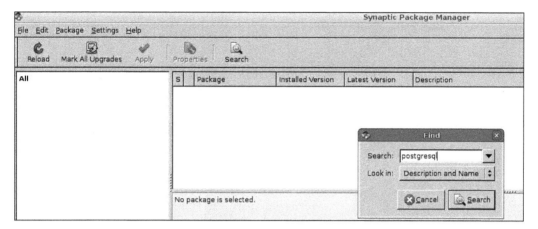

We check PostgreSQL.

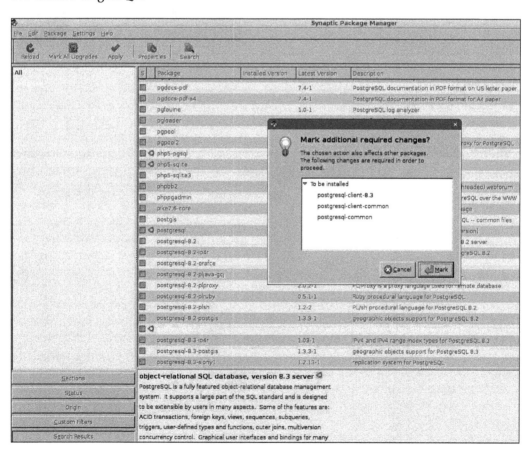

We look for the entry **pgadmin** and check it.

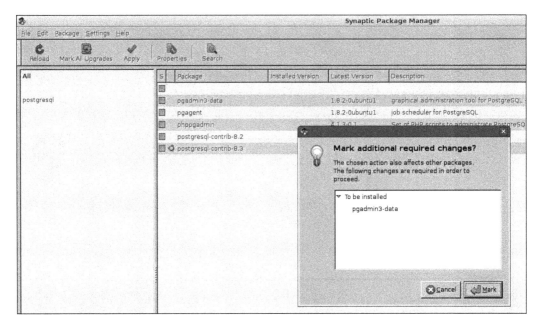

We install it.

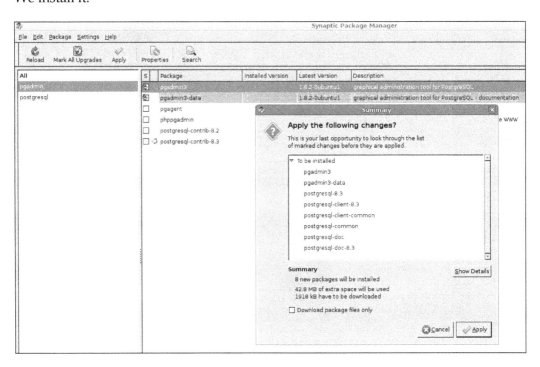

Now we have to set a password on **postgres**. In the shell we write:

sudo su postgres -c psql template1

postgres=# will appear.

We key in **ALTER USER postgres WITH PASSWORD 'postgres';** – in this way
we have set the password postgres to the user postgres; **postgres=#** will appear.
Finally again we key in **\q** to end.

In the following image we see the command in the shell:

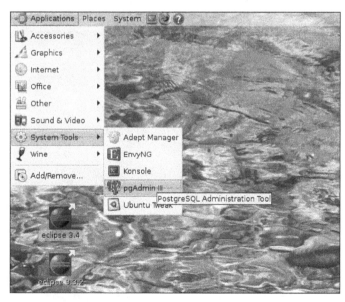

To start, we go to **System Tools | pgAdmin III**.

MacOSX

Let's see how to download and install PostgreSQL as a service on MacOSX.

Go to `http://www.postgresql.org/download/macosx` and you will reach the link.

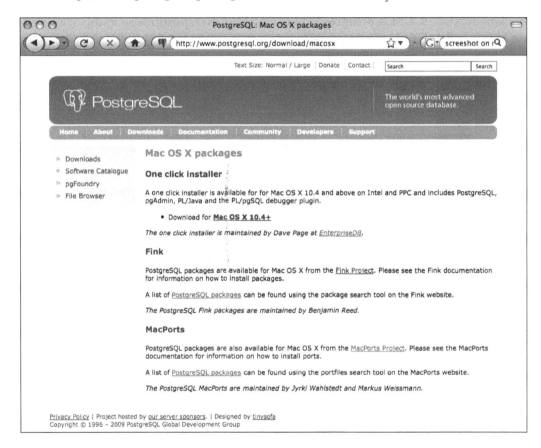

Download it, then unpack it and click twice on `postgresql-8.3.x-osx.app` to start the installation.

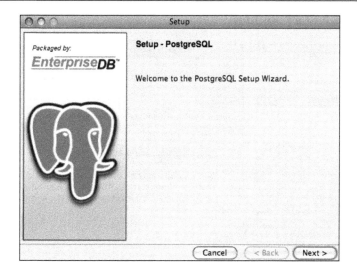

The installation path is the first choice.

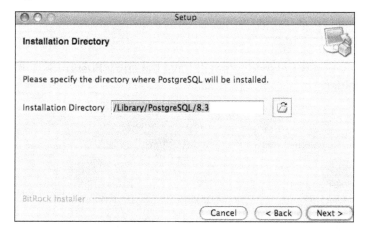

The installation is now ready to begin.

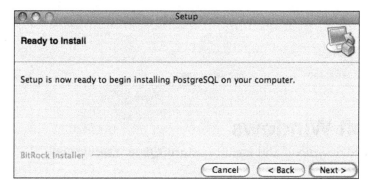

We disable **Launch Stack Builder**.

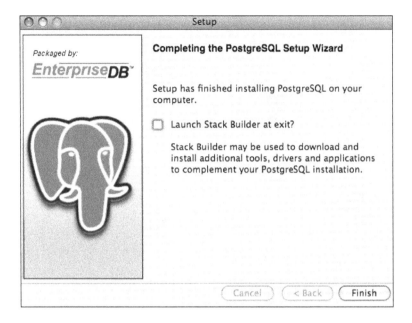

When the installation is finished, we will have the entry **PostgreSQL 8.3** in the Applications folder.

Microsoft Windows

Let's see how to download and install PostgreSQL as a service on Microsoft Windows.

Go to `http://www.postgresql.org/ftp/binary/v8.3.3/win32` and you will reach the link:

Download `postgresql-8.3.3-2.zip`, unpack it, and double-click on `postgresql-8.3.msi` to start the installation.

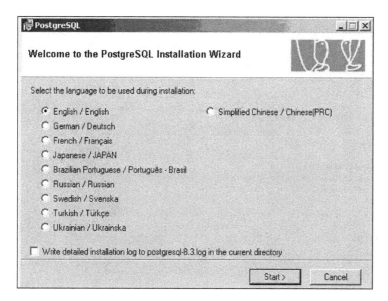

The setup wizard lets you select the installation language, installation path, and options.

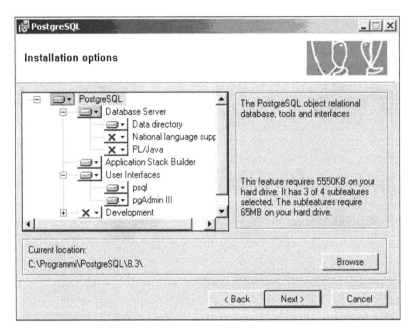

We will be asked if we want to install it as a service, and a user for the service is created (we could subsequently disable it).

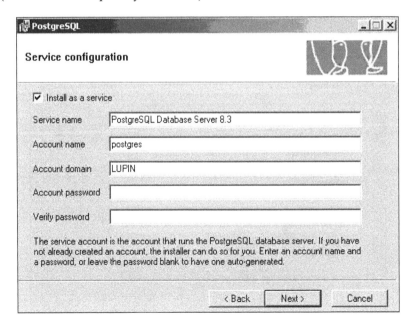

We choose the encoding **UTF-8** and the password for the user administrator.

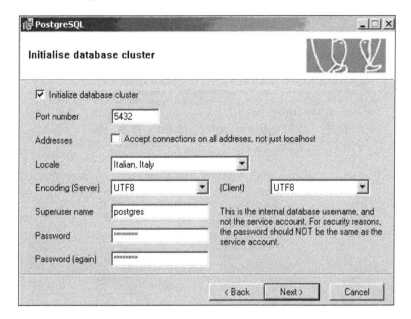

We choose to install **PL/pgsql**.

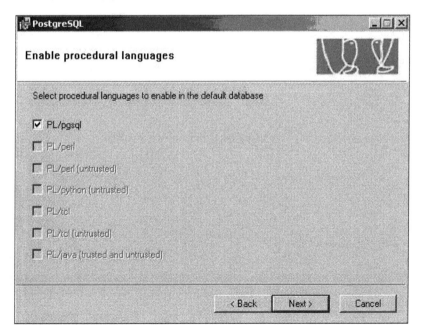

We enable **adminpack**.

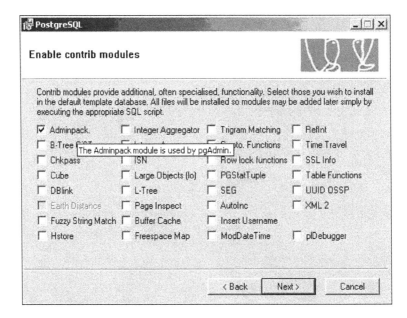

The installation is now ready to begin.

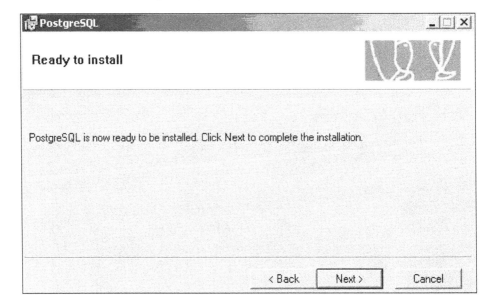

We disable **Launch Stack Builder**.

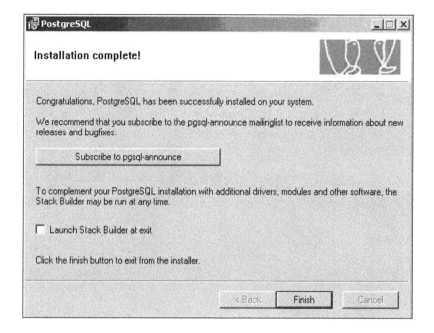

When the installation is finished, we will have the entry **PostgreSQL Database Server 8.3** in the services, as shown in the image:

and **pgAadmin** III in Programs:

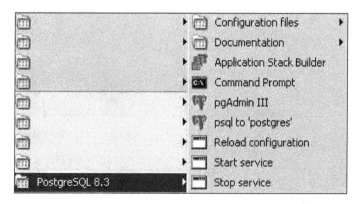

Common steps for Linux, Apple MacOSX, and Microsoft Windows

Connect to the database with the administration password and create the user **sffs** with your preferred password (such as sffs)

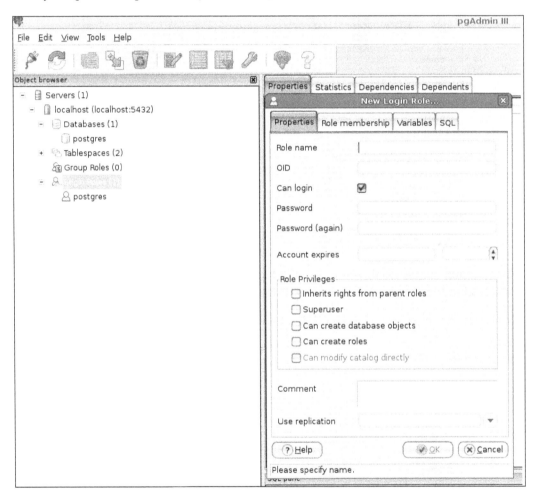

Create the database with name **sffs**.

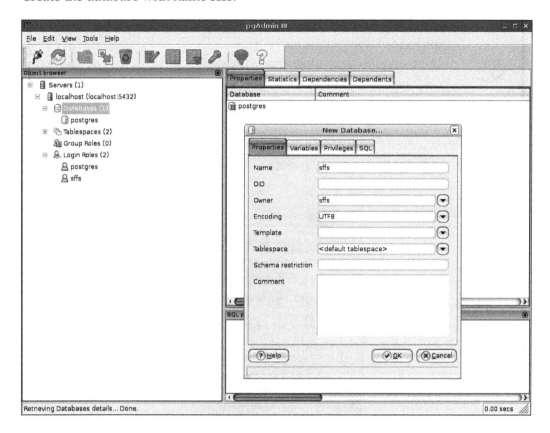

Open the SQL window and insert the text contained in `dump.sql` (in the `db` folder of the `SpringFreshFruitsStore` example application).

If you already have a PostgreSQL installation and you only create the database, check if you have to install pl/pgsql. In accordance, uncomment or comment the instructions:

CREATE PROCEDURAL LANGUAGE plpgsql;

ALTER PROCEDURAL LANGUAGE plpgsql OWNER TO postgres;

in the SQL script.

Launch the query and wait for the end of the operation.

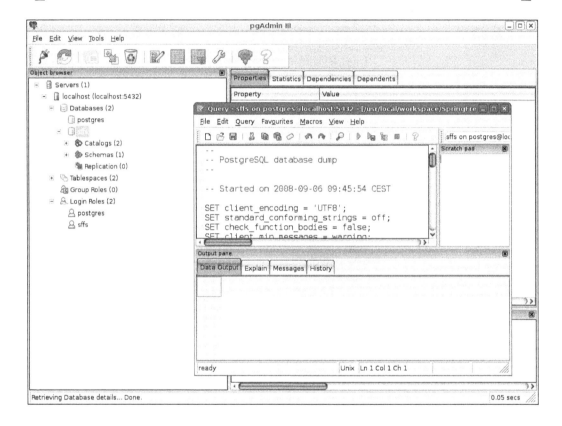

JDBC Driver

To connect the application to the database or to run the tests, the PostgreSQL JDBC driver JAR file is necessary.

To download it let's go to the web site `http://jdbc.postgresql.org`.

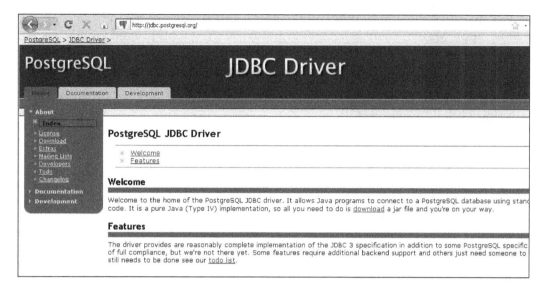

Choose the appropriate driver version for the PostgreSQL version installed.

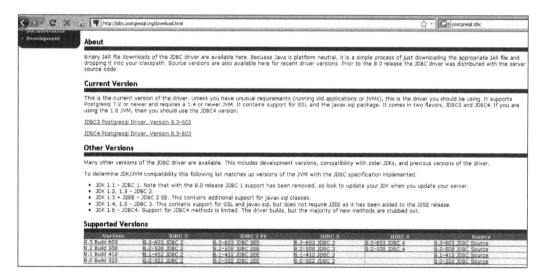

After choosing the JAR version and downloading the file, copy `postgresql-8.3-603.jdbc3.jar` in `<tomcat_dir>/lib` and in `libExt` in the `SpringFreshFruits` folder.

Summary

In this chapter, we saw how to set up the development environment on Ubuntu Linux, Apple MaxOSX, and Microsoft Windows XP. The tools needed are the JDK, Eclipse IDE with SpringIDE and AJDT plug-ins, SpringFramework, Apache Tomcat, and PostgreSQL to make our AOP application persistent and available on the Web.

It's now time to act in the world of Aspect-Oriented Programming, where we have been introduced by SpringAOP.

Have fun with Spring and AOP!

Index

M

O

P

R

U

UI controller
AddOrderItemController 224, 225
building 222
form controller, creating 225
methods, names 221
UiUtils, using 222-224

V

VO(Value Object) 183

W

weaving AOP components 18
within PCD, pointcut 122

X

XML Schema based configuration
advice 146
advisors 153
aspect 144
introduction 151, 152
pointcut 144-146
using 143

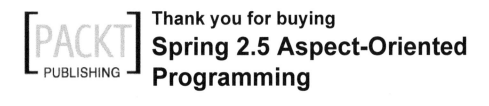
Thank you for buying
Spring 2.5 Aspect-Oriented Programming

Packt Open Source Project Royalties

When we sell a book written on an Open Source project, we pay a royalty directly to that project. Therefore by purchasing Spring 2.5 Aspect-Oriented Programming, Packt will have given some of the money received to the Spring project.

In the long term, we see ourselves and you—customers and readers of our books—as part of the Open Source ecosystem, providing sustainable revenue for the projects we publish on. Our aim at Packt is to establish publishing royalties as an essential part of the service and support a business model that sustains Open Source.

If you're working with an Open Source project that you would like us to publish on, and subsequently pay royalties to, please get in touch with us.

Writing for Packt

We welcome all inquiries from people who are interested in authoring. Book proposals should be sent to author@packtpub.com. If your book idea is still at an early stage and you would like to discuss it first before writing a formal book proposal, contact us; one of our commissioning editors will get in touch with you.

We're not just looking for published authors; if you have strong technical skills but no writing experience, our experienced editors can help you develop a writing career, or simply get some additional reward for your expertise.

About Packt Publishing

Packt, pronounced 'packed', published its first book "Mastering phpMyAdmin for Effective MySQL Management" in April 2004 and subsequently continued to specialize in publishing highly focused books on specific technologies and solutions.

Our books and publications share the experiences of your fellow IT professionals in adapting and customizing today's systems, applications, and frameworks. Our solution-based books give you the knowledge and power to customize the software and technologies you're using to get the job done. Packt books are more specific and less general than the IT books you have seen in the past. Our unique business model allows us to bring you more focused information, giving you more of what you need to know, and less of what you don't.

Packt is a modern, yet unique publishing company, which focuses on producing quality, cutting-edge books for communities of developers, administrators, and newbies alike. For more information, please visit our website: www.PacktPub.com.

Spring Web Flow 2 Web Development

ISBN: 978-1-847195-42-5   Paperback: 200 pages

Master Spring's well-designed web frameworks to develop powerful web applications

1. Design, develop, and test your web applications using the Spring Web Flow 2 framework

2. Enhance your web applications with progressive AJAX, Spring security integration, and Spring Faces

3. Stay up-to-date with the latest version of Spring Web Flow

4. Walk through the creation of a bug tracker web application with clear explanations

JasperReports for Java Developers

ISBN: 978-1-904811-90-9   Paperback: 344 pages

Create, Design, Format and Export Reports with the world's most popular Java reporting library

1. Get started with JasperReports, and develop the skills to get the most from it

2. Create, design, format, and export reports

3. Generate report data from a wide range of datasources

4. Integrate Jasper Reports with Spring, Hibernate, Java Server Faces, or Struts

Please check **www.PacktPub.com** for information on our titles

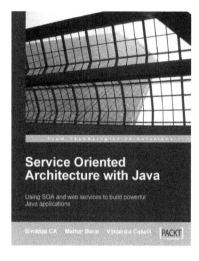

Service Oriented Architecture with Java

ISBN: 978-1-847193-21-6   Paperback: 192 pages

Using SOA and web services to build powerful Java applications

1. Build effective SOA applications with Java Web Services

2. Quick reference guide with best-practice design examples

3. Understand SOA concepts from core with examples

4. Design scalable inter-enterprise communication

Learning Dojo

ISBN: 978-1-847192-68-4   Paperback: 249 pages

A practical, comprehensive tutorial to building beautiful, scalable interactive interfaces for your Web 2.0 applications with Dijits

1. Learn real-world Dojo programming with detailed examples and analysis of source code

2. Comprehensive guide to available Dojo widgets (dijits) and how to use them

3. Extend Dojo by creating your own dijits

4. Highly practical, with hands on examples and short, clear explanations right from the start

Please check **www.PacktPub.com** for information on our titles

www.ingramcontent.com/pod-product-compliance
Lightning Source LLC
Chambersburg PA
CBHW062102050326
40690CB00016B/3171